how to use tools

By Alfred P. Morgan

219 Park Avenue South, New York, N.Y. 10003

Fourth Printing, 1973

Published by ARCO PUBLISHING COMPANY, Inc.
219 Park Avenue South, New York, N.Y. 10003

Copyright 1952, 1955 by Fawcett Publications, Inc.

*This book is a reproduction in part of the book Tools
and How To Use Them, copyright 1948 by Alfred P.
Morgan, published by Crown Publishers, New York, N.Y.*

Library of Congress Catalog Card Number: 56-11177

ISBN 0-668-00426-6

Printed in U.S.A.

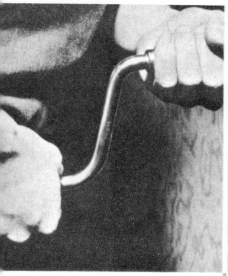

CONTENTS

791352

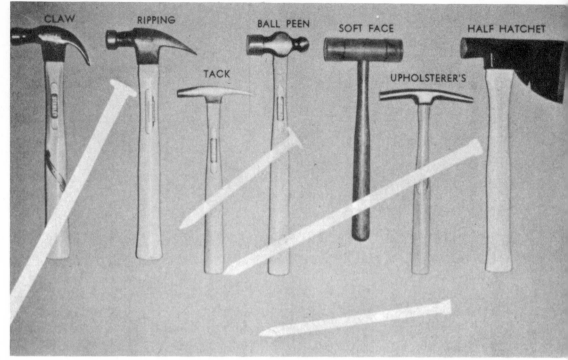

CLAW   RIPPING   BALL PEEN   SOFT FACE   HALF HATCHET

TACK   UPHOLSTERER'S

hammers and nails

It's easy to use a hammer correctly and to drive nails where you want them to go once you master these simple techniques.

ANYONE possessed of ordinary coordination can easily learn to handle tools efficiently. It is not difficult to use, or to learn how to use, most of the ordinary tools with skill. Do not be dismayed by the dexterity of a skilled workman. Practice and instruction will make you skillful also.

First, you must understand the tools you propose to use, their purposes and limitations; then, the proper way to hold them and apply them to the work.

To get the most out of a tool, we do not, for example, pick up a hammer and merely whack at a nail with it or push a saw back and forth to cut wood. We learn the *technique* of using each tool. Starting right is half the secret. If we start right, we soon acquire skill by practicing. If we start wrong, practice will not bring skill.

Striking a blow is not all there is to using a hammer. There can be artistry in its use or in the use of a saw, a wrench, a screw driver, a plane, or in fact of any other tool. The skilled mechanic is skilled in the use of his tools because he knows more about his tools than the novice and has learned the

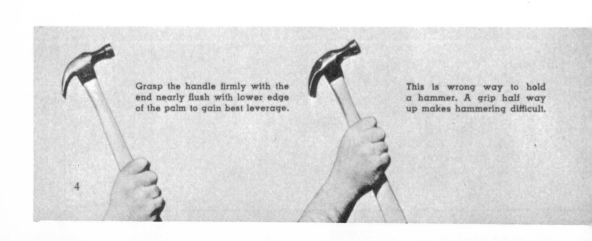

Grasp the handle firmly with the end nearly flush with lower edge of the palm to gain best leverage.

This is wrong way to hold a hammer. A grip half way up makes hammering difficult.

4

technique of using them. His tools have become extensions of his hands and brain.

You can learn how to use tools properly from a good mechanic and from a good book. Not all mechanics are good teachers.

It helps if you know why a tool is made the way it is and how it does the job it was intended for. How to hold a tool correctly is very important.

Some persons cannot drive a nail straight with the result that sometimes they hit fingers as well as the nail. That is because there is something to be known in order to drive a nail properly, and they do not know that something.

Let us consider first the three tools most commonly used in the household and by woodworkers, viz., hammers, screw drivers, and saws.

The Nail or Claw Hammer

The nail or claw hammer is a woodworker's tool which mechanics use principally to drive nails, wedges and dowels. The curved claws are used to pull out nails or rip woodwork apart. If the claws have a pronounced curve, the hammer was designed to be more efficient at pulling nails than ripping woodwork apart. If the claws are only slightly curved the hammer is better adapted to ripping than nail pulling. There is also a semi-ripping pattern of hammer, intended as a happy medium between the best ripper and the best nail puller.

A claw hammer designed for nail pulling is usually part of the tool kit of every household. Here it is used not only to drive and pull nails but often serves a great variety of other purposes ranging from homicide to cracking walnuts. A good mechanic does not put his hammer to quite such diversified use. He does not try to break kindling wood or drive cold chisels with it.

He chops kindling wood with a hatchet; he drives punches and cold chisels with a machinist's hammer.

We can divide nail hammers into two other classifications: those sold in the dime stores to the neophyte woodworker and would-be interior decorator and the hammers which mechanics use.

Specifications of a Good Hammer

The dime store hammer has a cast head, whose face is not accurately ground. It soon chips and loses its shape. It slips off the heads of nails. It is an ideal tool for driving nails crooked and hammering fingers.

Mechanics' nail hammers may be obtained from any tool and hardware supplier. The head of a first-class hammer is not cast. It is drop forged from tough alloy steel and is tempered and heat treated so that it is twice as strong as ordinary steel. A cast head is made by pouring white hot steel into a sand mold. A drop-forged head is made by hammering red-hot steel into a steel die. A cast head is brittle; a drop-forged head is really tough.

The head of a first-class hammer is accurately ground to shape. The face is usually ground smooth and slightly beveled at the edge to prevent chipping, although carpenters sometimes use a hammer having a face roughened by cross checkering which is often employed for nailing together the frame of a building. The smooth-faced slightly convex or "bell-face" hammer is the most generally useful.

A hammer handle is tough, seasoned, straight-grained hickory shaped to fit the hand at one end and tapered toward the head so as to give the hammer its "spring." An important quality of a hammer handle is spring which gives the mechanic better control of the tool and eases the strain on

Don't use metal face of nail hammer directly on woodwork in pounding joints together. Use a soft wood block to prevent marring woodwork surfaces.

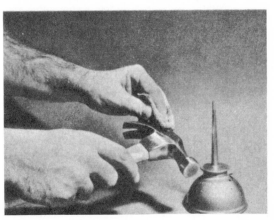

Take good care of your hammer. Use oil on a soft cloth to clean and polish the head occasionally. Oil a hammer which has been exposed to moisture.

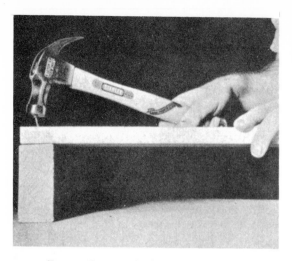

Keep nail perpendicular to face of hammer. If face is inclined at angle away from hammerer, a nail bends away from him after several strokes.

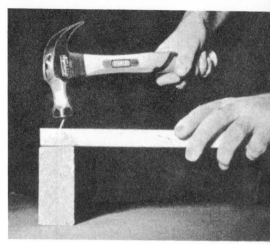

As the hammer is inclined the nail is bent. If hammer face is watched closely, most nail bending can be prevented. Always nail on a solid support.

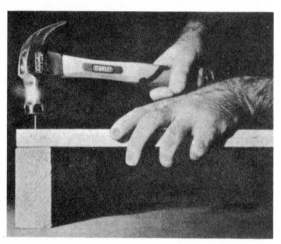

When hammer meets nail like this, the nail's not likely to bend. Keep wrist limber and relaxed for easy hammering. Note face is parallel to board.

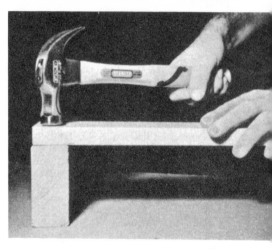

Last blow must meet the nail squarely to prevent hammer leaving mark in surface and yet sink nail head well into wood. Keep fingers away from nail.

his muscles. You can best appreciate this by driving a few nails with a hammer head fitted with a solid metal handle. Not only will it not feel right, but your muscles will soon be shocked and tired. That end of the hickory handle which is fitted into a hammer head is expanded into the tapered eye usually by one wooden wedge and two metal wedges so it won't come off easily.

Hammer Sizes

The size of a nail hammer is the weight of the head in ounces ranging from 5 oz. to 28 oz. The common sizes are 10 oz., 12 oz., 14 oz., 16 oz. and 20 oz. The lighter hammers are used for driving small nails. The heaviest is used for driving large nails into soft wood or ordinary nails into hard wood. When the hammer used is too light for the job it will cause a nail to bend. It should be so heavy that a large nail can be driven in completely with five blows. A 16 oz. hammer is a good choice for general use.

Plain-Face and Bell-Face

A smooth-face nail hammer may have either a bell face or a plain face. The face is the part of the hammer head which strikes against the nail. On a bell-face hammer it is slightly more convex than on a plain-face hammer. The novice cannot drive nails straight as easily with a bell-face hammer as with a plain-face hammer. However, there is a good reason why a bell-face hammer is frequently used. With it, an experienced mechanic can drive a nail flush, or even slightly below the surface of the wood, without leaving marks.

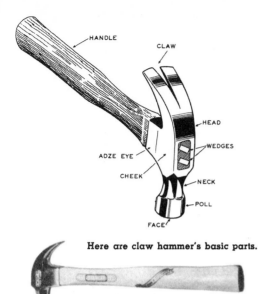

Here are claw hammer's basic parts.

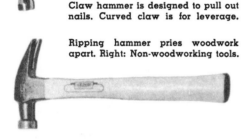

Claw hammer is designed to pull out nails. Curved claw is for leverage.

Ripping hammer pries woodwork apart. Right: Non-woodworking tools.

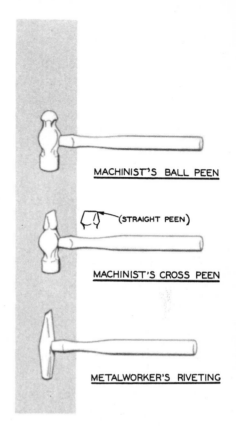

MACHINIST'S BALL PEEN

(STRAIGHT PEEN)

MACHINIST'S CROSS PEEN

METALWORKER'S RIVETING

Using the Claw Hammer

Unless you are a confirmed south-paw hold the hammer in your *right* hand. Grasp the handle firmly with the end practically flush with the lower edge of the palm. Grasp the nail near its point with the thumb and forefinger of the other hand. Place the point of the nail on the work at the exact spot where it is to be driven. Unless the nail is to be purposely driven at an angle it should be *perpendicular* to the surface of the work. Rest the face of the hammer at its center on the head of the nail, raise the hammer slightly and give the nail one or two light taps to start the nail and fix your aim. Then get your fingers out of the way and drive the nail into the wood.

The wrist and arm motion used in driving the nail depends upon the power of the blows required. Small nails require light blows which are struck almost entirely with a wrist motion. Slightly heavier, or medium blows are struck with both a wrist and a forearm motion. The heavy blows required to drive a large nail come from the wrist, forearm and shoulder. Do not attack a nail viciously. On the other hand, do not be timid. Nails are properly driven with a few positive, firm blows and not with either a pile-driving whack or a series of light taps. Always strike the nail with the center of the hammer face. Do not strike with the side or cheek. Dirt or grease on the hammer face will cause it to slip on the nail.

Sometimes the grain of the wood, a knot or a hidden obstruction will cause a nail to bend or go in crooked. Usually it is the fault of the workman.

When a nail is going in straight, strike so that when the hammer hits the head of the nail, the nail is perpendicular to the hammer face. Striking the nail with the face at a slight angle will force the head of the nail forward, sidewise or back depending upon the angle. This is the trick used to straighten up a nail which is not going in the right direction. Slightly changing the angle of the hammer face to the nail is one of the controls.

If a nail bends when it is driven, draw it out and throw it away. Start another in its place. If the second nail also bends, investigation is called for. If the nail appears to be striking a knot, a hidden nail or other metal, it will be necessary to withdraw it. Drive a new nail in a new place. Or drill a hole past the obstruction and try again.

NAIL INFORMATION

Listed below is the length, diameter, head size and approximate number to a pound of the various penny sizes of common nails and finishing nails.

COMMON NAILS

Size	Length	Diameter Gauge No.	Diameter of Head	Approx. Number to a Pound
2 d	1″	15	11/64″	830
3 d	1 1/4″	14	13/64″	528
4 d	1 1/2″	12 1/2	1/4 ″	316
5 d	1 3/4″	12 1/2	1/4 ″	271
6 d	2″	11 1/2	17/64″	168
7 d	2 1/4″	11 1/2	17/64″	150
8 d	2 1/2″	10 1/4	9/32″	106
9 d	2 3/4″	10 1/4	9/32″	96
10 d	3″	9	5/16″	69
12 d	3 1/4″	9	5/16″	63
16 d	3 1/2″	8	11/32″	49
20 d	4″	6	13/32″	31
30 d	4 1/2″	5	7/16″	24
40 d	5″	4	15/32″	18
50 d	5 1/2″	3	1/2 ″	14
60 d	6″	2	17/32″	11

FINISHING NAILS

Size	Length	Diameter Gauge No.	Diameter of Head Gauge No.	Approx. Number to a Pound
2 d	1″	16 1/2	13 1/2	1351
3 d	1 1/4″	15 1/2	12 1/2	807
4 d	1 1/2″	15	12	584
5 d	1 3/4″	15	12	500
6 d	2″	13	10	309
8 d	2 1/2″	12 1/2	9 1/2	189
10 d	3″	11 1/2	8 1/2	121
16 d	3 1/2″	11	8	90
20 d	4″	10	7	62

*The above tables are reprinted from the Catalog of U. S. S. American Nails. Courtesy of the American Steel and Wire Co.

SPECIAL PURPOSE NAILS

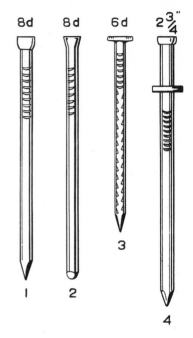

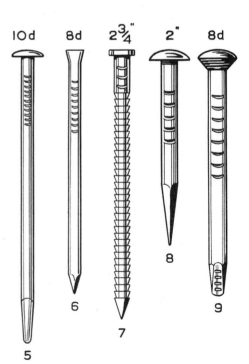

Here are a few of the more than 100 varieties of special purpose nails. 1. Common finishing nail. 2. Flooring brad for hardwood. 3. Barbed box nail. 4. Duplex head nail for concrete forms and scaffolding. 5. Clinch nail. 6. Flooring brad. 7. Fetter ring nail. 8. Hinge nail. 9. Boat nail.

COMMON NAILS

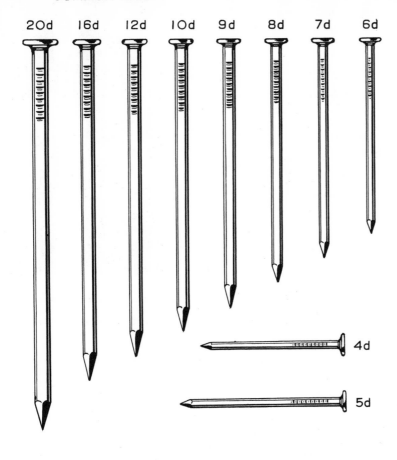

20d 16d 12d 10d 9d 8d 7d 6d

4d

5d

These are the common nails which the carpenters use to fasten together the framework of a building. The nails have flat heads and diamond-shaped points. The full size sketches can be used to identify 4d to 20d common nails. A 4d nail measures one and a half inches long and a 20d nail is four inches long. A chart of handy nail facts for reference is at far left.

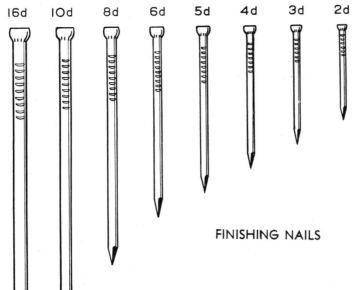

16d 10d 8d 6d 5d 4d 3d 2d

The finishing type nails are used to hold trim and finishing woodwork in place. The full size sketches can be used to identify 2d to 16d finishing nails. These nails are usually driven below the surface of wood so that the heads will not show. A finishing nail has a diamond point and a brad head which is easily driven into wood with the nail set, then concealed with putty.

FINISHING NAILS

Courtesy American Steel and Wire Company

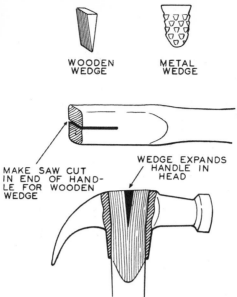

WOODEN WEDGE

METAL WEDGE

MAKE SAW CUT IN END OF HAND-LE FOR WOODEN WEDGE

WEDGE EXPANDS HANDLE IN HEAD

Loose hammer head is dangerous. Drill and split out old handle. Pare new handle to fit head; then drive on head by hitting handle on solid surface.

Metal or wooden wedges are hammered in to expand end of hammer handle so that head cannot fly off. Be careful not to split handle with wedges.

Using the Bell-Face Hammer

As already mentioned, the head of a nail can be driven slightly below a wooden surface without leaving any hammer marks on the surface by using a bell-face hammer. It is necessary for the face of the hammer to be parallel to the surface of the wood and for the head of the nail to be in the center of the face when it is struck.

The Ripping Hammers

Nail hammers are made with two types of claws. One is designed for pulling nails, the other for ripping woodwork apart. Claws designed for nail pulling are more curved than ripping claws. The flat, only slightly curved, claw of a ripping hammer is designed to slip under the edges of the boards and timbers and pry them apart.

Nail Sets

In fine work where the nail head must not show or must be inconspicuous, it is driven well below the surface with a nail set. The hole in the wood over the nail head can then be filled flush with the surface with putty, plastic wood or sawdust mixed with glue. The slender, small headed nails, called finishing nails, are usually set below the surface. Use a nail set for this.

Nail sets are made in several sizes, usually 1/32″, 2/32″ and 4/32″, the size being indicated by the diameter of the small end of the tapered shank. Notice that the end of a nail set is often "cupped" or hollowed. This helps prevent it from "walking" or slipping on the nail. Use a nail set of a size which will not enlarge the hole made by the head of the nail.

It is rather simple to "set" a nail. Hold the nail set between the thumb and forefinger and press the small end firmly against the head of the nail. Rest the little finger on the work to steady your hand and prevent the nail set from slipping. Drive the nail head about $\frac{1}{16}$″ below the surface of the wood with a light tap of the hammer. The resulting hole made by the head of the nail can then be concealed by filling it with putty, plastic wood or a mixture of sawdust and glue.

How to Draw a Nail

In order to pull out a nail with a claw hammer, it is necessary for the head of the nail to be above the surface of the work far enough so that the claws of the hammer can be slipped underneath. The slot between the claws should go around the nail and under the nail head. Then raise the hammer handle until it is nearly vertical. If the nail is short, this will withdraw it from the work. If the nail is long and the hammer handle is pulled past the vertical position, it will bend the nail, enlarge the hole and mar the work. Moreover when the hammer handle passes the vertical position, most of the leverage is lost and a great deal of force is required to draw out the nail any further.

Here is the simple remedy. Slip a piece of wood between the hammer head and the work so that the handle is again nearly horizontal and the leverage is increased. This will also apply the pulling force of the claws in the proper direction so that the nail is drawn out without enlarging the hole which it formed when driven into the wood. When long nails, only partially driven into work, must be pulled out, it may be necessary to start the pulling operation with a piece of wood under the hammer head in order to get the proper leverage.

Tack Hammers

Tacks and small nails (brads) can be driven with a light nail hammer, but in many instances a tack hammer will prove most efficient.

Useful Facts About Nails

To the person equipped with a good twenty-five-cent cast-iron hammer "a nail is a nail." If he makes fine distinctions when he buys nails, he specifies "small nails" or "large nails" or perhaps "medium-size nails." In the dictionary a nail is defined as "a slender piece of metal having a head, and used for driving into wood." But a nail is much more significant than either said person's or the dictionary's opinion of it. It is an important tool used to assemble or hold together a job. There are more than 100 different varieties of nails in common use and this figure does not include the different sizes of each variety. Each has a particular quality which makes it the best to use for certain work.

Today, nails are produced by automatic machines from wrought iron, steel, copper, brass, bronze, Monel metal and other alloys in hundreds of scientifically designed forms, sizes and shapes. The simple form of the ordinary nail has been modified to meet many specialized requirements. Changing the general proportions and the shape and size of the head and point produces special nails for fastening flooring, shingles, laths, wallboard, baskets, egg crates, fruit boxes, boats, barges, etc.

Common Nails

All hardware stores carry in stock common nails and finishing nails. Common nails have flat heads and diamond points. They are the nails which a carpenter uses to nail together a building's framework.

Finishing Nails

The nails used to hold trim and finishing woodwork in place are usually driven below the surface of the wood so that the heads do not show. It would be difficult to drive the large flat head of a common nail below the surface, so a carpenter employs finishing nails to accomplish this. Finishing nails have diamond points and brad heads. A brad head is a very small head and can be driven into the wood with a nail set.

Brads

These are small diameter diamond-pointed, brad-headed nails which are smaller in diameter than finishing nails. They are used in cabinet making and other fine work. Brads are also made of various metals and in a variety of finishes.

Wire Nails

Wire nails are diamond-pointed, flat-headed nails which are smaller in diameter than common nails. They are used in light wood which a common nail might split.

Nail Sizes

Brads and wire nails are sized according to their length and diameter. You can buy little ones only $\frac{3}{16}$" in length. The next larger size is ¼" long. They range from ¼" by ⅛" to 3" long. The diameter is measured by the American Steel and Wire Gauge and ranges from No. 24 gauge to No. 10 gauge.

Some of the special nails, for example, those used for brick siding, felt roofing, plasterboard, hinge nails, clout nails, and boat spikes are graded in sizes according to their length in inches. But common nails, finishing nails and a great many others are designated by the penny system.

The Penny System

This rather clumsy way of designating the sizes of nails originated in England in the dim past and has persisted in the nail industry ever since. No one knows how this curious designation began. One explanation is that two penny, three penny, six penny, etc. nails became known as such from the fact that one hundred cost two pennies, three pennies, four pennies, etc. Both the ancient and modern abbreviation for penny is "d." But whatever the origin of the penny system of designating nails may have been, the fact remains that a 2d nail is 1″ long and each 1 d added increases the length ¼″ until the 12d size is reached. A 10d nail is 3″ long. The next three sizes larger are the 12d (3¼″ long), the 16d (3½″ long), and the 20d (4″ long). After the 20d, come the 30d, 40d, 50d and 60d sizes and these are respectively, 4½″, 5″, 5½″ and 6″ long.

Holding Power of Nails

The usefulness of any nail, regardless of size, depends on its holding power in any given variety of wood. When manufactured, the shank of a nail is therefore roughened near the head to give it greater holding power. Box nails, which must have great holding power when driven into end grain, are roughened or barbed along the entire shank. Some varieties of nails are also coated with an adhesive cement.

The holding power of a nail is dependent on the closeness of the fibers of the wood into which it is driven. A nail has greater holding power when driven into heavy woods than it has in light woods. Green wood, or wood which is not well seasoned, has a higher holding power than dry wood. If a nail is driven into green wood, its holding power decreases as the wood seasons and dries out.

A nail must be properly selected for the work it is to do so that there is no chance for it to split the wood or unnecessarily distort the fibers. The type of nail that distorts the fibers of the wood the least will have the greatest holding power.

The tendency of a nail to split the wood into which it is driven is determined by the shape of the point and the diameter of the nail in relation to the thickness and variety of the wood. A large nail will split a thin or narrow piece of wood. Very sharp points and long diamond points on nails are likely to split hard dense woods. For that reason, a skilled woodworker sometimes uses a file to blunt the point of a nail which he intends to drive into hard wood. Light weight and soft woods which have little tendency to split can be advantageously fastened with sharp pointed nails, somewhat better holding power being secured.

The common nail has a moderately sharp point with short angles and consequently might be termed an all around nail. It results in only a moderate amount of splitting. Its holding power in soft woods can sometimes be improved by filing the point sharper and its tendency to split hard woods can be reduced by filing the point blunt.

New Handles for Hammers

Well-seasoned hickory makes the best hammer handles. Some mechanics prefer to make their own handles for hammers, hatchets and axes. But hardware stores carry machine-made hickory handles in stock so that when a hammer handle breaks it is not difficult to obtain a new one.

That portion of the broken handle which remains in the hammer head must be knocked out. This is not always easy because the end is expanded by the wedges so that it fits the head very tightly. Drilling into the end of the handle with a $\frac{3}{16}$″ to $\frac{5}{16}$″ diameter twist drill to remove as much wood as possible and then splitting out

Where the nail head must not show, a finishing nail may be driven below surface of wood with a nail set. Drive nail head 1/16″ into the wood.

Resulting hole made by head of nail can be concealed by pressing putty, plastic wood or a mixture of sawdust and glue into it with putty knife.

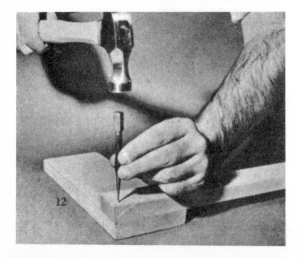

12

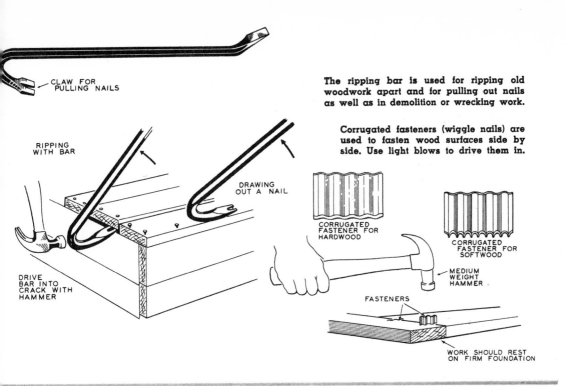

CLAW FOR PULLING NAILS

The ripping bar is used for ripping old woodwork apart and for pulling out nails as well as in demolition or wrecking work.

Corrugated fasteners (wiggle nails) are used to fasten wood surfaces side by side. Use light blows to drive them in.

RIPPING WITH BAR

DRAWING OUT A NAIL

CORRUGATED FASTENER FOR HARDWOOD

CORRUGATED FASTENER FOR SOFTWOOD

MEDIUM WEIGHT HAMMER

DRIVE BAR INTO CRACK WITH HAMMER

FASTENERS

WORK SHOULD REST ON FIRM FOUNDATION

small pieces will remove the old handle.

It may be necessary to scrape or pare the end of a new handle slightly before it will go into the head. This can be done with a knife, chisel, or wood rasp. The handle must fit *very tightly* in the head. The small end of the handle should be inserted in the adze eye, or opening in the head, and the opposite end of the handle struck sharply against the bench top or other solid surface until the handle is in place. Then the end of the handle is expanded in the hammer head by the insertion of wedges so that the head cannot fly off. A hammer with a head which is loose upon the handle is a very dangerous tool. From one to three wedges are generally used. The wedge in the original handle is usually wood, either maple or hickory. Metal wedges of various sizes can be purchased at any hardware store.

When a wooden wedge is used, a saw cut about as long as the wedge should be made with a fine saw into the end of the handle before it is inserted in the head. The wedge is driven into this slot. Of course no wedge should be driven in until the head is on the handle as far as it should go.

Corrugated Fasteners

These useful devices, often called "wiggle-nails" are used for holding two wood surfaces together side by side. They can be used in making window screens, screen doors, window frames, flower boxes, etc., and for tightening up loose joints or cracks in woodwork. They are made with both a plain and a saw edge. The corrugated fastener with a plain edge is used for hard woods. The saw edge fastener is for the soft woods.

There is a trick in driving a wiggle-nail. It is to use a medium weight hammer and strike light blows which are evenly distributed over the outside edge. It is essential that the work which is being fastened together rest on something solid while the fastener is driven in.

Ripping Bars

Of course a ripping bar is not a hammer, but since it is used, like a hammer, to pull out nails and rip woodwork apart, it is included in this chapter. It provides the necessary leverage to pull large nails.

There are several varieties of ripping bars. The most common type is the goose-neck pattern. It is drop forged from high grade hexagon tool steel and will not easily bend or break. The goose-neck has two claws like the curved claws of a hammer and is an efficient nail-puller. The chisel-pointed end can be forced into cracks to pry and rip in the same manner that a crow-bar can. A ripping bar is a very useful tool for opening heavy crates and cases and for demolition or wrecking work. •

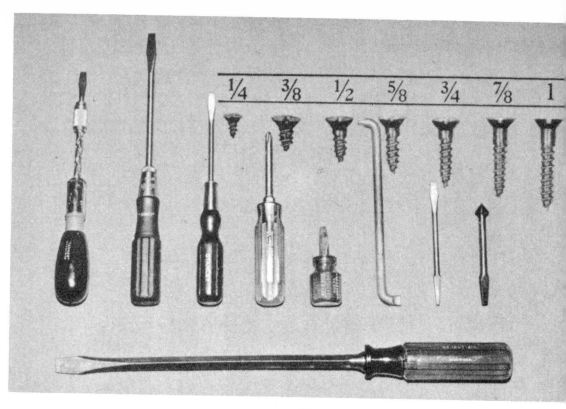

1/4	3/8	1/2	5/8	3/4	7/8	1

screws and
screw drivers

Apparently a simple operation, driving a screw is really an art.

Below is first step in correctly driving wood screw. Locate position of screw hole, mark with brad awl. Awl mark will center drill and prevent it from "walking."

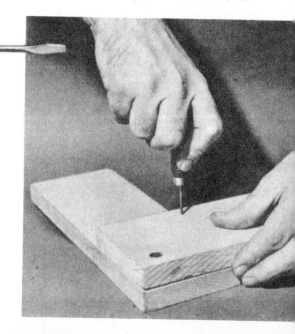

Screws have much greater holding power than nails. They also have the further advantage that work held together by them is easily taken apart and put together again without damaging the pieces. Screws are not used to the exclusion of nails because they are more expensive and take more time to drive.

The common wood screws are made of soft steel and of brass. Steel screws are usually called iron screws. The flathead iron screws generally have a bright finish but

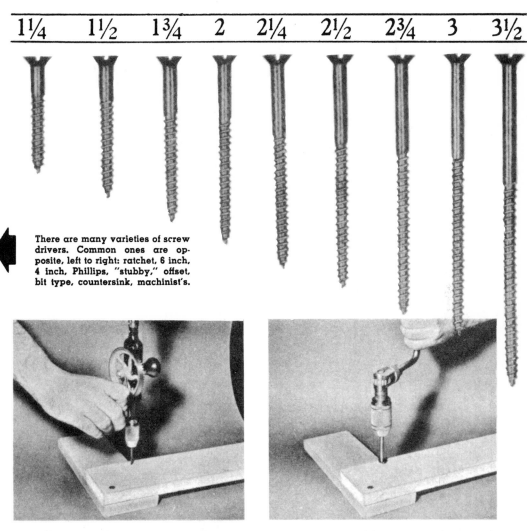

| 1¼ | 1½ | 1¾ | 2 | 2¼ | 2½ | 2¾ | 3 | 3½ |

There are many varieties of screw drivers. Common ones are opposite, left to right: ratchet, 6 inch, 4 inch, Phillips, "stubby," offset, bit type, countersink, machinist's.

The second step consists of drilling through at least one board. Otherwise, the wood might split.

To assure flat head screw being flush to surface, make countersink hole slightly smaller than head.

The right and wrong ways to drive a screw are shown below. Always hold the tool perpendicular.

Longer or thicker screws may require use of the brace and bit type of screw driver. Hold it straight.

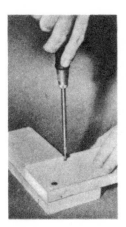
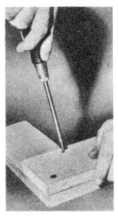
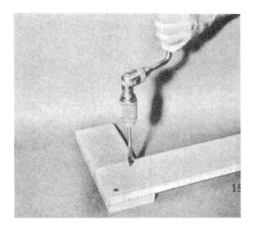

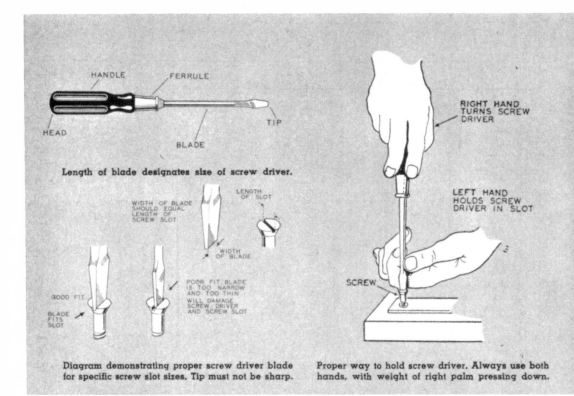

Diagram demonstrating proper screw driver blade for specific screw slot sizes. Tip must not be sharp.

Proper way to hold screw driver. Always use both hands, with weight of right palm pressing down.

are also plated with nickel, brass, cadmium or (galvanized) zinc. Round-head iron screws are blued or nickeled.

A screw driver is used primarily for tightening or loosening slotted screws. It is a tool which is often abused in the hands of a non-mechanic. It is difficult to convince some people that a screw driver is not a handy combination of small crowbar, chisel and can opener. Misusing a screw driver usually spoils it for driving screws.

All screw drivers are somewhat alike in general appearance but their sizes and shapes vary in design and construction according to work for which they were intended. For example, opticians' and watchmakers' screw drivers which are used for fine precision work are small in size and are turned with the tips of the thumb and forefinger. But heavy, square-shanked machinists' screw drivers are ruggedly made and are often turned with a wrench in order to apply extra force.

As in most things, there is an art in the apparently simple operation of driving a screw or removing one already in place. If improperly used, a screw driver may slip and damage the work or "chew up" the slot in the head of the screw. A screw with a damaged slot is usually very difficult to drive in or take out. Incidentally, if you damage the slot in a screw, take it out and

throw it away. Do not use it again; replace it with a new one.

Screw Driver Sizes

Screw drivers are made in many different sizes and styles. A mechanic always has several sizes. At least two or three sizes should be in every household tool kit. The size of a screw driver is indicated by the length of the blade. A 4-inch screw driver has a blade four inches long; a 6-inch screw driver has a blade six inches long, etc. The width of the blade also varies. A blade with a narrow tip is intended for small screws. If it has a wide tip, it is meant for large screws. There is no all-purpose screw driver; a screw driver must fit the job.

Screw Drivers in a Tool Kit

Too much emphasis cannot be placed upon the fact that the *tip of a screw driver blade* should fit the screw slot. In order to drive screws of several different sizes, it is necessary to employ several sizes of screw drivers. The thickness of the blade should fit snugly in the screw slot and the width of the blade should be about the length of the slot. If too wide, the blade tip may mar the work around the screw head. If too narrow or not thick enough, the screw slot

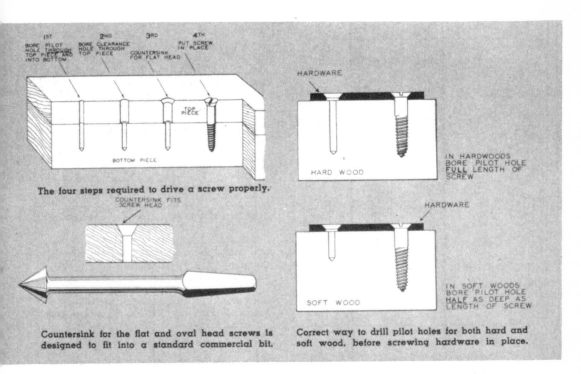

The four steps required to drive a screw properly.

Countersink for the flat and oval head screws is designed to fit into a standard commercial bit.

Correct way to drill pilot holes for both hard and soft wood, before screwing hardware in place.

and the tip of the blade will become burred. A blade that fits well can be kept in the screw head slot much more easily than one which does not fit.

More power can be applied with less effort with a long screw driver than with a short one. There is less danger that it will slip out of the slot. Of course limited space sometimes makes it impossible to use a long screw driver. Very short screw drivers called *stubbies* or *babies* are made for use in cramped spaces.

The handle, the steel in the blade and the method of construction in a quality screw driver are much superior to the equivalent parts in a cheap tool. The blade of better steel will not become twisted or burred as easily. Moreover the tip of a good screw driver is ground so that the sides are practically parallel. A blade which tapers out from the tip too quickly has a tendency to raise out of the slot. It costs more to grind the sides of the blade parallel than it does to produce a blade with taper. A correctly ground blade is found only on the more expensive screw drivers.

Driving Screws

Use the *longest* screw driver available which is convenient for the work and whose blade *fits* the screw slot. Center the tip of the blade in the screw slot. Hold the handle of the screw driver firmly in the right hand with the head of the handle against the palm and the thumb and fingers grasping the handle near the ferrule. To drive a screw *in*, turn it *clockwise* which means in the same direction that the hands of the clock move. To remove or withdraw a screw, turn it in the opposite or counterclockwise direction.

When taking a fresh grip on the handle with the right hand, steady the tip of the screw driver and keep it pressed in the screw slot with the left hand. The left hand fingers should grasp the blade of the screw driver just above the tip. Relax their grip when the screw driver is turned. Tighten it while renewing the grip on the handle for a new turn.

A little soap rubbed into the threads of a wood screw makes it easier to drive. A drop of oil or a little graphite will do the same thing for a machine screw. Graphite and oil smeared in the threads of a steel machine screw will often prevent it from becoming rusted in and will make it easier to remove when necessary.

To Remove a Tight Screw

When a tight screw is to be removed and it cannot be turned at the first attempt, often it can be started if it is first given a *slight* twist in a clockwise direction, that is,

17

Standard Wood Screw Diameters

Number	Basic	Diameter Maximum	Minimum
0	.060	.064	.053
1	.073	.077	.066
2	.086	.090	.079
3	.099	.103	.092
4	.112	.116	.105
5	.125	.129	.118
6	.138	.142	.131
7	.151	.155	.144
8	.164	.168	.157
9	.177	.181	.170
10	.190	.194	.183
11	.203	.207	.196
12	.216	.220	.209
14	.242	.246	.235
16	.268	.272	.261
18	.294	.298	.287
20	.320	.324	.313
24	.372	.376	.365

in the direction which will drive it in. It is sometimes helpful if the screw is worked both ways. In other words, it should be backed out as far as it will go easily and then turned part way back in. It will usually back out a little farther each time this operation is repeated, until it is all the way out.

When a tight screw is to be withdrawn, a screw driver with a blade that has parallel sides and which fits the screw slot perfectly, *must* be used. Otherwise the slot of the screw will be "chewed" so that the job is doubly difficult. If a stubborn screw with a damaged slot can be backed out part way, it is sometimes possible to turn it the rest of the way with a pair of pliers.

Pilot Holes for Screws

If a wood screw is driven in without first boring a pilot hole for the threaded part, the wood may split and in some instances the screw head may be twisted off. Holes for small screws can be made with a small brad awl. Bore the holes for large screws with bits or twist drills. If the wood is soft (pine, spruce, basswood, tulip, etc.) bore the hole only about half as deep as the threaded part of the screw. If the wood is hard (oak, maple, birch, etc.) the hole must be almost as deep as the screw.

In hard wood, if the screw is large or is a brass screw, it is necessary to bore a pilot hole slightly smaller in diameter than the threaded part of the screw and then enlarge the hole at the top with a second drill of the same diameter as the unthreaded portion of the screw.

Fastening Wood with Screws

When two pieces of wood are to be fastened tightly together with screws, two sets of holes must be drilled. The holes are drilled so that the threaded portion of the screw "bites" or "takes hold" only in the under piece of wood. The piece on top is clamped to the lower piece only by the pressure of the screw head. There are five steps in the operation:

1. Locate the position of the screw holes and mark them with a brad awl. The awl mark will center the drill and prevent it from "walking" away from the spot.

2. Bore a pilot hole, slightly smaller in diameter than the threaded portion of the screw, all the way through the upper piece of wood and into the lower piece half the length of the threaded part of the screw.

3. Enlarge the pilot hole in the upper piece of wood by drilling it out to the same diameter (or slightly larger) than the shank or unthreaded portion of the screw.

4. If flat head or oval head screws are to be used, countersink the clearance hole in the upper piece of wood to match the diameter of the heads of the screws. If round head screws or cup washers are used, do not countersink.

5. Drive all screws firmly in place and, after they are all in, tighten each of them.

To Fasten Hardware

Certain hinges, striking plates, etc., require that the wood underneath be recessed before they can be mounted. Locate the position of the hardware on the work and score a line around it with the point of a sharp penknife blade. Using this line as a guide, cut the recess with a chisel. Locate the position of the screws, mark with a brad awl and drill holes of the proper size for the screws. Drive the screws in place tightly.

When the work does not need to be recessed to fit the hardware piece, the proper procedure is:

1. Lay the hardware on the work in the correct position and mark the screw holes.

2. Bore pilot holes which are slightly smaller in diameter than the threaded portion of the screws. If the wood is soft, bore the pilot hole only as deep as half the length of the threaded part of the screw. If the

wood is hard, bore the hole nearly as deep as the length of the screw. If the screws are short only a pilot hole will be needed, but long screws require a clearance hole of the same diameter and length as the shank or unthreaded part of the screw.

3. The size of the screws should be the largest size that will slip easily through the holes in the hardware unless the holes are countersunk. If countersunk, oval head or flat head screws to fit the countersink should be used. If the holes in the hardware are not countersunk, round head screws should be used.

4. Drive all the screws in but do not tighten them completely until all are in place.

Twisting Off of Brass Screws

Since a brass screw is not as strong as a steel screw, the head and shank will twist off more easily. This is apt to occur when a brass screw is driven into hardwood. Rubbing the threads on a cake of soap before the screw is put in place will help avoid this. A more certain method is to drive in a steel screw of the same size first. The steel screw is then removed and the brass screw put in its place. The steel screw cuts a thread in the wood into which the brass screw will go easily.

How to Conceal Screws

Screws are sometimes set below the surface of the wood and concealed by a wooden plug. The planking on a boat is usually fastened to the boat frames in this manner. Wooden plugs of various diameters, cut from mahogany, oak, pine, white cedar and cypress, can be purchased from dealers in boat supplies and at some hardware stores. They can be cut with a tool called a plug cutter. This tool fits into an ordinary brace. Plugs should be cut from the same kind of wood as that in which they are to be inserted and the grain should match as closely as possible. They should be cut so that the grain runs across the plug and not lengthwise.

First bore a hole at least ⅜" deep with an auger bit of the same size as the wooden plug. Then bore the proper pilot and clearance holes for the screw. Put the screw in place and drive it in as far as it will go with a screw driver. Select a suitable plug, put some glue on its sides and insert it into the hole with the grain on the end of the plug running in the same direction as the grain

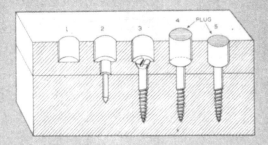

Left: How to conceal screws with wooden plugs.

1. Bore hole to fit plug. 2. Bore pilot and clearance holes for screws. 3. Drive screw in place. 4. Drive plug in, using glue on it. 5. After glue has dried, pare off top of the plug, then plane flush.

Right: Fastening hardware with extra-long screws.

Both pilot hole and clearance hole are often necessary when long screws are used to fasten hardware that requires extra strength for holding. Pilot hole is first drilled about two thirds the length of screw; then clearance hole.

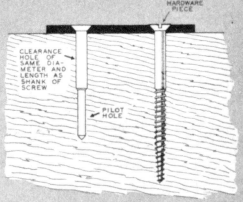

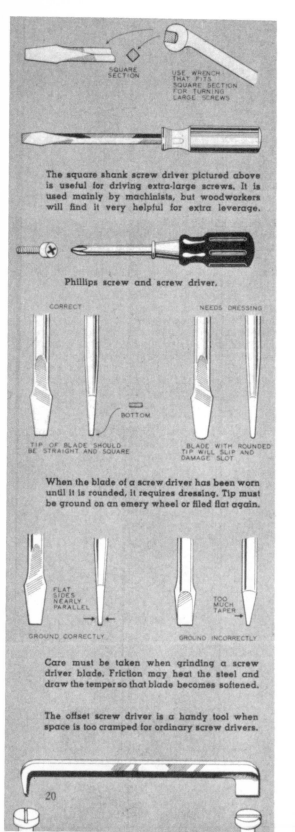

The square shank screw driver pictured above is useful for driving extra-large screws. It is used mainly by machinists, but woodworkers will find it very helpful for extra leverage.

Phillips screw and screw driver.

When the blade of a screw driver has been worn until it is rounded, it requires dressing. Tip must be ground on an emery wheel or filed flat again.

Care must be taken when grinding a screw driver blade. Friction may heat the steel and draw the temper so that blade becomes softened.

The offset screw driver is a handy tool when space is too cramped for ordinary screw drivers.

on the surface of the work. Drive the plug in as far as it will go. When the glue has dried, use a chisel or a plane to pare the plug off level with the surface.

Misusing Screw Drivers

Until this point in our discussion we have talked about the common form of screw driver. This has a long, slim, steel shank with a wood or plastic handle and is used to loosen or tighten ordinary wood screws and small machine screws.

The handle is usually fastened to the shank by a steel pin through the ferrule (the metal band around the handle where the shank enters).

The ordinary screw driver will withstand considerable twisting strain but it is not intended for prying or chiselling. If used for prying, it will bend and it is usually difficult to make it perfectly straight again. A screw driver which is even slightly bent is difficult to keep in the slot of a screw.

When a screw driver is used as a substitute for a chisel or a punch and you hammer the handle, there is a good chance that the handle will split. If you must pry with an ordinary screw driver or hammer on the handle, use judgment so as not to strain it or, better still, keep an old screw driver on hand just for such purposes.

The tip of a screw driver blade is hardened to prevent it from becoming worn and burred. The tip is harder and more brittle than the rest of the shank. It will break if strained too much.

While it is a common practice, starting a screw with a hammer damages both screw and wood.

On the other hand, there is a rugged screw driver which will withstand a great deal of hard use and considerable abuse. It is used by automotive mechanics, machine repair men and assemblers. The shank goes all the way through the handle so that you can tap on it, if the occasion requires, without splitting the handle. When a rusty screw must be removed and the slot is full of rust, the tip of the blade may have to be seated in the slot by hitting the handle with a hammer. This is permissible if the steel shank extends through the handle.

Some heavy duty machinists' screw drivers have a handle with a double grip so that both hands can be used to apply the force necessary to tighten or loosen an obstinate screw. There are also heavy duty screw drivers having a square shank which is extra large and strong so as to stand up under hard use. The shank is square so that you can use a wrench on it and apply enough turning force to loosen a large rusted screw.

Phillips Screws and Screw Drivers

Phillips screws have two slots which cross at the center. They are used to considerable extent in radio sets and on the moldings and trim of automobiles. Their advantage is that the screw driver cannot slip out of the slot and damage the finish. Phillips head screws require a Phillips screw driver. The tip of the blade is shaped like a cross and fits into both slots. It is necessary to use more downward pressure

Safety hint: Never guide a screw driver tip with your fingers. It's one way to slash them painfully.

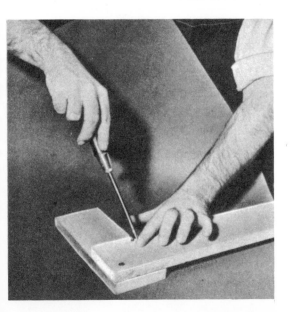

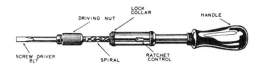

The ratchet screw driver.

The brace provides greater leverage and can be used with screw driver blade or countersink tool.

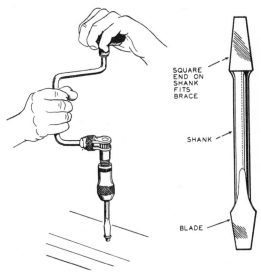

Large screws can be driven or withdrawn almost effortlessly with brace and screw driver bits. These are made in many widths with square shank ends.

Below is shown a method for measuring wood screws. Diameter or gage is measured across the shank; lengths are determined as illustrated.

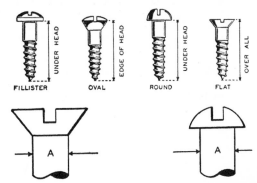

to keep a Phillips screw driver in the crossed slots than to keep the blade of an ordinary screw driver in the slot of an ordinary screw.

Dressing a Screw Driver Blade

Dressing is a term which mechanics use to mean putting in order or adjusting. Since a screw driver is not a cutting tool, it does not need to be resharpened. It must, however, be dressed or kept in condition by occasionally grinding or by filing with a flat file.

If filed, the screw driver must be held in a vise. The tip should be made straight across the end, at right angles to the shank and the sides. The faces near the tip should be made parallel or almost parallel to each other. If the tip is rounded or beveled and the sides are not nearly parallel, the screw driver will slip or climb out of and damage the slot.

When a screw driver is dressed on an emery wheel, the novice should remember not to hold the blade against the wheel too long. The friction may heat the steel and draw the temper so that the blade becomes soft. When the blade is being ground, dip it in water frequently to cool it. If the blade becomes so hot that it discolors (blue or yellow) the temper has been damaged.

Offset Screw Drivers

Hidden screws or screws located where there is not sufficient space to use an ordinary screw driver can often be manipulated with an offset screw driver. This tool is usually made from a piece of round or octagonal steel with two blades at right angles to one another at opposite ends. In a very cramped place it may be necessary to use both ends of the screw driver, alternately turning the screw a short distance with one end and then the other.

Screw Driver Bits

Large screws can be driven or withdrawn more easily with a screw driver bit and a brace than with a screw driver. The brace provides more leverage than a screw driver. A screw driver bit is a screw driver blade with a square shank at one end so that it will fit in the chuck on a brace. Bits are made in several widths from $\frac{3}{16}''$ to $\frac{3}{4}''$ to fit screws from No. 4 to No. 26 and larger. The bit should fit the slot of the screw snugly and should be of the same width as the head of the screw. It is important for the bit blade to be in good shape. A twisted blade or one with a rounded or beveled tip will climb out of the screw slot and damage the screw so that it cannot be turned. A screw driver bit is dressed and kept in good shape by filing or grinding in the same manner as the common screw driver.

Wood Screws and Machine Screws

Screws may be divided into two general groups; those designed for fastening wood and those made for metal. The former are called wood screws, the latter machine screws. A wood screw cuts its own thread into the material into which it is screwed. A machine screw does not cut its own thread. It must be provided with a threaded hole. Both hole and thread must fit the screw. A machine screw has no holding power unless a hole is first drilled and threaded for it.

The two most common wood screws are the flat head and round head, so-called because of the shape of their head. Wood screws are sized according to diameter and length. The length is indicated in inches or fractions thereof. The diameter is indicated by a number. The smallest diameter is No. 0 and the largest common size is No. 24. The most generally used sizes are Nos. 3 to 16.

Standards for screws have been established by co-operation between the manufacturers and the U. S. Bureau of Standards so that standard screws of all screw manufacturers are alike.

In addition to flat head and round head wood screws there are also oval head and fillister head screws. The length of a flat head wood screw is the over-all length, but the length of round and fillister head screws is measured from the point to the under side of the head. The length of an oval head screw is measured from the point to the edge of the head.

Lag Screws and Hanger Bolts

Lag screws have square heads like machine bolts and are driven in place or withdrawn with a wrench instead of a screw driver. They are used in heavy construction where great strength is required. They are also used to fasten machinery and heavy metal parts to beams, walls and wooden floors. A pilot hole should be drilled for a lag screw. When two pieces of timber are to be held together by lag screws, both a pilot hole and a clearance hole should be drilled as though ordinary wood screws were being used. A metal washer should be placed under the head of a lag screw so that the head will not cut its way into the wood when it is tightened.

Lag screws are sized according to diameter and length.

The common diameters are ¼″, $\frac{5}{16}$″, ⅜″, $\frac{7}{16}$″, ½″ and ⅝″. Common lengths range from 2″ to 6″ in half-inch steps and from 6″ to 12″ in one-inch steps. Lag screws are made in black iron, galvanized iron, forged bronze and Everdur bronze.

The head of a hanger bolt is a hexagonal nut which can readily be removed with a wrench. Hanger bolts are used for fastening machinery and other heavy metal pieces to a wooden foundation. If a lag screw is driven in and out of the same hole several times, it loses some of its holding power. In order to remove a machine fastened with hanger bolts, it is unnecessary to withdraw the whole bolt. Only the nut which forms the head is unscrewed. Thus a machine secured with hanger bolts may be removed and replaced innumerable times without the bolt losing any of its holding power. •

Table Showing Sizes of Holes to Bore for Wood Screws

	Size of Screw				
	No. 4	No. 5	No. 6	No. 7	No. 8
Diameter of Gimlet, Auger or Twist Bit to use for Clearance Hole	1/8″	1/8″	5/32″	5/32″	3/16″
Size Twist Drill to use for Clearance Hole	No. 34	No. 30	No. 28	No. 24	No. 19
Diameter of Gimlet, Auger or Twist Bit to use for Pilot Hole	1/16″	3/32″	3/32″	1/8″	1/8″

	Size of Screw			
	No. 9	No. 10	No. 11	No. 12
Diameter of Gimlet, Auger or Twist Bit to use for Clearance Hole	3/16″	3/16″	7/32″	7/32″
Size Twist Drill to use for Clearance Hole	No. 16	No. 11	No. 6	No. 2
Diameter of Gimlet, Auger or Twist Bit to use for Pilot Hole	1/8″	1/8″	5/32″	5/32″

14 12 10 9 8 7 6 5 4 3 2 1

The full-size sketches of wood screws, above, may be used to identify sizes varying from Nos. 1 to 14. The chart in the center of this page, covering sizes from 0 to 24, indicates the standard limits allowed.

At right are two types of wood screw designed to be driven with a wrench. They are used in heavy work, where great strength is required: for example, to fasten heavy machinery to wooden beams.

LAG SCREW

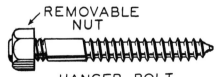

REMOVABLE NUT

HANGER BOLT

how to use
a hand saw

Sawing is not merely pushing a saw to and fro. To cut accurately, you have to use your eye and your head as well as your muscles.

1 Rip saw is used for cutting board lengthwise in direction of grain.

2 Crosscut saw is designed to cut across board, to saw across grain.

3 Mitre box saw, a type of back saw, is used in sawing joints and angles.

4 Back saw of small type is employed in cabinet making and fine joinery.

5 Dovetail saw, smallest back saw, for model making and dovetailing.

6 Keyhole saw cuts sharp curves and keyholes, starting from drilled hole.

7 Compass saw is larger version of a keyhole saw, cuts curves and holes.

8 Coping saw is used to cut patterns and intricate curves in thin boards.

PRACTICALLY everyone is familiar with the standard hand saw. Some men and boys will consider it as presumptuous to tell them how to saw as it would be to tell them how to walk or run. But whereas walking may consist of moving your legs back and forth, sawing is not merely pushing a saw to and fro.

Accurate sawing requires a knack which is acquired by knowledge and practice. When you have the knack it is easy to cut a piece off a 10- or 12-inch plank to accurate length and find upon checking it with a try square that the end is at 90 degrees with the top, bottom and sides.

The Right Saw for the Job

The wooden portion you grip in your hand when sawing is the handle. The toothed steel portion which extends from the handle and does the cutting is the blade.

To the skilled mechanic there is only one saw intended for each specific job. The stair builder and the boat builder use special saws in their work, which neither the carpenter nor ordinary woodworker needs. The correct tool always makes work easier. It saves time and energy and produces better results.

The grain of wood must be taken into consideration in all woodworking operations. All wood has grain. The same saw will not cut equally well across the grain and with the grain. Therefore there are two types of hand saws for wood. One, called a *rip* saw, is made to saw in the direction of the grain, which usually runs lengthwise in a piece of wood. The other, called a *crosscut* saw, is used for cutting across grain.

You can distinguish between a rip saw and a crosscut saw by examining the teeth. A rip saw usually has larger teeth than a crosscut saw of the same length. In both types the teeth are set alternately to the left and right so as to cut a kerf (the slot which the saw forms) which is wider than the thickness of the blade. The teeth on a rip saw are given less set than the teeth on a crosscut saw. If you look closely at them you will see that they are shaped like chisels. In fact, they cut exactly like a gang of small vertical chisels arranged in a row.

The teeth of a crosscut saw are sharpened at a bevel so that they are pointed like the end of a knife blade. This provides two lines of sharp points which cut across the wood fibers like knives. The teeth then force out the wood between the two cuts.

There are four common sizes of hand saws. The size is the length of the tooth edge measured in inches. The popular sizes are 24″ and 26″.

The coarseness or fineness of a saw depends upon the size of the teeth and is designated by the number of tooth points per inch. The saw having few teeth—5, 5½, 6 or 7 points to the inch—will cut fast but make a rough cut. Rip saws usually are in this category. The common hand crosscut saw can be obtained with either 8, 9, 10, 11 or 12 points per inch.

Green or wet wood can best be cut across grain with coarse teeth (6 or 7 points per inch) having a wide set. Dry, seasoned wood requires fine teeth (10 or 11 points per inch) having a narrow set. A fine-tooth saw is better for smooth, accurate cutting.

For general work, a 24″ or 26″ rip saw with 5½ or 6 points to the inch, and a 24″ or 26″ crosscut saw with 8 or 9 points to the inch, are most widely used.

Quality saws are taper ground so that the steel blade is thinner at the back than at the toothed edge. A tapered blade makes a saw easier to push back and forth in the kerf.

The Care of Saws

Moisture on the blade of a saw, unless the surface is well protected by a film of oil, produces rust almost immediately. Rust will pit and roughen the smooth sides of a saw blade. Both sides must be smooth in order for a saw to be in perfect working condition. At the first appearance of any rust spots on a saw blade, rub them off with fine emery cloth and apply a coat of light oil. Keep your saws in a dry place and hang them up when not in use. Especially in the summer, an unoiled saw blade will rust if it is not used constantly. When you lay a saw down, do so carefully. Do not drop it.

A dull saw makes hard work of sawing. A saw cuts with ease when properly sharpened and set. Keep it that way.

Sawing

Before a piece of wood can be sawed to accurate size or shape, it must be marked with a line which will serve as a guide for the saw cut. Rough work can be marked with a pencil. Use a try square as a guide for the pencil if the cut is to be made at right

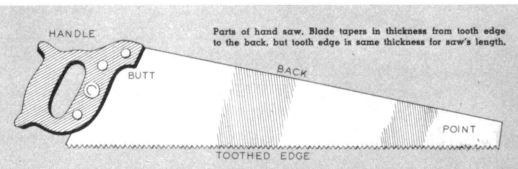

HANDLE

BUTT

BACK

POINT

TOOTHED EDGE

Parts of hand saw. Blade tapers in thickness from tooth edge to the back, but tooth edge is same thickness for saw's length.

angles and a sliding T-bevel if the cut is to be cut at an angle other than 90 degrees.

A pencil line is easy to see, but when drawn on wood it is too thick for close work. For accurate work or small work, the mark should be scored into the wood with a scratch awl. The point of a knife blade can also be used. A marking gauge is frequently used in laying out work for sawing, especially when making a mortise, a tenon or a rabbet.

In sawing, allowance must be made for the width of the saw cut or kerf. Do not saw directly on the marked line. Accurate sawing is always done on the waste side of the line. Sawing on the line or on the wrong side of the line makes the stock too short. If you leave too much wood, it can be planed or chiseled off. But if you leave too little, there is no "putting on tool" which will put the wood back in place.

How to Use a Crosscut Saw

Start the kerf by drawing the saw backward across an edge of the stock on the waste side of the line. Guide the blade carefully with the tip or the first joint of the left thumb, bearing in mind that if you are careless you may cut yourself. In crosscutting, a 45° angle between the saw and the work will give the best results. It may be necessary to draw the saw back several times before the kerf will be properly started. Continue to guide it with your thumb so that the kerf is started at the exact point where you wish the cut to begin. Draw the blade back slowly. A too rapid motion may cause the saw to jump.

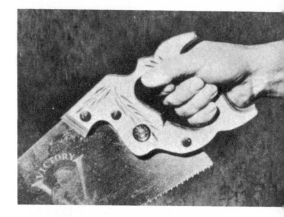

Here is a good grip for crosscut or rip saw. Some workers prefer to extend index finger to guide saw.

How to Use a Rip Saw

If the rip saw is a coarse one it will have a few fine teeth at the end farthest from the handle, which end, incidentally, is usually referred to as the point of the saw. The cut should be started with the fine teeth at the point of the saw by drawing them back several times in the manner already described for starting the crosscut saw. When ripping, an angle of 60 degrees between the blade and the work gives the best results. The teeth of either the crosscut or the rip saw will cut most efficiently only when the blade is held approximately at the angle suggested.

After a little practice, you'll almost automatically adjust the saw to the correct angle when you start to saw.

Reflections in polished blade can be used to ascertain its correct position. In sawing at right angle (line D, left), image B of wood's edge reflected on side of blade will appear continuous with the real edge AC. When sawing at 45° (along line D, right), image B of wood's edge reflected on blade will be perpendicular to the edge AC below.

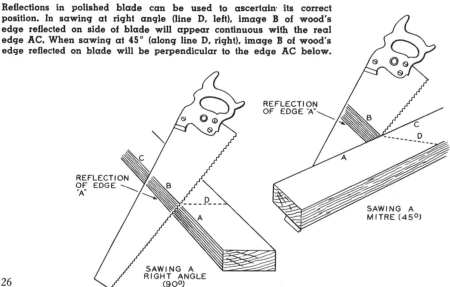

REFLECTION OF EDGE "A"

B

C

D

A

SAWING A RIGHT ANGLE (90°)

REFLECTION OF EDGE "A"

B

C

D

A

SAWING A MITRE (45°)

Hints for Sawing

The piece to be sawed must be held firmly in a vise, or on a workbench, a box or a pair of horses. Small work often can be held firmly on a bench or table by the pressure of the left hand. A bench hook for this purpose is a great convenience. Pieces of considerable length are best supported on a pair of saw horses, or on two boxes or two chairs, and held firmly by one knee.

As a saw progresses across the grain of a board, the weight of the board tends to close the cut and bind the saw so that you can no longer push the blade back and forth. If the waste end is a short, light piece you can hold it up with your left hand while sawing and prevent the slot from closing on the blade. You will need an assistant to hold a long or heavy piece. Moreover, if you do not support the waste end properly, it will break off just as you are finishing the cut and take a large splinter from the corner of the other piece with it. The splinter can be glued back in place but it is preferable to avoid such poor workmanship.

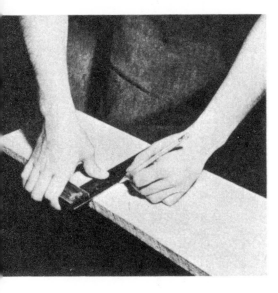

To do accurate sawing, first draw guide line with try square to help get a straight and square cut.

Start cut. Draw saw back a few times across edge of stock on waste side of line. Use thumb as guide.

Use slow, easy stroke at first, remembering that saw cuts only on down stroke. Keep fingers clear.

Develop accuracy. Check saw position often with try square till you can saw straight without it.

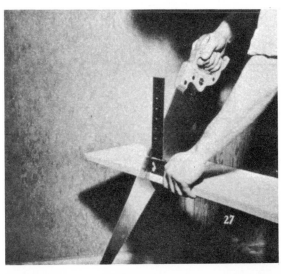

27

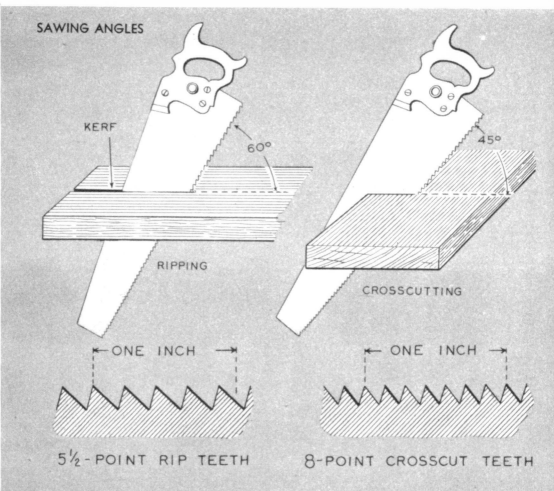

SAWING ANGLES

KERF

60°

RIPPING

45°

CROSSCUTTING

←— ONE INCH —→

←— ONE INCH —→

5½-POINT RIP TEETH

8-POINT CROSSCUT TEETH

At the top are shown the correct angles for rip and crosscut sawing. For average rip saw work, a 5½-point saw is satisfactory. For ordinary crosscut sawing, an 8-point crosscut saw is good.

The proper position for sawing permits long easy strokes using nearly the full length of the blade. Take your time, and be careful not to jerk the saw back and forth. It is difficult to keep the kerf beside the marked line where it belongs if much of the cutting is done with only a few inches of the blade.

Watch your grip on the handle closely when you are learning to saw. It should be firm but not tight. The saw should run freely. A tight grip prevents the free running of the saw and tends to swerve the blade away from the line. The thumb should be against the left side of the handle. Keep the index finger extended along the right side of the handle to help guide the blade. If the blade starts to cut into the marked line or to move too far away from it, twist the handle slightly in order to draw it back to the correct position for even sawing.

To keep the saw at right angles to the surface of the work is the most difficult thing to learn in sawing. The beginner should make an occasional test with a try square to keep the saw in a perfectly vertical position and to help develop the knack of sawing square. Check the position of the blade with the try square from time to time until the tests show that you can get along without it. That stage in your skill will not be reached the first few times that you use a saw. It will come only with careful practice. Accurate sawing is done with long, easy, relaxed strokes, guided by the hand and eye, and is mastered only with considerable practice.

All the cutting action of the teeth on a hand saw takes place on the forward or pushing stroke of the saw blade. Do not try to make the teeth cut on the backward or pulling stroke. Exert a little downward pressure of the wrist on the forward stroke and do not apply any pressure on the return stroke. Do not try to guide the blade on the return stroke. Relax and lift it more than pull it. If the tip of the blade vibrates when the blade is brought back on the return stroke, you are not allowing the saw to run freely but are bending or twisting it slightly.

Look carefully for nails in the path of the saw when second hand lumber is used or repair work is done. A hand saw will not cut nails. If it is drawn or pushed over a nail, the sharp points and edges will be knocked off the teeth.

Back Saws for Fine Accurate Work

A back saw is a thin-bladed crosscut saw with fine teeth, stiffened by a thick steel rib on the back edge. A dovetail saw is a small edition of a back saw. Both tools are used for cutting light stock, moldings and picture frames and for dovetailing, tenoning, pattern making, fine joinery, cabinet work and model making.

Back saws range in size from a blade length of 8″ with 16 points to the inch to a blade of 16″ with 12 points to the inch. A popular size for fairly smooth accurate cutting of light stock, making mitres, tenons, etc., is the 12″ with 14 points per inch, a compromise of the two extremes.

Dovetail saws range in length from 6″ to 12″ and have 17 points per inch.

Mitre Box Saws

Mitre box saws are long back saws (20″ to 28″) made for use with a mitre box.

The simplest form of mitre box is made of three pieces of wood fastened together so as to form a trough, open at the top and both ends. It has several vertical saw slots in the sides which act as guides for the saw blade and hold it at the proper angle to make either a square or 45-degree cut. A 12″ or 14″ back saw can be used with the average, small homemade mitre box. The long mitre box saws are made for use with the more elaborate adjustable factory-made mitre boxes.

To saw off a piece of wood square or at an angle of 45 degrees in a wooden mitre box, put the work in the box in position so that the cut to be made lines up with the proper slots in the box. Hold the work firmly

CROSSCUT TEETH

Examine the teeth of your crosscut saw. The teeth are sharpened at a bevel, pointed like the end of a knife blade to make cuts.

RIP TEETH

Now look at the teeth of your rip saw. Note they have less set than crosscut saw and that they are a series of small chisels.

CROSSCUT

1ST   2ND   3RD   4TH

Teeth of crosscut saw cut across fibers like two rows of knives. Teeth then force out wood between two cuts, clearing way for next cut.

RIP

1ST TOOTH   2ND   3RD   4TH

When cut is made with rip saw, then alternately-set teeth chisel small bits of wood from first one side of the cut then the other.

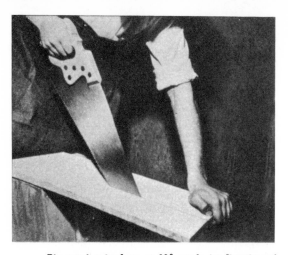

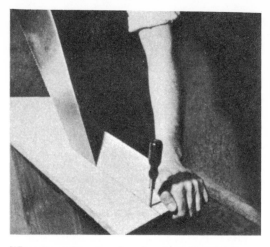

Rip sawing is done at 60° angle in direction of grain which usually runs lengthwise in the board.

When rip sawing a long board, a screw driver blade placed in cut prevents pinching of the saw blade.

against the bottom and the back of the box as pictured in the drawing. Start the cut slowly and carefully, using the back stroke and holding the handle of the saw upward until the kerf is established. Then begin sawing, gradually lower the handle until the blade is horizontal and finish the cut with it in that position.

When a back saw is used without a mitre box, it's best to hold the work in a vise.

Practice for Back Saw Skill

Pattern makers and cabinet makers use back saws with great skill for light or fine work and for fitting and dovetailing. Their tool kits usually contain at least two back saws, one filed for crosscutting, and the other filed for ripsawing or cutting with the grain of the wood.

The woodworking beginner who will carefully practice with a back saw can learn to use this tool with skill in a few hours.

The guide line for sawing with a back saw is always scored with a knife. A pencil line is not fine enough for the accurate work which can be done with a back saw.

Good exercise for practicing with a back saw is to cut thin sections from the end of a block of wood. Take a block of white pine about 1¾" square and from 12" to 16" long. Lay it out by scoring lines with a try square and a sharp-pointed pocketknife on the front upper and back surfaces. The lines should be about ¼" apart and cut at least $\frac{1}{32}$" deep. These lines are the guide lines for cutting the sections. The thumb of the left hand is used as a guide for the saw in starting the saw cut on the far edge of the stock. In starting the saw cut the handle of the

ACQUIRE SKILL WITH A BACK SAW

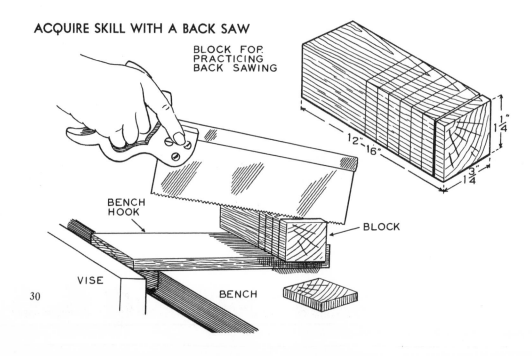

BLOCK FOR PRACTICING BACK SAWING

BENCH HOOK

BENCH

VISE

BLOCK

12"–16"

1¼"

¾"

BLOCK

saw is raised slightly. As the cut progresses, the saw is lowered gradually to a horizontal position. The saw cut through the block should be true to each of the three lines and the kerf should be close to but just a hair outside the knife line. If the sawing is done accurately, the saw teeth should not scratch any of the knife cuts but at the same time should be so close that there is no wood left projecting beyond the knife cut which must be smoothed down with plane or chisel.

A simple trick which will aid in getting a back saw started so as to make a straight and accurate cut is to cut a triangular groove on the waste side of the scored line. The groove can be made with either a pocketknife or chisel.

Compass and Keyhole Saws

The narrow tapered blade of a compass saw is used for cutting curves or cutting holes started from a hole bored in the work. This tool comes with a fixed blade or with a removable blade which can be used in

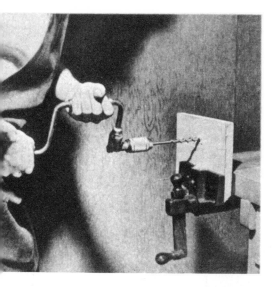

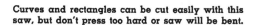

To cut a hole with a compass or keyhole saw, first drill a hole large enough to admit the saw point.

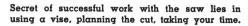

Start cutting from the side of the hole, slowly and accurately. Always stay inside the guide line.

Curves and rectangles can be cut easily with this saw, but don't press too hard or saw will be bent.

Secret of successful work with the saw lies in using a vise, planning the cut, taking your time.

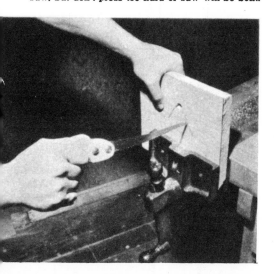

reverse position for undercutting. The teeth have considerable set so that they cut almost equally well with or across the grain. The blade length varies from 10″ to 16″. The teeth usually have 8 or 9 points to the inch.

A keyhole saw is like a compass saw but smaller. Usually it has a straight handle. Its 10″ or 12″ removable blade with 10 teeth to the inch is made very narrow for small work in close quarters, such as cutting keyholes, sharp curves, fret work, etc.

When dismantling old woodwork for repairs or alterations, a compass saw or keyhole saw sometimes is used to start a kerf which is enlarged until a hand saw can be

Back saw and a mitre box are almost indispensable when fine or accurate 45° angle sawing is required.

Start work with coping saw in same way as for a compass saw. Mark guide line, then drill hole.

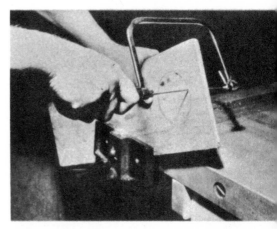

Fine coping saw blade is "threaded" through hole and then fastened in the saw frame under tension.

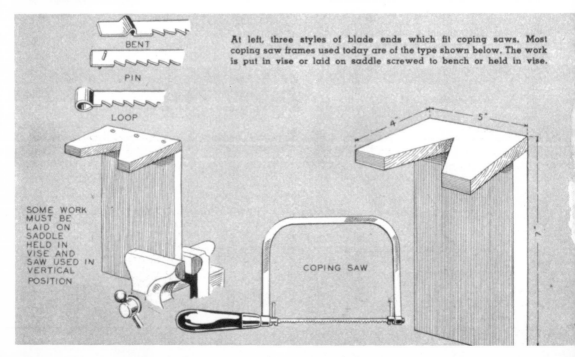

BENT

PIN

LOOP

At left, three styles of blade ends which fit coping saws. Most coping saw frames used today are of the type shown below. The work is put in vise or laid on saddle screwed to bench or held in vise.

SOME WORK MUST BE LAID ON SADDLE HELD IN VISE AND SAW USED IN VERTICAL POSITION

COPING SAW

4″

5″

inserted. First, a hole is bored with an auger bit; then a compass or keyhole saw is inserted in the hole and the kerf started. When the cut is long enough, a regular hand saw is brought into use.

To cut a keyhole in a door or drawer, first mark the outline of the hole in the desired position. Bore a hole through the door or drawer large enough to pass the blade of the keyhole saw. Then cut along the marked line with the saw.

Coping Saws

A coping saw takes narrow blades ⅛″ wide which are held in a frame similar to that of a hacksaw and which may be replaced quickly when dull. A coping saw is used to cut curves and intricate patterns in thin wood. Carpenters sometimes use this tool for shaping or "returning" the ends of molding.

It is customary to place the blades in the frame with the teeth pointing toward the handle so that they cut when the handle is pulled and not when it is pushed. This is the opposite of an ordinary saw and is the way Chinese and Japanese hand saws work. The arrangement gives better control of the small blade.

There are two types of coping saws. One has a frame made of heavy wire and takes blades having a loop at each end which fits into a slot in the frame. The blades are pulled out straight and held under tension by the spring of the frame. The other type of coping saw has a rigid frame and the blade is kept under tension by a threaded stretcher which is adjusted by turning the handle. The blade is fitted at its ends with pins which slip into slots in the stretcher at each end of the frame. If the blade is strained tight in the frame, it may be turned to prevent snapping when making sharp turns while sawing.

A coping saw is usually worked up and down so that the blade moves vertically. The work is supported on a saddle which is held in a vise or screwed to a workbench. It consists of two pieces of board fastened together so as to form an L. The short board is cut with a V shaped notch about 3 or 4 inches wide and the same depth. The work to be sawed is marked with the design to be followed by the saw and held on the saddle so that the saw blade can work up and down in the notch. Since the cutting is done on the down stroke, the work is not lifted from the saddle by the motion of the blade. The work is turned and shifted from time to time to keep the saw blade in the V notch and to accommodate the curves as they are encountered. •

Never lay or throw saws on floor or against other tools for teeth may be dulled or bent out of line.

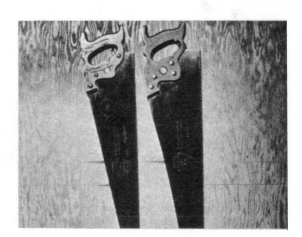

A good workman hangs his saws up on the workshop wall after using them. Nails serve for hooks.

Blade sides must be smooth. Rust quickly roughens and pits blade. Rub light oil on it occasionally.

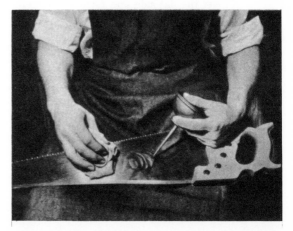

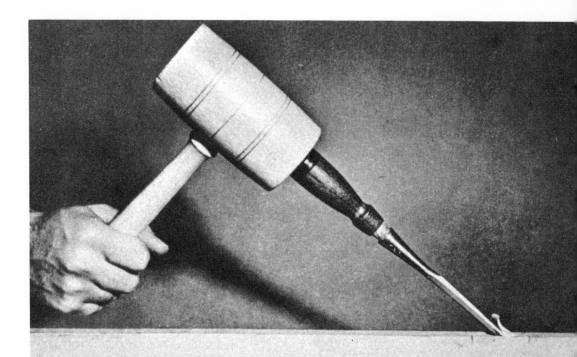

how to use wood chisels

Here are some interesting facts about the

chisel, a highly versatile woodworking tool.

THERE are chisels for cutting wood and chisels for cutting metal. Chisels for cutting metals are called cold chisels. Woodworking chisels cannot be used to cut metal and cold chisels are of no value as woodcutting tools.

The chisel is one of the most important and most used woodworking tools. It is indispensable in the construction of most wood joints made by hand. The modern woodworker's chisel is a tapered steel blade forged from special chisel steel and heat-treated to hold a keen cutting edge. One side of the blade is flat; the other is beveled to meet the flat side and form an efficient, sharp cutting edge.

Chisels are used so frequently in hand woodworking that only the best quality should be purchased.

Take good care of your chisels. You'll keep chisels sharp longer if you hang them up in a rack when the job's done.

Although chisels for woodworking are made in many sizes and shapes to suit the work they are to perform, they may be divided into three general classes, known as tang, socket and everlasting chisels.

Tang Chisels

The blade of a tang chisel is tapered to a projecting shank called a tang and forced into a wood handle or inserted in a molded plastic handle. The handle is reinforced against splitting by a metal ferrule and may have a leather tip. Tang chisels are designed for carving, paring and other light work. They are not built to withstand the blows of a heavy mallet or a steel hammer. They may be driven with a light wooden or composition mallet without danger of splitting the handle, but primarily they are intended only for work in which they are driven by the pressure of the hand.

Socket Chisels

One end of the steel blade of a socket chisel is formed into a funnel-shaped socket that fits over the tapered end of a wood or composition handle. Socket chisels are of heavier construction than tang chisels. The blade is thicker. They can be driven with a heavy mallet. If the handles wear out, new handles can be easily fitted on.

34

Everlasting Chisels

Many carpenters and woodworkers who work away from a bench and must carry their tools to the job save space and weight in their tool kits by omitting a mallet. They use a nail hammer to drive chisels. It takes a great deal of force to cut vertically into such woods as yellow pine and oak. Driving a tang or socket chisel with a hammer will eventually spoil the handle.

An everlasting chisel is made so that it may be driven with a steel hammer. The head of the handle where the hammer strikes, the shank, ferrule and blade are all one piece of steel so that a blow struck on the head is transmitted directly to the cutting edge of the blade.

Other Chisels

Differences in the length and thickness of the blade give chisels special qualities which make one better adapted to certain work than another. Consequently there are several varieties of chisels known as paring, butt, firmer, framing, pocket and mortise chisels whose differences lie in the proportions of their blades. Any variety of chisel may have either straight edges or beveled edges, depending on the type of design.

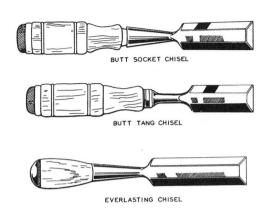

BUTT SOCKET CHISEL

BUTT TANG CHISEL

EVERLASTING CHISEL

Socket and Everlasting are driven with mallet or hammer. Use hand pressure only with Tang chisels.

Glazier's chisel, 2 inches wide, is used for cleaning out old putty and for loosening window sashes.

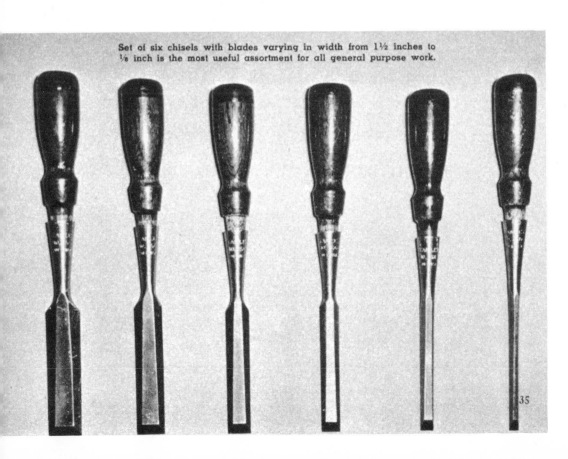

Set of six chisels with blades varying in width from 1½ inches to ⅛ inch is the most useful assortment for all general purpose work.

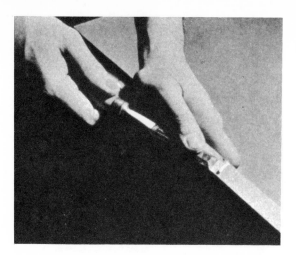

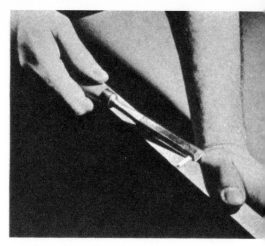

Correct way to use a chisel. Note fingers are kept back of cutting edge. Secure work so it can't move.

It's easy to cut yourself accidentally with the chisel. Use proper technique and prevent accidents.

The Beveled-edge Chisel

The beveled-edge chisel is the preferred one. It is lighter and will reach into angles and under projections which are difficult to reach with a square-edged tool.

The Paring Chisel

The blade of a paring chisel is lighter and thinner than the blade of other chisels. It is used mainly for hand chiseling or paring.

The Firmer Chisel

The firmer chisel has a long, strong blade which makes it adaptable for both heavy and light work. There should be one of these all-around chisels in your shop.

The Butt Chisel

The butt chisel is different from other chisels only in that it has a shorter blade (usually 2½" to 3" long when new) and consequently can be used in places inaccessible to a longer blade.

The Mortise Chisel

The mortise chisel is used for chiseling mortises and consequently must be driven with a hammer or mallet. In chiseling a mortise the blade is used not only for cutting but also as a lever to force the chips out. Since it receives hard use the blade of a mortise chisel is made thick and strong just below the handle.

If a mortise is first bored so that most of the wood is removed with an auger, it may be cleaned out and squared up with an ordinary firmer chisel. In that case a special mortise chisel is unnecessary.

Experience will soon teach the workman the most convenient size of chisel to use on a particular job. The chisel should always be smaller than the job. For example, in chiseling a recess 1" wide in a piece of wood, the chisel used should not be 1" wide; a ⅜" or ½" chisel is the proper tool. The reason is that in general a chisel should not be pushed straight forward but moved laterally at the same time that it is pushed forward.

Chisel Sizes

All varieties of chisels are made with blades varying from ⅛" to 1" in steps of ⅛" and from 1" to 2" in steps of ¼". For most purposes the ¼", ½", ¾" and 1" widths suffice. A collection of nine or ten chisels which includes two or three paring chisels and six or seven firmer chisels is all that most professional woodworkers need and should satisfy the most particular amateur craftsman. Blade widths from ⅛" to 1½" are the most useful for general woodworking purposes.

Glazier's Chisel

The carpenter or glazier uses the glazier's chisel for loosening window sashes that stick, cleaning out old putty and smoothing sash for glass. The blade is usually about 3¼" to 3½" long and 1¾" to 2" wide. The sides of the blade are not beveled. It is better to have a chisel especially for this work if only to avoid spoiling the keen edge or breaking the blade of a regular paring or butt chisel.

How To Use a Chisel

You do not gain time by making haste with a chisel. There is always danger of unintentionally splitting the work if you take too large a cut. Whenever possible, other tools such as saws, planes and augers should be used to remove as much of the waste wood as possible and the chisel employed for finishing purposes only. This saves time and effort.

On rough work, the power which drives a chisel is usually the blow of a hammer or mallet. On fine work the driving power is applied entirely with the right hand. Most of the control is exercised by the left hand.

It is probably easier to cut yourself accidentally with a chisel than with any other tool, and the cut of a chisel can be wicked. The best safeguard against injury is to *hold the tool properly. Keep both hands back of the cutting edge at all times.*

A safety precaution which will not only help to protect the mechanic but also make the work easier is *always secure the work* which is to be chiseled so that it *cannot move in any way.*

When starting a cut with a chisel always cut away from the guide line and toward the waste wood so that any splitting which takes place will occur in the waste and not in the finished work. Do not start *on* the guide line. Start slightly away from it, so that there is a small amount of material to be removed by the finishing cuts. Never cut toward yourself with a chisel.

Make the shavings thin, especially when finishing. Examine the grain of the wood to see which way it runs. Cut with the grain. This severs the fibers and leaves the wood smooth. Cutting against the grain splits the fibers and leaves the wood rough. Such a cut cannot be controlled.

Chiseling may be done by cutting either horizontally or vertically. Vertical chiseling cuts are usually made across grain.

Paring

If the cutting edge of a sharp chisel is examined under a magnifying glass, it will appear saw-toothed. If the chisel is slanted slightly in the direction of the cut, the minute teeth will cut more easily and smoothly. This gives a shearing cut which should be used whenever possible, both with the grain and on end grain. Cutting *fine* shavings with a shearing cut is called *paring,* in the parlance of the workshop.

To Cut Horizontally with the Grain

The chisel handle is grasped in the right hand with the thumb extended toward the blade. The cut is controlled by holding the blade firmly with the left hand, knuckles up and the hand well back of the cutting edge. The right hand is used to force the chisel into the wood and push it away from the work. The left hand pressing downward on the chisel blade regulates the length and depth of the cut. For a roughing cut hold the chisel with the bevel down. To make a finishing cut, work with the bevel up for best results.

As already explained the chisel cuts more easily and leaves a smoother surface when the cutting edge is held at a slight diagonal to the direction of the cut or is given a slight sliding motion. This can be done by holding the tool so that it is turned a bit to one side as it is pushed forward or by moving it slightly from left to right at the same time that it is advanced.

The cutting edge of a chisel tends to follow the direction of the wood fibers. The cut cannot be controlled in chiseling against the grain. There is danger of splitting and damaging the work. Consequently a chisel cut should *always* be made with the grain. With cross-grained wood it is necessary to work from both directions so as to cut only with the grain.

Remember, chiseling should not be hurried and only fine shavings should be cut. If thick shavings are cut the tool may

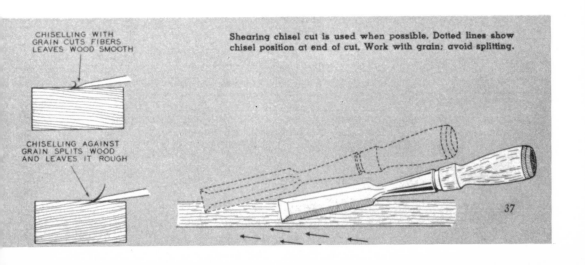

CHISELLING WITH GRAIN CUTS FIBERS LEAVES WOOD SMOOTH

CHISELLING AGAINST GRAIN SPLITS WOOD AND LEAVES IT ROUGH

Shearing chisel cut is used when possible. Dotted lines show chisel position at end of cut. Work with grain; avoid splitting.

37

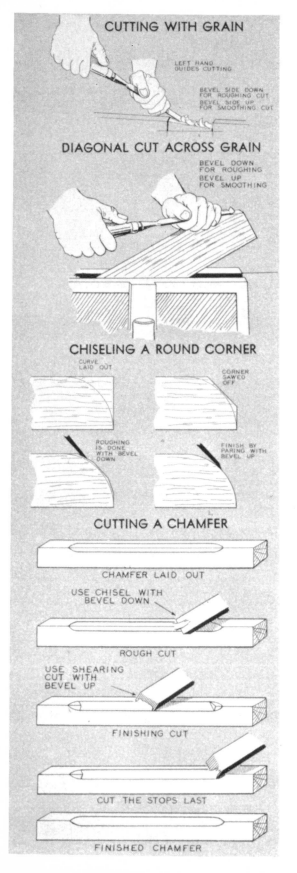

CUTTING WITH GRAIN

LEFT HAND GUIDES CUTTING

BEVEL SIDE DOWN FOR ROUGHING CUT
BEVEL SIDE UP FOR SMOOTHING CUT

DIAGONAL CUT ACROSS GRAIN

BEVEL DOWN FOR ROUGHING
BEVEL UP FOR SMOOTHING

CHISELING A ROUND CORNER

CURVE LAID OUT

CORNER SAWED OFF

ROUGHING IS DONE WITH BEVEL DOWN

FINISH BY PARING WITH BEVEL UP

CUTTING A CHAMFER

CHAMFER LAID OUT

USE CHISEL WITH BEVEL DOWN

ROUGH CUT

USE SHEARING CUT WITH BEVEL UP

FINISHING CUT

CUT THE STOPS LAST

FINISHED CHAMFER

dig in and split off a piece of wood which was never intended to be cut.

Chamfering with a Chisel

A chamfer is made by flattening the sharp corner between two surfaces which are at right angles to each other. A plain chamfer runs the full length of the edge and is usually made with a plane. A stopped chamfer does not run the full length of the edge. If a stopped chamfer is long enough, part of it can be planed and the ends finished with a chisel. A short stopped chamfer must be made entirely with a chisel. This assures accuracy.

A chamfer is usually made at 45 degrees. Guide lines which mark its edges should be made with a pencil. In the case of a 45 degree chamfer the guide lines will be the same distance back from the edges on both surfaces of the wood.

A marking gauge, scratch awl or penknife should not be used to make the guide lines for a chamfer because they produce marks in the wood which are difficult to remove.

To cut a stopped chamfer hold the chisel with the edge parallel to the slope of the chamfer and cut with the grain as in ordinary horizontal paring. Begin chiseling at the ends and work toward the center. The ends of the chamfer may be either flat or curved. If flat, use the chisel with the bevel up. If curved, you must always work with the bevel down.

Unless the grain of the wood is quite straight, there is some danger of splitting off too much wood if a roughing cut is used. Rather than risk spoiling the work, it is better for the novice to use light smoothing entirely, holding the chisel diagonally, even if this does take more time to remove the surplus stock. The experienced mechanic can often safely remove most of the surplus wood from the chamfer with roughing cuts and then finish with a number of light, smoothing cuts.

To Cut Diagonally Across the Grain

To cut a straight slanting corner, as shown in the illustration, as much waste wood as possible is first removed with a saw. The work is then clamped in a bench vise with the guide line horizontal and the chisel used in the same manner as in horizontal chiseling with the grain. Here again it is necessary to chisel with the grain and to hold the chisel so that the cutting edge is a bit diagonal to direction of the cut.

To Chisel a Round Corner

To cut a round corner on the end of a piece of wood, first lay out the work, then remove as much of the waste as possible with a saw. Use a chisel with the bevel down to make a series of straight cuts tangent to the curve. In making these cuts the chisel is moved sideways across the work at the same time that it is moved forward. The curve is finished by paring with the beveled side of the chisel up.

Convex curves are chiseled in the same manner as a round corner.

To Cut Horizontally Across Grain

To make any of the lap joints in woodworking, the wood between the saw cuts is removed with a chisel. This calls for cutting horizontally across the grain of the wood. The work should be held in a vise. Most of the waste wood is removed by the chisel with the bevel held down.

On light work the pressure of the hand or light blows on the end of the chisel handle with the palm of the right hand will provide sufficient driving force. On heavier work a mallet must be used. To avoid splitting at the edges, cut from each edge to the center and slightly upward so that the waste stock at the center is removed last.

The finishing cuts are made with the flat side of the chisel down. A mallet should not be used in making the finishing cuts, even on large work. The pressure of the right hand is all that is required to drive the chisel which is guided by the thumb and forefinger of the left hand. The thumb and forefinger act as a brace and also give the chisel a sideways paring motion as it is pushed forward.

The finishing cuts should also be made from each edge toward the center. Do not cut all the way across from one edge or the far edge may be split off.

Chiseling Practice

As an exercise for gaining skill in the free use of chisels there is nothing better than making a few lap joints. The simple half-lap or middle-lap joint is a good starting point for the beginner.

White pine is the best material to use in the beginning. When a perfect joint can be made in white pine, the novice should test his workmanship on other woods with coarser grain.

The first operation is to cut a groove on the waste side of the knife cuts which are the guide lines for the shoulders of the joint. The grooves should be cut with the beveled side of the chisel up. The shoulders of the joint are cut down almost to the horizontal guide line with a back saw. The saw is started in the grooves which help produce a straight cut.

A few extra saw cuts made between the shoulder cuts and without the aid of starting grooves will make the chiseling out of the waste stock easier and prevent material from splitting off below the horizontal or depth guide line. The waste material is cut away with the chisel held bevel down. Work from both sides to avoid splitting wood off at the edges. Take only light cuts.

The joints are finished by paring with a very sharp chisel held bevel up and with the flat side of the chisel in contact with the wood. Only very light cuts are taken. When both parts of the joint are pared down to the guide line they are fitted together and checked. Any irregularities or high spots are removed with the chisel. The two parts should fit together firmly and snugly. It should not be necessary to force them together.

The beginner should continue to make these joints until he can do so accurately and easily. Then some dovetail joints should be attempted. The mechanic who can make good dovetail joints is no longer a novice with the chisel.

Vertical Chiseling

Vertical chiseling means cutting at right angles to the surface of the wood. Usually it involves cutting across the wood fibers as in chiseling out the ends of a mortise or making a gain or stopped dado joint.

When vertically chiseling across grain a mallet may be used to drive the chisel. If the wood is maple or other hardwood, a mallet is necessary. But if the edge is with the grain, to drive the chisel with a mallet is to risk splitting the wood.

A shearing cut is the only one that will probably make much progress in cutting across grain. The chisel should be brought from a position slightly to one side of vertical to vertical as it is driven down, or, the cutting edge should be slid to one side as it is pressed down. Either method will produce a shearing cut.

To Cut a Concave Curve

In cutting a concave curve, it may be possible to conserve time and effort by removing most of the waste wood with a

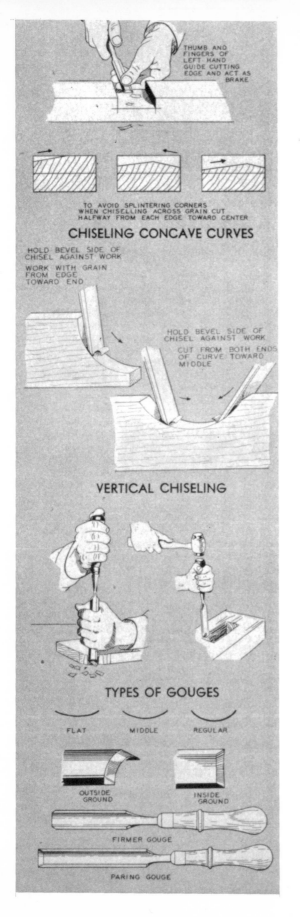

THUMB AND FINGERS OF LEFT HAND GUIDE CUTTING EDGE AND ACT AS BRAKE

TO AVOID SPLINTERING CORNERS WHEN CHISELLING ACROSS GRAIN CUT HALFWAY FROM EACH EDGE TOWARD CENTER

CHISELING CONCAVE CURVES

HOLD BEVEL SIDE OF CHISEL AGAINST WORK
WORK WITH GRAIN FROM EDGE TOWARD END

HOLD BEVEL SIDE OF CHISEL AGAINST WORK
CUT FROM BOTH ENDS OF CURVE TOWARD MIDDLE

VERTICAL CHISELING

TYPES OF GOUGES

FLAT   MIDDLE   REGULAR

OUTSIDE GROUND   INSIDE GROUND

FIRMER GOUGE

PARING GOUGE

coping saw or a compass saw. Smooth and finish the curve by chiseling. The chiseling must be with the grain. The left hand is used to hold the bevel side of the chisel against the work. The right hand should press down on the chisel and at the same time draw back on the handle to drive the cutting edge in a sweeping curve. It is difficult to control the depth in this sort of cut. Care must be used to take only light cuts or the work may be damaged.

To Cut Vertically Across Grain

The work should be clamped or otherwise secured so that it cannot move under the pressure of chiseling. If care is used, much of the waste wood can be removed by driving the chisel with a mallet. Vertical chiseling which can be carried to the workbench should be done with a cutting board or bench hook between the work and the bench, never directly on the bench top. Then the cutting edge of the chisel will not mar the bench at the end of its stroke.

A shearing cut should be used in cutting vertically across the grain. Always cut with the grain so that the waste wood will split *away* from the guide marks. If part of the chisel is kept pressed against the portion just cut, it will guide that part of the chisel cutting a new portion of the surface.

Vertical Chiseling on End Wood

Use a bench hook or cutting board under the work. Remove as much waste wood as possible with a saw. Observe the direction of the grain and start to cut at an edge to avoid splitting the wood. Use a shearing cut and make the shavings thin.

Thin shavings can be made without the aid of a mallet. Grasp the handle of the chisel in the right hand with the thumb pressing down on the top of the handle. Use the left hand to guide the tool, and to supply some of the driving force if much pressure is required to do the job.

Gouges

A gouge is a chisel with a concave blade which gives it a curved cutting edge. Firmer gouges are ground with the bevel either on the outside or the inside. Paring gouges are ground with the bevel on the inside only. The curve of a paring gouge is flatter than the curve of a firmer gouge and may be had in three styles, called the flat sweep, medium sweep and regular sweep in widths from ⅛″ to 2″.

Gouges are used for cutting hollows and grooves, shaping core boxes (used in foundry work) and paring the ends of irregular surfaces which must be matched together. A gouge with an inside bevel is handled in the same way as a chisel with the bevel up. A gouge with an outside bevel is used in the same manner as a chisel with the bevel down.

A gouge is always started at the edge of a cut and driven toward the center. In gouging out a large hollow, the depth of each cut can be kept under better control if the cutting is done across grain.

A bent-shank gouge is used to cut a long groove. The bent shank raises the handle clear of the work. This gouge can be used at a very low angle to the work surface and allow room for the fingers under the handle.

Woodcarving

Woodcarving is one of the great arts. Men devote a lifetime to it and it is too large a subject to more than mention in this book.

When roughing out large work the woodcarver sometimes uses the chisels and gouges, etc. of the carpenter but for the actual carving, he has special tools called carving tools. These are chisels and gouges which differ from the ordinary in that the blades taper toward the tang instead of having parallel sides and surfaces. The taper gives them clearance back of the cutting edge.

There are many different sizes and shapes of carving tools. The cutting edge of the chisels may be either square or oblique with the blade and the blade may be straight or bent. The carving gouges are made with eleven different sweeps or curves. The V-shaped carving gouges are called parting tools and the narrow, deep, U-shaped gouges are known as veiners. The larger deep gouges are fluters and those with a flat curve are called flats.

The handle of small carving tools is ball shaped and made to fit in the palm of the hand. The blade is grasped between the thumb and forefinger.

The average craftsman desiring to carve small models or simple designs in low relief needs only a small assortment of carving tools. A keen razorlike edge should be maintained on all carving tools by frequently honing them on an oil slip stone. It is necessary to observe the grain of the work and to cut insofar as is possible only with the grain.

When carving a design such as a low relief, the design is outlined on the wood with pencil. The first cutting is done with a parting tool or a small gouge by making a shallow cut along the background side of the outline of the design. The background is then cut down with a flat gouge and whatever other tools may be necessary to conform to the design. The surface of the design is modeled and shaped with whatever tools are necessary in order to follow the form. A little experience will soon give the novice judgment in selecting the proper tools to use in the various stages of the carving. There are many helpful books devoted wholly to woodcarving. •

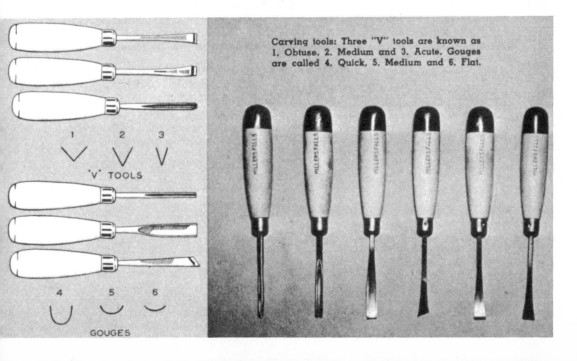

Carving tools: Three "V" tools are known as 1. Obtuse. 2. Medium and 3. Acute. Gouges are called 4. Quick, 5. Medium and 6. Flat.

1   2   3

"V" TOOLS

4   5   6

GOUGES

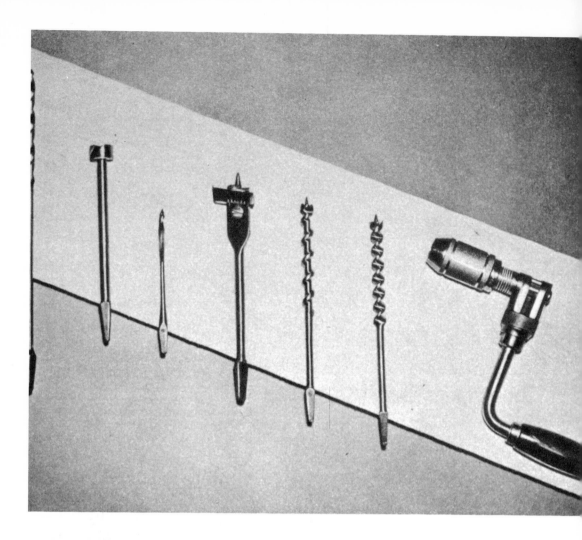

drilling holes in wood

You can consider yourself a craftsman when you have learned how to drill holes smoothly in wood.

W HEN a hole is to be drilled in wood, the size, location and purpose of the hole determine whether an auger bit, expansion bit, Forstner bit, fluted drill, gimlet or a twist drill should be used.

Auger Bits

The common auger bits are sized by $\frac{1}{16}''$ and are made in sizes to bore holes $\frac{1}{4}''$, $\frac{5}{16}''$, $\frac{3}{8}''$, $\frac{7}{16}''$, $\frac{1}{2}''$, $\frac{9}{16}''$, $\frac{5}{8}''$, $\frac{11}{16}''$, $\frac{3}{4}''$, $\frac{13}{16}''$, $\frac{7}{8}''$, $\frac{15}{16}''$ and $1''$ in diameter. Holes which are smaller than $\frac{1}{4}''$ in diameter are bored with a twist drill or double fluted drill.

Small holes are also made with gimlet bits and bradawls. Small holes are bored mainly for wood screws.

Although auger bits are made up to $2''$ diameter, sizes larger than $1''$ diameter are not common. Holes larger than $1''$ diameter are therefore generally bored with an extension bit or a Forstner bit.

The size of an auger in fractions of an inch is usually stamped on the shank, or a number is used which indicates the diameter of the hole that the auger will bore, in 16ths of an inch. For example, a No. 4 auger will bore a hole 4/16″ in

Bit brace is the basic tool for drilling holes in wood. Hold the brace with the palm and fingers in the left hand and turn it slowly with right hand.

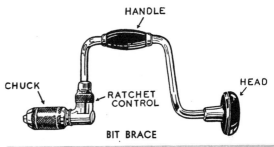

diameter, or, in other words, ¼". A $\frac{5}{16}$" auger is marked 5; a ½" auger is marked 8, and so on.

Differences in Augers

The cutting parts of an auger are the *screw*, the *spurs* or *nibs* and the *lips*.

The screw centers the bit and draws it into the wood. The screws have different pitches. They are made *fast*, *medium* and *slow*. The fast pitch cuts fast and has a coarse thread. The slow pitch cuts slowly and has a fine thread. An auger bit with a screw having a medium pitch is most serviceable for all around work. Fast and medium screws work best in boring end wood or resinous wood because they do not clog up as easily as a fine-threaded screw. An auger bit with a slow thread bores the smoothest hole.

The spurs or nibs on the auger score the circumference of the hole and the lips cut the shavings. The twist or thread of the bit lifts the shavings out of the hole; it is a conveyor. Three types of auger bits whose differences lie in their threads will be found

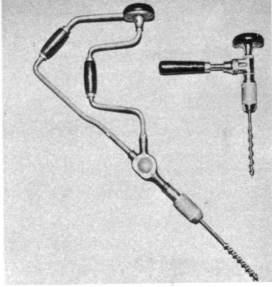

Use the corner brace, left, or short brace where it's impossible to drill with regular brace. With these, you can drill near perpendicular surfaces.

in general use in woodworking shops. They are called *single twist*, *double twist* and *straight core* or *solid-center* auger bits. The boring actions are similar.

The single twist and straight core bore faster and clear themselves of chips more rapidly than the double twist type. They also bore *hard* and *gummy* woods better. They are the auger bits most generally used in the home workshop.

The double twist auger bit bores more slowly than one having a single thread but at the same time it cuts more accurately and smoothly. The hole which it bores is truer in size than the hole made by a single thread auger. It is best for boring *soft* woods. Cabinetmakers use the double twist.

There are tricks to boring holes in wood which will become familiar to you as the characteristics of each type auger bit are learned in practice and actual use.

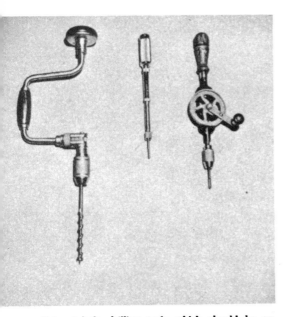

Trio of hole drilling tools which should be on every woodworker's tool panel: Brace with a bit, automatic push drill, hand drill with fluted drills.

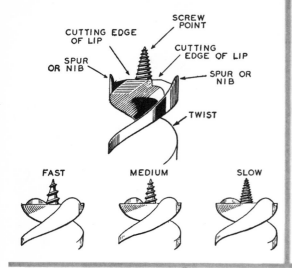

SCREW POINT
CUTTING EDGE OF LIP
SPUR OR NIB
CUTTING EDGE OF LIP
SPUR OR NIB
TWIST

FAST   MEDIUM   SLOW

Special Purpose Auger Bits

Dowel bits are short auger bits about one half the length of ordinary auger bits. They are, as their name implies, used for drilling holes for dowel pins.

Ship augers are auger bits from 18″ to 24″ in length. Some have no screw or spur. They are used to bore through thick timbers and through planks edgewise. They are also called car bits.

Gimlet bits are gimlets with a square shank so as to fit a brace. They are used for boring holes ranging in size from $\frac{1}{16}$″ to $\frac{3}{8}$″ needed when screws are to be inserted in hardwood. The size varies by 32nds of an inch and is stamped on the

The cutting end of an auger bit. Screw centers and draws bit into wood. Spurs score circle and lips cut out wood. Screw pitch controls bit speed.

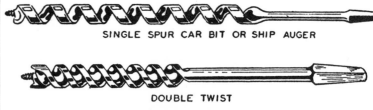

SINGLE SPUR CAR BIT OR SHIP AUGER

DOUBLE TWIST

SINGLE TWIST SOLID CENTER

Types of auger bits: the single twist is best for fast work. Double twist cuts more smoothly and accurately. Ship augers are very long type bits.

Bore from both sides to prevent bit from breaking through. Boring from both sides produces the smooth, clean edged hole you need for a neat job.

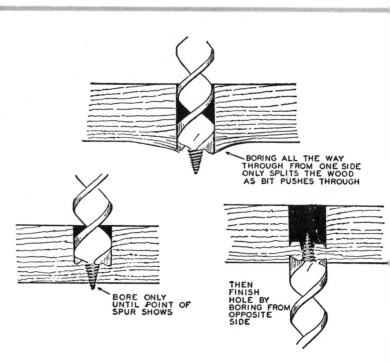

BORING ALL THE WAY THROUGH FROM ONE SIDE ONLY SPLITS THE WOOD AS BIT PUSHES THROUGH

BORE ONLY UNTIL POINT OF SPUR SHOWS

THEN FINISH HOLE BY BORING FROM OPPOSITE SIDE

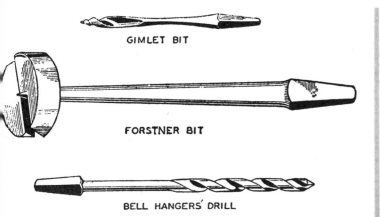

GIMLET BIT

FORSTNER BIT

BELL HANGERS' DRILL

Gimlet bit is used for boring screw holes. The Forstner bits bore much smoother holes than auger bit. Bell hangers' drill is not damaged by metal.

To start a hole in wood, find the center mark and score it with an awl. Then set the point of the lead screw in this mark, turn brace and apply pressure.

tang. A gimlet bit may be damaged if it is not kept perpendicular to the work in the early stages of drilling. Also it's best not to apply heavy pressure.

Forstner bits have no twist and neither screw nor spurs. The cutting is done by two lips and a circular steel rim. The rim centers the bit and scores the circle which forms the circumference of the hole bored by the bit. Forstner bits cut very accurately. They are made in sizes up to 2 inches in diameter. The sizes are indicated in 16ths of an inch and are stamped on the tang. Forstner bits have special uses and advantages over the ordinary auger bits. These are:

1. They will bore well in end wood. An auger bit does not bore well in end wood.
2. They will bore a larger hole where a smaller hole has already been bored. This cannot be done with an auger bit without first plugging the smaller hole.
3. They will bore holes in thin wood near an end which the screw on an auger bit would split.
4. They will bore straight holes through knots and cross-grained wood.

Absence of a screw makes Forstner bits more difficult to center than auger bits. Centering them is made easier if a circle is drawn on the work with a pair of dividers equal to the size of the hole to be bored and located in the same place.

The Forstner bit is started so that its rim coincides with the circumference of the circle. When boring holes completely through stock a piece of waste wood should be clamped to the back to prevent splitting as the bit cuts through the work.

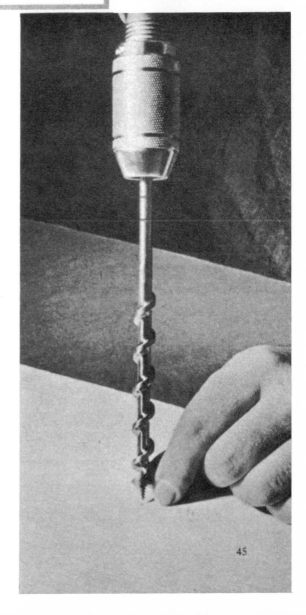

45

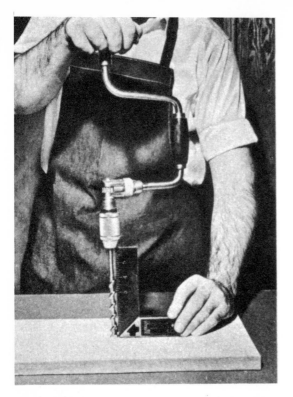

As soon as spurs of auger bit hit wood's surface, check the position of the auger with try square to make sure you bore perpendicular to surface.

Twist Drills for Wood and Metals

Twist drills for wood have a tapered shank to fit in a ratchet brace. They are used to make holes in wood for screws, nails, bolts and small dowels and are obtainable for drilling holes of the following diameters:

$\frac{1}{16}''$	$\frac{7}{32}''$	$\frac{1}{2}''$
$\frac{3}{32}''$	$\frac{1}{4}''$	$\frac{9}{16}''$
$\frac{1}{8}''$	$\frac{5}{16}''$	$\frac{5}{8}''$
$\frac{5}{32}''$	$\frac{3}{8}''$	$\frac{11}{16}''$
$\frac{3}{16}''$	$\frac{7}{16}''$	$\frac{3}{4}''$

Twist drills *for wood* are not tempered hard enough to make holes in metal. If misused in this way, they will lose their sharp edges quickly and may be damaged severely. Special bit stock drills, designed and tempered to make holes in soft metal, which will fit into a ratchet brace, are often used by woodworkers to make holes in both wood and soft metal. These are especially useful in repair work where hidden nails or unexpected metal may be encountered in drilling into wood.

Probably more auger bits are ruined by boring into nails or other metal hardware than by any other means. Use one of these twist drills and save your bits.

Boring Holes with Brace and Bit

It has been said that there are two kinds of holes which can be bored in wood. One kind is bored straight; it both goes in and comes out at the intended place. The other is crooked, ending where it is not supposed to, thus surprising the driller.

Many a man who considers himself handy with tools bores crooked holes. But it is easy to bore a hole which both starts and ends where it should. It is merely necessary to "sight" the auger or drill from two points 90 degrees apart. One sight is made when beginning the hole and two more after the hole is fairly well started. The auger will go wherever it is sent. Sighting takes only a few seconds. The method will be explained in a moment.

The Brace

A brace is a crank used to turn and guide auger bits and drills. It can also be used as

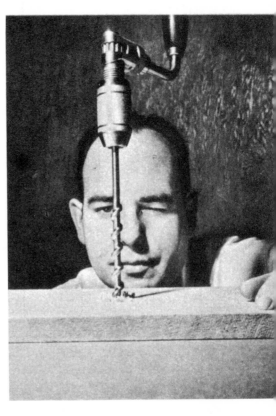

When spurs have cut into the wood some distance, take a sighting from two positions 90° apart to determine if you are holding bit perpendicular.

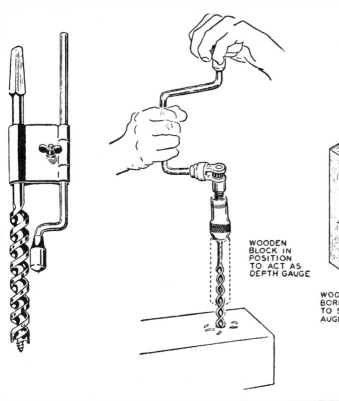

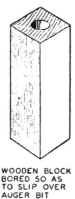

WOODEN BLOCK IN POSITION TO ACT AS DEPTH GAUGE

WOODEN BLOCK BORED SO AS TO SLIP OVER AUGER BIT

There are depth gauges on the market for boring holes, left; but wooden block can be bored and cut to proper length to butt up against chuck, serves nearly as well.

a powerful screw driver. By placing a screw driver bit in the chuck on the brace, screws can be driven or withdrawn with much less physical exertion than would be required for the same work done with a screw driver.

The best brace has a ball-bearing handle which makes it easy to turn and a ratchet-driven chuck for holding the bits. The ratchet may be locked or made to operate in either direction. The ratchet makes it possible to use the brace in confined spaces where there is not room enough to turn the brace a full 360 degrees. A universal chuck which will hold all sizes of regular square shank bits, No. 1 Morse taper shank bits and round shanks from ⅛" to ½", is desirable. Prices of the various styles of braces vary with quality.

How to Use a Brace and Bit

To use a brace and bit, first make certain that the chuck is screwed up tight. Then go to work. Hold the brace with the palm and fingers of the left hand and turn it with the right. Of course, if you are a southpaw you will find it more natural to reverse this position by holding the brace with your right hand and turning it with your left.

At a bench it is usual to hold the brace and bit either vertically or horizontally,

unless, of course, the hole is to be bored at an angle to the surface of the work. A vertical or horizontal position helps your eyes to more accurately sight the brace and bit at right angles to the surface of the piece which is to be bored.

When a hole is to be bored in wood, its exact center should be located on the work and marked with a bradawl. The point of the lead screw on the auger is placed in this mark. Then the handle of the brace is turned slowly in a clockwise direction, at the same time pressure is exerted on the head of the brace. The lead screw will bite into the wood the same as an ordinary wood screw.

When hard woods are bored, it is necessary to apply more pressure to the head of the brace than is used when boring soft woods. The pressure of the hand and the pull of the lead screw both force the auger bit into the wood. As soon as the spurs touch the work, the eyes are brought down to that level where the auger can be sighted from two positions 90 degrees apart to determine whether it is perpendicular to the surface of the work. Both sights cannot be made from the same position.

Sighting from one position will show whether or not you are holding the auger bit perpendicular to the work in one plane; sighting from the other position will show the same thing with respect to another

47

plane at right angles to the first. If the auger is not perpendicular in both planes, shift the position of the brace head until it is. Then hold the brace head steady, apply the proper amount of pressure and start boring your hole slowly.

If you are not sure of your eye, that is if you cannot judge a perpendicular accurately, test the position of the auger

of the work. As soon as it does, *stop* turning the brace. Remove all pressure from the head of the brace and turn the handle slowly in the opposite direction (counterclockwise) so as to back out the lead screw from the wood in which it is imbedded. Continue to turn the brace counterclockwise so as to withdraw the auger as soon as the lead screw is free. Now turn the work

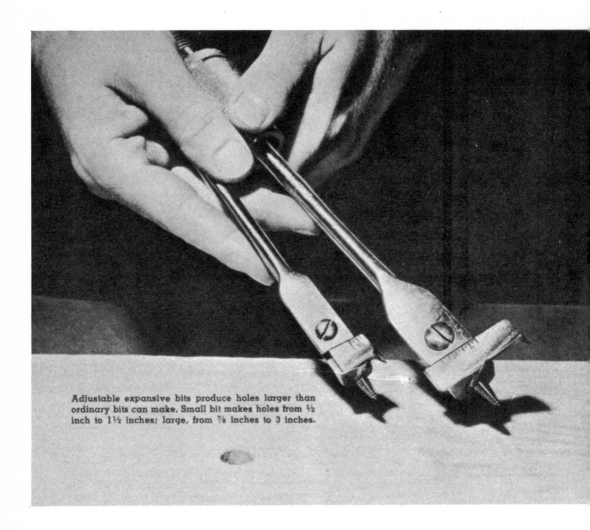

Adjustable expansive bits produce holes larger than ordinary bits can make. Small bit makes holes from ½ inch to 1½ inches; large, from ⅞ inches to 3 inches.

bit in two planes with a small try square.

When the spurs and cutting edges of the auger bit have started to bore into the wood, sight the work once more. If the auger is still perpendicular in both planes continue boring until it is near the bottom of the hole. At this point, turn the brace slowly. Watch closely for the bottom of the lead screw to come through the under side

over and do boring from the opposite side.

Boring from one side splits the wood when the auger breaks through. Boring from two sides results in a smooth, clean edged hole; if you have sighted the auger accurately, the hole will have come through where you wanted it to.

You can bore from one side only, without danger of splintering when the auger

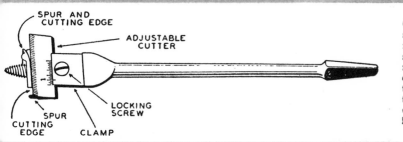

Close-up of expansive bit shows how width adjustment is set. A loosening screw allows spur to be moved. Scale is set to width desired, then screw is re-tightened. Always make a test bore in scrap wood to check diameter before boring hole in finished work.

comes through, by clamping a block of wood tightly on the back of the work in position so that the auger will cut into it after it has completed the hole in the work. And don't forget, boring holes is easier if you turn your brace slowly.

Boring at an Angle

Boring holes at a slight angle is no more difficult than boring them at right angles to a surface. If you sight an auger or a drill at an angle, it will go where you aim it.

If the angle of the hole is only slightly away from the perpendicular or horizontal, there will be no difficulty in starting the auger and getting it to bite into the wood. It is a good plan to lay the angle out on a piece of thin wood or cardboard and use this in sighting. If the auger is kept parallel to the line indicating the angle, the drill will go where it should.

When a hole is to be bored at a considerable angle away from the perpendicular to a surface, it is difficult to start the auger without a guide. The guide is made by boring a vertical hole through a block of wood, using the same size auger bit that is to be used in making the finished hole. The bottom of the block is then sawed off at the proper angle and clamped or fastened with finishing nails to the work to be bored.

The center of the hole in the bottom of the block must be directly over the starting point at the center of the hole about to be bored. Then if the auger is inserted in the hole in the block, you can bore the hole while the block holds the auger at the proper angle and prevents it from slipping.

It is easy to calculate the angle to be given the bottom of the block. Deduct from 90 the angle of the hole to be bored. The remainder is the number of degrees the angle of the bottom of the block should have. For example, if a hole is to be bored at an angle of 60 degrees, deduct 60 from 90 and the answer will be 30 degrees. Make

the angle of the bottom of the block 30 degrees. This is so simple to do. Try it.

Extension or Expansive Bits

When holes larger than one inch in diameter are to be bored in wood, a carpenter or cabinetmaker employs an extension or expansive bit. This fits into a brace like an ordinary auger bit but has an adjustable cutting blade which can be set to bore holes of any diameter within its range. It is used in the same manner as the auger bit. Two sizes are made. The small size will produce holes from ½" to 1½" in diameter. The large size makes holes ⅞" to 3" in diameter.

The spur and cutting lip is fastened to the shank by a screw passing through a small steel clamp. Loosening this screw makes it possible to move the spur and adjust the bit. The screw must be firmly tightened again so that the spur cannot slip while the hole is being bored.

The accuracy of the adjustment should always be tested by boring a hole in a piece of waste wood and measuring its diameter. Not until this check has been made, should the bit be used to bore a hole in the finished work.

Boring through from one side only with an extension bit may split the wood. It is better to bore until the tip of the spur or lead screw appears on the under side. Then turn the work over and finish the hole by boring through from the opposite direction.

Automatic Push Drill

This tool speeds up the drilling of small holes in wood. When the handle is held with one hand and the sliding sleeve moved back and forth with the other hand, the chuck and drill will revolve. Carpenters use a push drill frequently to make holes for screws used in fastening hinges, locks and other hardware fittings. The hollow handle usually contains a set of straight

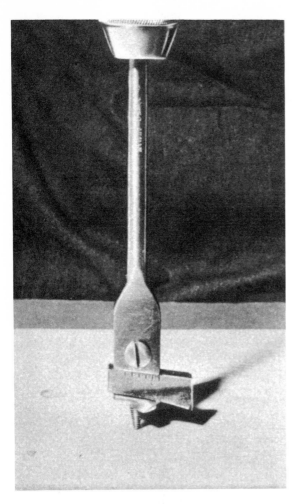

Large expansive bit is set for 2 inches. Start to turn brace slowly, hold bit exactly perpendicular, and lead screw will pull spur into wood smoothly.

shank and may be driven by a hand drill or an electric drill. Power driven drills are used for high-speed production. The 3-jaw chuck with which the ordinary hand drill is fitted takes drills up to ¼″ in diameter. To drive twist drills of larger diameter by hand, a breast drill should be used. The chuck on this tool will usually take straight shank drills up to ½″ in diameter. A few drops of oil on a breast drill makes the job easier.

When drilling with a Morse twist drill it is necessary to hold the driving mechanism steady and drive the drill perfectly straight. Otherwise the drill may be bent or broken. The shank of the drill is soft and will bend but the body of the drill is

Avoid splitting. Put old board under work. Bore till lead screw goes through. Turn work over, center the bit, finish by boring hole from opposite direction.

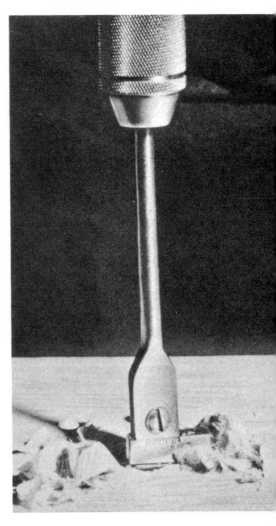

flute drills ranging in size from $\frac{1}{16}$″ to 11/64″. It is a handy tool.

Countersink Bit

This tool is used to shape the top of a screw hole so that the head of a flat head screw may be driven flush with, or slightly below, the surface of the work. There are two types. One has a tapered shank to fit a bit brace; the other has a straight round shank to fit a hand drill.

The Hand Drill

When small diameter, accurate holes are to be drilled in wood, Morse twist drills are used. These are made with a straight

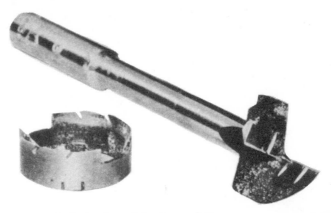

Another bit for boring large holes in wood is the PTI bit which is made in sizes from ⅝ inch to 2 inches by 1/16ths. Work can be drilled without pilot hole or centering. The spur can be taken off shank for sharpening.

Automatic push drill is used with straight type fluted drills. It's the handiest drill to make the pilot holes for screws used to hold hardware.

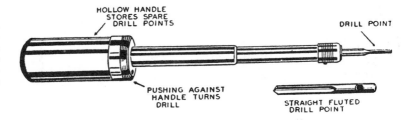

tempered and will break if sufficiently strained.

When driven rapidly, a small twist drill will bite into wood very fast but if it is pushed ahead too quickly, the chips will not clear out properly. When this occurs, the drill becomes hot. If the wood is hard and the chips clog in the drill flutes, the drill may break or may become hot enough to char the wood and spoil its own temper. A burnt twist drill will no longer hold a keen cutting edge.

Withdraw the drill several times to clear the chips from its flutes before a hole in hard wood is fully drilled. The chips will usually fall out when the drill is withdrawn but it is sometimes necessary to push them out with a small nail or an awl. If the flutes are jammed with chips, the drill squeaks as it revolves. The drill should be withdrawn and cleared immediately.

Morse twist drills are especially useful whenever a good job of setting a screw is to be done. Two drills are necessary then. The first part of the hole is drilled to the depth of the length of the smooth shank of the screw with a drill of the same diameter as that shank. The second part of the hole is made with a drill which is smaller than the threaded part of the screw. The screw will go in easily.

Breast Drills

These are larger and more strongly built editions of the hand drill. The chuck will usually take straight shank drills up to ⅜″ in diameter and sometimes will receive a ½″ diameter drill. Breast drills are fitted with a plate instead of a handle. The chest or abdomen of the operator pressing against this plate provides the pressure which feeds the drill. Two sets of driving gears make it possible to change the speed ratio by shifting driving wheel spindle. •

Jack plane used diagonally is good for leveling off rough surfaces prior to fine planing.

planes

It's easy to use any plane once you know how to assemble and adjust it.

ALMOST everyone who has watched a carpenter using a plane has had an urge to get his own hands on the tool and make his own shavings. However, the technique of planing involves more than making shavings. Know how is necessary. It is necessary to know how to adjust, how to hold and how to push one of these indispensable tools in order to produce good workmanship. In principle, a plane is a kind of chisel set in a block of wood or metal which acts as a guide to regulate the depth of the cut. A chisel-like plane "iron" does the cutting. This must have a keen edge and be correctly adjusted, and the whole tool must be controlled properly.

There are several types of planes. Each has a special purpose. The three most common are: the block plane, the smoothing plane and the jack plane. All are made on the same principle but differ in size and in use. The general purpose of a plane is to smooth off rough surfaces and bring woodwork to exact size after it has first been roughed out to approximate size. For example, it is not possible to make a close fit with a hand saw alone. A hand saw does not cut to accurate size and it leaves a rough, uneven surface. But the sawed edges can be smoothed with a plane and brought to close dimensions.

There are also planes for special purposes, such as the rabbet and cabinetmaker's planes used for cutting rabbets, tongues, grooves and moldings; low angle planes, circular planes, scrub planes, etc. All are described in this section.

Old-fashioned planes were made with

52

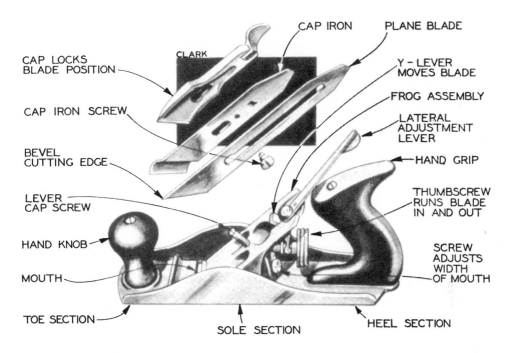

CAP LOCKS BLADE POSITION

CAP IRON SCREW

BEVEL CUTTING EDGE

LEVER CAP SCREW

HAND KNOB

MOUTH

TOE SECTION

CLARK

CAP IRON

PLANE BLADE

Y – LEVER MOVES BLADE

FROG ASSEMBLY

LATERAL ADJUSTMENT LEVER

HAND GRIP

THUMBSCREW RUNS BLADE IN AND OUT

SCREW ADJUSTS WIDTH OF MOUTH

SOLE SECTION

HEEL SECTION

COMPONENT PARTS OF COMMON HAND PLANE

wood frames. The modern plane has a cast iron frame, which is preferable.

Holding the Work

While being planed, work should be so firmly secured that it cannot move. Accurate planing requires the use of both hands to guide the tool when the jack, smoothing, fore or jointer plane is used. A skilled woodworker can hold a short length of board on its edge with one hand and use the other to drive the plane, but such ability comes only with experience. The novice will find that the most efficient way to hold work when planing is to clamp it in a vise.

The most desirable bench for woodworking is one provided with two quick-acting vises. One vise is attached to the front of the bench and the other to the right end. The vises may be of either wood or iron, the latter, equipped with an adjustable dog, being preferable. The vise dog is a square steel pin which can be moved up and down in a slot in the vise jaw. The dog can be set flush with the top of the jaw or raised above it.

A row of holes into which a bench stop can be pushed should be cut in the top of the bench. The row should be in line with the dog on the end vise and parallel to the front edge of the bench. This arrangement permits boards to be clamped between the dog on the end vise and a bench stop located in one of the holes.

A hole for a bench stop near the left-

Here's how to produce a shaving of approximately same thickness from beginning to end of stroke.

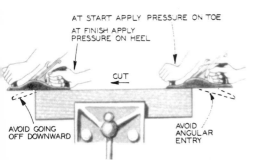

AT START APPLY PRESSURE ON TOE

AT FINISH APPLY PRESSURE ON HEEL

CUT

AVOID GOING OFF DOWNWARD

AVOID ANGULAR ENTRY

Block plane is smallest of common planes. It's used to smooth end grain and shape small boards.

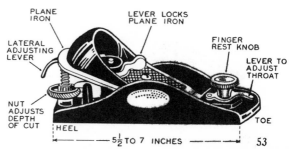

PLANE IRON

LEVER LOCKS PLANE IRON

FINGER REST KNOB

LATERAL ADJUSTING LEVER

LEVER TO ADJUST THROAT

NUT ADJUSTS DEPTH OF CUT

HEEL

TOE

$5\frac{1}{2}$ TO 7 INCHES

53

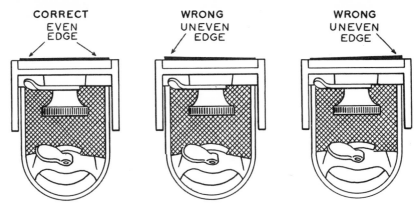

CORRECT	WRONG	WRONG
EVEN EDGE	UNEVEN EDGE	UNEVEN EDGE

Unevenly projecting edge makes uneven shaving. Planes at right need lateral lever adjustment.

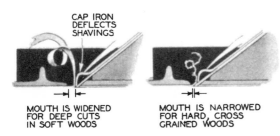

CAP IRON DEFLECTS SHAVINGS

MOUTH IS WIDENED FOR DEEP CUTS IN SOFT WOODS

MOUTH IS NARROWED FOR HARD, CROSS GRAINED WOODS

The plane iron cap stiffens the iron and curls the shavings as they come up through the throat.

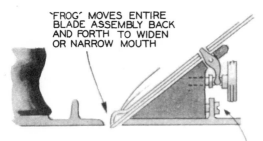

'FROG' MOVES ENTIRE BLADE ASSEMBLY BACK AND FORTH TO WIDEN OR NARROW MOUTH

FROG' SET SCREW

Screw is turned in or out to adjust mouth for planing hard or soft woods. See previous sketch.

Correct grip for a block plane allows one hand operation to grip, push, and guide it properly.

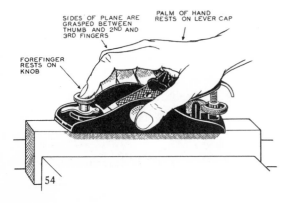

SIDES OF PLANE ARE GRASPED BETWEEN THUMB AND 2ND AND 3RD FINGERS

PALM OF HAND RESTS ON LEVER CAP

FOREFINGER RESTS ON KNOB

hand front edge of the bench is also useful. It provides a firm rest against which a board can be held for planing when close accuracy is not needed.

A thin strip of wood nailed across the bench can also be used as a stop.

The Block Plane

This is the smallest and the simplest of the three common planes. It is held in one hand and in general it is used to plane small pieces of wood and end grain. Because the plane iron (the chisel-shaped cutter) is set at a lower angle than that of other planes, it will cut end grain better. It is the proper tool to use for making chamfers on small pieces of wood, for planing the ends of moldings and trim and for shaping the hulls and spars of model boats.

Before discussing the adjustment and handling of the block plane, let us examine one. It has a chisel-shaped plane iron set at a low angle in an iron frame. Notice particularly that the iron is a single blade. The plane iron in a jack plane or a smoothing plane is double, for reasons which will be explained later. The blade in a block plane is locked in position by a lever cap or a lever cam. This detail will vary slightly in planes produced by different manufacturers. Moving the lever cap screw or the lever, whichever the plane may have, in one direction will lock the plane iron. Moving the lever or screw in the opposite direction unlocks the blade so that it can be removed from the frame.

There is a slot in the plane bottom which is known both as the throat and as the mouth. The width of the throat is adjustable on some planes. The sharpened lower edge of the plane iron can be moved in or out of the mouth by means of an adjusting screw. Turning this screw controls the thickness of the shavings. The shavings curl up through the throat.

The sharpened edge of the plane iron is beveled on one side only. It is set in the frame with the bevel *up*. In the jack and smoothing planes, because the iron is at a greater angle, it is set bevel *down*.

How to Adjust a Block Plane

Hold the plane bottom side up in the left hand with the toe or front of the plane toward you and the bottom level with the eye. Sight along the bottom and with the right hand turn the adjusting screw until the sharp edge of the blade or plane iron projects *slightly* through the throat and above the bottom of the plane. The most common mistake made by the novice in attempting to adjust a plane is setting the blade too far out. You should be able to see only its edge or to feel it just perceptibly by moving the fingertips very lightly across the bottom of the plane. If the blade is sharp, it will make thin shavings when properly set. Furthermore, much better results will be obtained if the plane is adjusted in this manner.

The blade's adjustment made to regulate the thickness of the shavings is called the vertical adjustment. The lateral adjustment is made to produce even shavings. It is meant to prevent one edge from being thicker than the other. To make a lateral adjustment, loosen the lever cap screw or the lever cam slightly and sight along the bottom of the plane. Press the upper end of the blade (near the adjusting screw) to the right or left, whichever is necessary to bring the cutting edge of the blade parallel with the bottom of the plane. Do not set one corner of the blade farther out of the throat than the other.

How to Hold a Block Plane

One hand only is used to guide and push a block plane. The sides of the plane are grasped between the thumb and the second and third fingers. The forefinger should rest in the hollow of the finger rest at the front of the plane. The finger rest is usually the hollowed out top of the thumbscrew which locks the throat-adjusting lever. The lever cap should rest under the palm of the hand. This position is necessary to guide the plane correctly.

If your hand and eye are skillful enough to guide the plane firmly and accurately, you will have no trouble. You may, however, have to practice a great deal before you can plane properly. Press down and forward at the beginning of the stroke and *maintain the same pressure* throughout the forward motion. An even pressure is essential. Beginners are likely to bear down hard at the beginning of a planing stroke, lighten the pressure toward the center and bear down again at the end. Some do the opposite—bear down harder at the center than at the ends. The result of either of these mistakes will be a convex or concave surface instead of a straight one. Practice planing on pieces of scrap wood.

As you know, all wood has a grain (direction in which the fibers run) and the grain seldom runs perfectly parallel with a surface. You must take this into consid-

Block plane in action shows correct grip. This plane is excellent for fitting or finishing work.

Long surfaces require a jack, fore or jointer plane, all alike except in size. Use both hands.

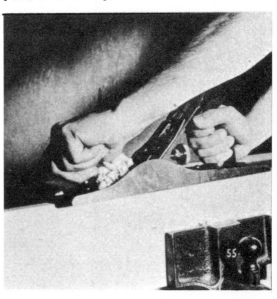

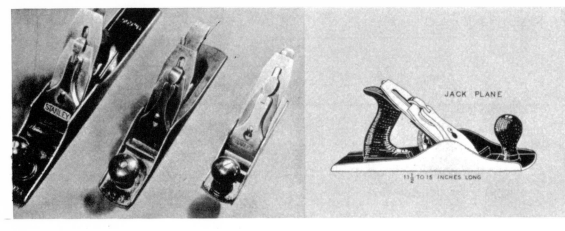

From left: Fore plane is 18 inches; jack plane is 14 inches; and the smooth plane is 10 inches.

Jack plane is the larger plane used most often to straighten long, rough edges before smoothing.

eration when planing. To plane a wood surface smooth, it is necessary to plane *with* the grain, *not against* it. If the wood is torn and roughened by a sharp plane set to make thin shavings, you are planing against the grain. Reverse the work and plane from the opposite end. If the grain is irregular, it may be necessary to plane one portion of a surface in one direction and the other portion in the opposite direction. When cross grain or curly grain is encountered, the plane iron must be very sharp and set to cut a very thin shaving.

It is necessary to plane *end*-grain halfway from each edge. If you push a plane all the way across end-grain, the corners and the edge will split off. You should never plane from the center to the corner on end-grain. There are several "tricks" which can be used in end-planing to avoid breaking corners at the end of the stroke. One of them is to use a wider piece of stock than the finished piece and cut the corner off slightly at a bevel, shown in the page 57 sketch, in order to relieve pressure on the last wood fibers. After end-planing, the edge can be planed to eliminate the bevel. Another method is to clamp a piece of wood on the edge of the board which is at the end of the plane stroke. This piece should be on the same level as the piece you are planing. You can hold the two pieces together either with the clamp or in a vise.

Jack, Fore, Smoothing, Jointer Planes

The first few cuts on a long surface require a long plane. The bottom, called the sole, covers so much area that it rides over any hollows in the work and cuts only on the high spots until the surface is even. Therefore it is easier to straighten a long edge or surface with a long plane than with the shorter variety. After the roughness has been removed with a long plane, the work can be finished with a smaller plane called a *smoothing* plane.

Long planes are called jack, fore or jointer planes depending upon their length. The sole of a jack plane is usually from 11½″ to 14″; the sole of a fore plane is 18″ and the sole of a jointer plane is 22″ or 24″. Among these three, the jack plane is used most often. Since all three are alike except for the length of sole, our discussion of a jack plane will apply equally well to the other two. Note the relative sizes of the planes shown on these two pages.

If the grain is torn or roughened by the plane, reverse the direction in which plane is pushed.

Don't work from the center of end grain to edges for the wood will almost be certain to splinter.

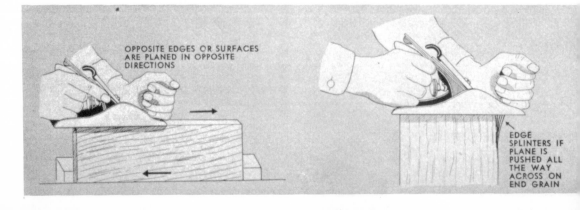

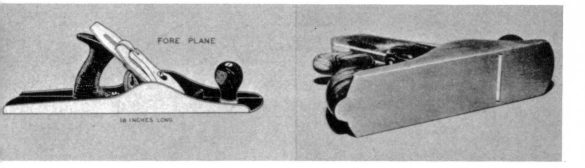

Long fore plane covers so much linear area that it rides over hollows, cuts high spots down level.

When a blade is adjusted for cutting, always lay plane on its side to protect the sharpened edge.

Planing with a Jack Plane

At the back of a jack plane is a handle somewhat like a saw handle. A knob is fixed to the front end. It is a tool to be used with two hands. The work must be secured so that it will not move while being planed. At the start of the planing stroke, take a position directly behind the work with the left foot forward. As you push the plane, shift the weight of the body gradually to the left foot. If the work being planed is long, it may be necessary to take one or two steps in order to finish the stroke.

Proper Adjustment of Plane Iron

The jack, smoothing, fore and jointer planes each has a plane iron cap clamped to the cutting blade. This has a double purpose. It stiffens the iron and breaks and curls the shavings as they come up through the throat. The breaking and curling and the action of the toe (this is the portion of the sole forward of the throat) prevent the wood from splitting ahead of the cutting edge and are the reasons for the cutting edge producing a smooth surface.

The position of the plane iron cap in re-lation to the plane iron is adjustable and can be shifted by loosening the clamping screw. A correct adjustment is essential. For general work, the edge of the plane iron cap should be about 1/16" back of the cutting edge of the plane iron. It should be as near the cutting edge as possible when cross-grained or curly wood is planed.

The thickness of the shaving is adjusted by sighting along the bottom of the plane and turning the adjusting screw until the blade projects about a hair's breadth. The blade is pushed out when the adjusting nut is turned so that it moves toward the handle. Turning the adjusting nut so that it moves in toward the blade draws the blade in, decreases thickness of shaving.

The plane must be set so that it makes a shaving of even thickness. This is done with the lateral adjusting lever. Sight along the bottom of the plane and move the lever to the right or left, whichever direction may be necessary in order to make the cutting edge parallel to the bottom.

Types of Smoothing Planes

A smoothing plane is used to smooth the surface of work after the rough surface and

The correct way to plane end wood grain is shown here. Start at each end; finish cuts in center.

Also to avoid splits: bevel waste edge of excess stock area; work toward bevel; plane off waste.

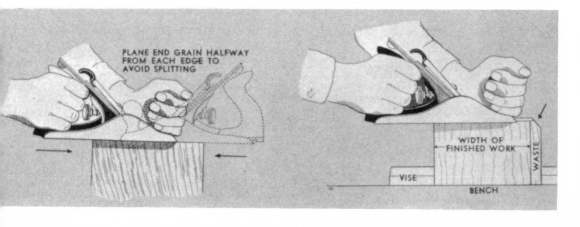

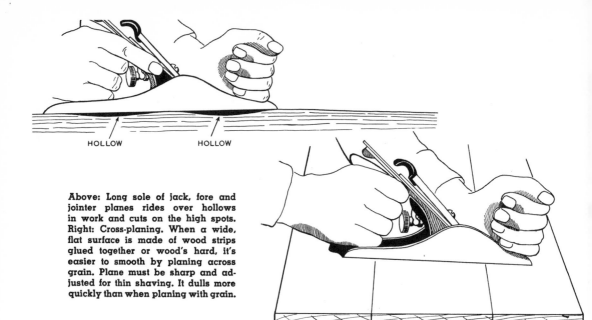

HOLLOW   HOLLOW

Above: Long sole of jack, fore and jointer planes rides over hollows in work and cuts on the high spots. Right: Cross-planing. When a wide, flat surface is made of wood strips glued together or wood's hard, it's easier to smooth by planing across grain. Plane must be sharp and adjusted for thin shaving. It dulls more quickly than when planing with grain.

unevenness have been removed with a jack plane. It is considerably larger than a block plane but smaller than a jack plane. It will not cut end grain as well as a block plane because the blade is set at a greater angle.

A smoothing plane is made exactly like a jack plane but has a shorter sole. This may be from 5½" to 10" long. You should own at least one smoothing plane.

A smoothing plane has a plane iron cap attached to the plane iron to curl and break the shavings. It has a handle and a knob and is used with two hands in the same manner as a jack plane. It should also be set in the same way. The edge of the plane iron cap should be about 1/16" back of the cutting edge of the plane iron for general work and as near to the cutting edge as possible for curly and cross-grained wood. The cutting edge of the plane iron should

project about the thickness of a hair through the throat and be parallel to the bottom of the plane. This adjustment is made by sighting along the bottom of the plane and shifting the adjusting nut and lateral adjusting lever as may be necessary.

The cutting edge on the blade of a smoothing plane must be kept very sharp and be set to make a fairly fine shaving. If the throat of the plane becomes clogged, stop planing and clear it immediately. Use a wooden splint for this purpose. Never use a screw driver or anything made of metal because it will dull or nick the cutting edge if it is dragged across it.

Hold the plane as square as you can while you work and remember that since this plane has a short sole you can quickly make "hollows" and "rounds" with it if you do not apply the proper pressure to

Low angle plane (only 12° angle) cuts across grain smoothly on boards too heavy for block plane work.

Model maker's plane is only four inches long, and it is used for both flat and curved fine planing.

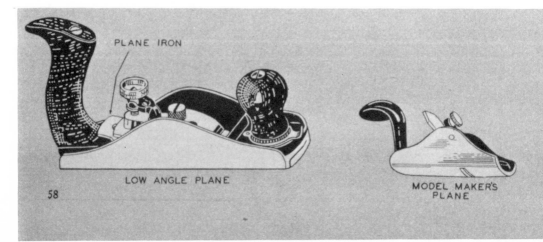

PLANE IRON

LOW ANGLE PLANE

MODEL MAKER'S PLANE

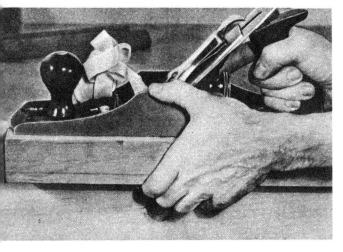

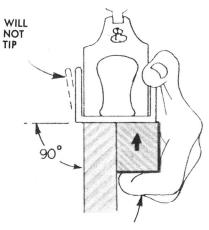

WILL
NOT
TIP

90°

GRIP WOOD STRIP
TIGHTLY TO PLANE
SOLE, AS GUIDE

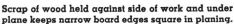
Scrap of wood held against side of work and under
plane keeps narrow board edges square in planing.

make an even shaving. At the beginning of any stroke, you should put a little more downward pressure on the knob with your left hand than you do on the handle with your right hand. When the stroke has been started, the pressure of both hands should be equal until toward the end. At the end, all the downward pressure should be exerted on the handle and practically none on the knob. This should result in a shaving of approximately the same thickness from the beginning to the end of the stroke.

It does not take much planing to dull a keen edge on a plane iron. You should be able to resharpen your own plane. Complete instructions for removing the blade, grinding and whetting it and putting the plane together again are given in another part of this book. Planes can be quite troublesome if not kept well sharpened.

Roughing or Scrub Planes

These tools are specially designed to save time and energy when it is necessary to remove a considerable amount of wood from a board—not enough to slice away with a rip saw but a great deal to plane away with a jack plane. They are made in two sizes—9½" long with a cutter 1¼" wide and 10½" long with a cutter 1½" wide. The blade is heavy and rounded so that it will bring a board down to rough dimensions quickly. A smoothing plane or a jack plane can be used to finish the job if necessary.

A roughing or scrub plane is handled in the same manner as a jack plane. Carpenters frequently use it to back out base boards, clean up rough and gritty timbers, true up sub-flooring, bring large timbers

The scrub plane removes wood rapidly and is used to bring work to rough dimensions for fine planing.

This oddly-shaped, edge-trimming block plane is used to trim and square off the edges of boards.

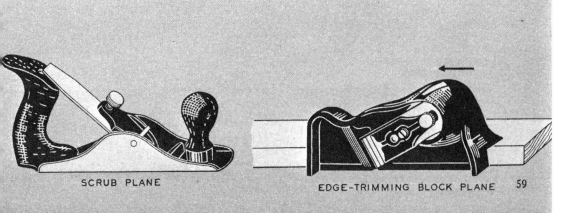

SCRUB PLANE   EDGE-TRIMMING BLOCK PLANE   59

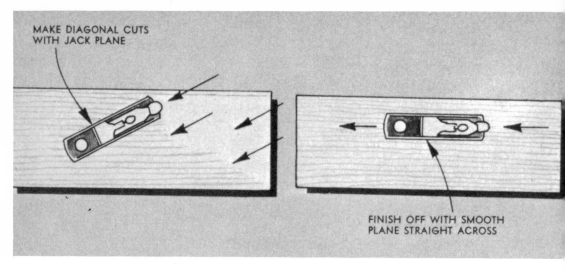

MAKE DIAGONAL CUTS
WITH JACK PLANE

FINISH OFF WITH SMOOTH
PLANE STRAIGHT ACROSS

Use a jack plane on wide rough boards, cutting diagonally to level off high spots, smooth wood.

After rough planing has leveled off board, then the smaller smooth plane is used for smoothing.

to rough size, etc. The scrub plane is quite useful in doing remodeling work and in reclaiming pieces of used lumber.

Special Low Angle Planes

While a block plane does very nicely in cutting across the grain of ordinary boards and small or medium-sized pieces of wood, it is too small to work efficiently on timbers or other large pieces. When more power is required for cutting across the grain on heavy wood than can be applied to a regular block plane, a special low angle plane is used. This handles like a smoothing plane so that the power of both arms can be applied. The blade is set at a very low angle (12 degrees). A blade having a low angle cuts across hardwood more easily than a blade with a greater angle.

Edge Trimming Block Plane

This is a time saver for the professional woodworker and a godsend to the amateur craftsman who has difficulty in planing square. The bottom of the plane consists of two surfaces at right angles. The cutter is at an angle so that it works on a skew. This plane will trim or square the edges of boards up to $7/8''$ thick to a square or close fit without any effort required to keep the tool square with the edge. Wood blocks of various bevels may be attached to the bed of the plane so that accurate bevels can be planed on the edge of a board.

Model Maker's Plane

This is also known as a violin plane. It is a small tool, being only $3''$ to $4''$ long.

Circular planes, either convex or concave, are used in smoothing curved edges. The planes have flexible steel bottoms which can be adjusted to fit curved area to be planed. Note adjustments.

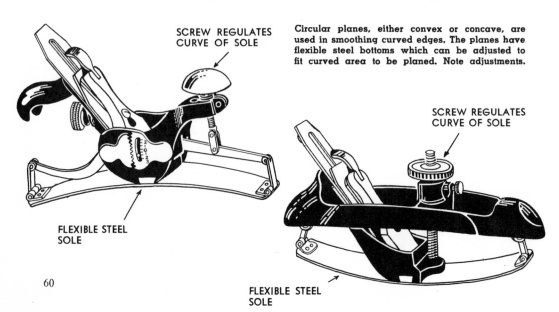

SCREW REGULATES
CURVE OF SOLE

FLEXIBLE STEEL
SOLE

SCREW REGULATES
CURVE OF SOLE

FLEXIBLE STEEL
SOLE

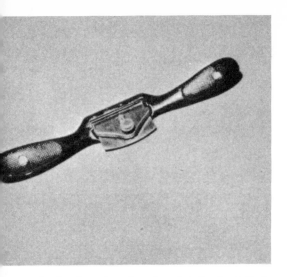

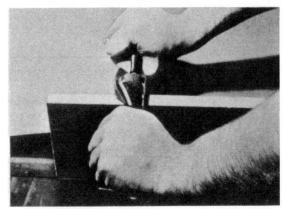

Spoke shave is not a plane but it cuts similarly to a plane. Blade is sharpened like a plane iron.

Held with both hands, the spoke shave is pulled toward operator in making chamfers, curved edges.

The bottom is curved in both directions and the sharpened edge of the blade is rounded to conform with the curve of the bottom. The plane can be used to remove wood from any flat surface, from a convex surface of any radius and from concave surfaces down to a 12-inch minimum radius.

Rabbet Planes

A rectangular recess cut out of the end or edge of a piece of wood is called a rabbet. Rabbets are used to form grooved joints in furniture, door, window and box construction and in other forms of woodwork. Rabbets can be cut by hand with a saw and chisel or planed with a special plane called a rabbet plane. The bottom of a rabbet plane is cut away so that the edge of the cutting iron is in line with the side of the plane. See drawing below.

A rabbet plane is a two-handed tool that is pushed in the same manner as a smoothing plane or jack plane. The piece to be rabbeted should have a strip of wood clamped across it to act as a guide for the side of the plane. When fitted with a properly shaped cutter, it is also used to cut the groove or bead on woodwork edges.

Circular Planes

There are planes which will smooth a circular edge, either concave or convex. They are built with a flexible steel bottom which can be adjusted to form a curve so that concave and convex surfaces down to a minimum radius of 20 inches can be planed. The same tool cannot be used for both convex and concave work. •

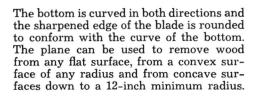

BEAD

END VIEW

STRIP CLAMPED TO BOARD AS GUIDE FOR THE RABBET PLANE

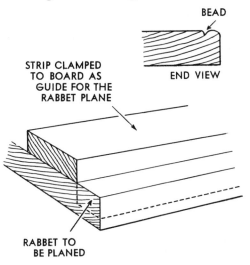

RABBET TO BE PLANED

Rabbet planes are used to work out square corners or laps. Cutting edge of plane iron below is set at right angles to side of plane. Skew-iron type is set diagonally and cuts more easily and smoothly.

RABBET

END VIEW

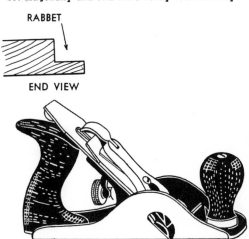

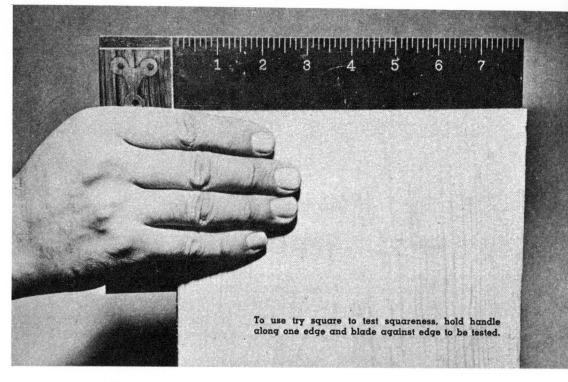

To use try square to test squareness, hold handle along one edge and blade against edge to be tested.

laying out and measuring

Accuracy in measuring and marking is the trademark of an experienced woodworker and the fine results he produces.

CUTTING wood to *exact* dimension is the basis of all good woodworking. Chisels, planes, saws, etc., are only a means to this end. Before any accurate cutting process can be undertaken successfully, guiding lines must be marked upon the work.

The plan and measurements for the work may be taken from a blueprint or sketch or they may exist only in the mind of the workman. But in either case, a full-sized reproduction of the various angles, curves and details of the plan must be marked on the lumber which is the raw material. This measuring and marking process is called laying-out or setting-out. It is absolutely essential to a good piece of work. In an industrial woodworking plant, it is usually performed by the foremen.

The tools used for laying out are rules, squares, gauges, dividers, pencils, knife blades and sliding T bevels.

The rules used by woodworkers are usually of the folding type so that they can be carried in a pocket. They are from 2' to 8' long and are usually graduated to show feet, inches and fractions of inches on both sides. They are also available with inch divisions on one side and metric divisions on the other side of the rule.

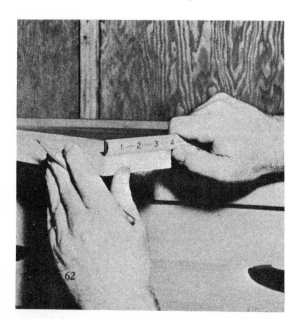

Zig-zag folding rule held on edge will be accurate up to two feet. Beyond two feet, it must be laid flat.

62

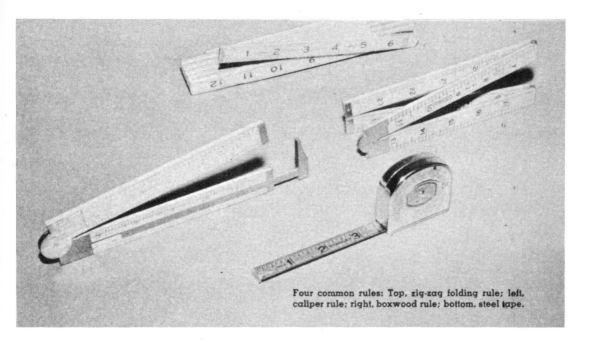

Four common rules: Top, zig-zag folding rule; left, caliper rule; right, boxwood rule; bottom, steel tape.

Caliper Rule

The caliper rule will measure the diameter of dowels, drills, and the thickness of boards, tenons, etc., more accurately than an ordinary rule. Some caliper rules are made for both inside and outside calipering. They can therefore be used to measure accurately the diameter of holes, the width of slots, etc.

Using a Rule

The joints of a folding rule should be lubricated with light machine oil occasionally to prevent rust and stiff joints which might break when the rule is opened or closed after exposure to moisture.

To measure distances of more than 2′ the rule is laid flat on the surface to be measured. When a folding rule is laid on a flat surface, the rule itself is flat and therefore accurate. It is inaccurate to measure any great length with a folding rule held on edge. Since the rule is flexible, to hold it perfectly straight in this position is difficult in many instances.

When laying out accurate measurements of less than 2′, the rule is placed on edge and the distance marked with a fine pencil point or the tip of a penknife blade.

Rules which have been used considerably are sometimes worn at the ends. It may be more accurate to measure from the 1-inch mark of an old rule.

Dividers

This tool is sometimes called a compass. Its principal use is to scribe small circles. It is also a handy instrument for picking up a measurement and transferring it to the work. For example, suppose it is necessary to lay out a number of lines 3″ apart on a piece of board. If the dividers are set to 3″ and are used to locate the lines, the distances between them will all be equal.

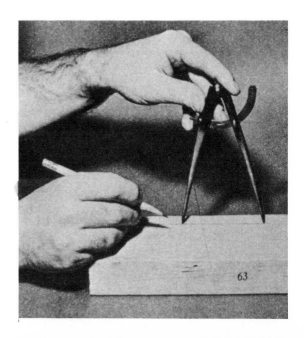

Dividers are handy for picking up a measurement and transferring it to the work. Also called compass.

63

SQUARES

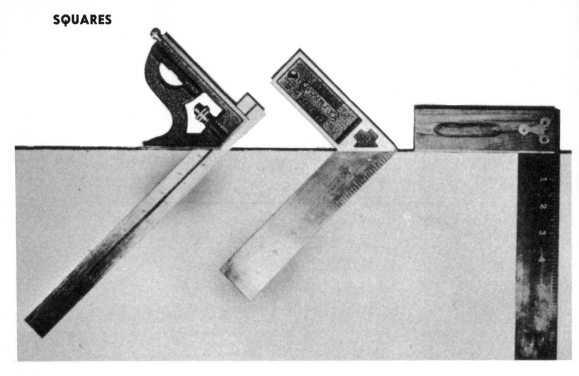

From left: Adjustable try and mitre square with level; fixed mitre and try square; fixed try square.

Carpenter's Square

The carpenter's steel square usually measures 24"x16" or 24"x18". The 24" side is called the body and the 16" or 18" side, at right angles to the body, is called the tongue. The flat sides of the body and tongue are graduated in inches and fractions of an inch. Both the body and tongue may be used as a rule and also as a straight edge in laying out operations.

Besides the inch and fractional graduations on the square, the following tables are marked on it: rafter or framing table, board measure, octagon scale, brace measure and hundredths scale.

The square is as important a tool to the carpenter, as the slide rule is to the engineer. He performs many of his calculations with the aid of the graduations and tables marked on its sides and uses it to lay out the guide lines for cutting rafters, oblique joints, stairs, etc.

The cabinetmaker, jointer and amateur craftsman has little or no use for the tables on a carpenter's square or some of its special applications. They use it for laying out and squaring up large stock and large patterns and for testing the flatness and squareness of large surfaces. In their hands, it is handled much like the try square.

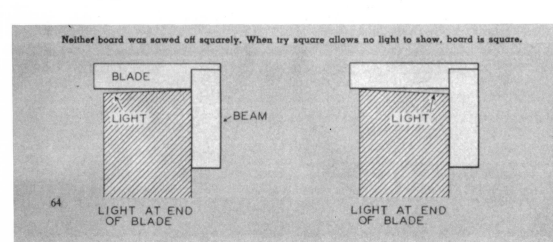

Neither board was sawed off squarely. When try square allows no light to show, board is square.

BLADE

LIGHT

BEAM

LIGHT

LIGHT AT END OF BLADE

LIGHT AT END OF BLADE

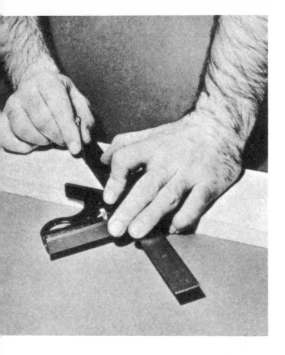

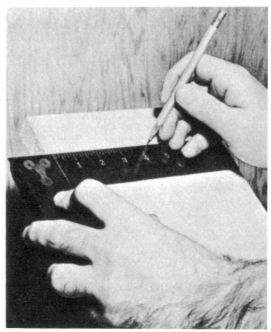

Adjustable try and mitre square has sliding blade; it permits marking off 45° as well as 90° angles.

Use fixed try square to draw 90° straight line for sawing; also for checking cut board for squareness.

Try Squares

The common try square consists of two parts at right angles to each other, a thick wood or iron stock and a thin steel blade. The best try squares are made with the blades graduated in inches and fractions of an inch. The blade length varies from 2″ to 12″.

A more convenient but slightly more expensive form of try square is the adjustable type whose blade can be locked in its seat at any point along its length. The iron stock is provided with a level.

A try square is a necessity in the woodworker's tool kit. It is used constantly for laying-out and to determine whether edges and ends are true with adjoining edges and with the face of the work after it has been sawed, planed or chiseled.

Pencil Versus Knife

A pencil is satisfactory for marking guide lines for roughing out woodwork. But because of the wide, relatively indefinite mark it produces, it cannot be used to lay out the accurate lines required in cabinet work and jointing. Such work should be laid out with the blade of a pocketknife or bench knife. The tip of the blade should be used. This makes a clean,

Try square will indicate if surface is true or not. Light shows at points where trueness is wanting.

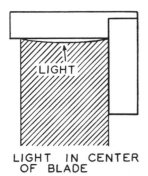

LIGHT IN CENTER
OF BLADE

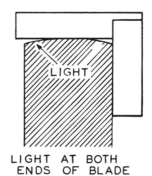

LIGHT AT BOTH
ENDS OF BLADE

accurate line for the meeting sides of joints which must fit smoothly.

Squaring Lines Across a Board

When a board is to be cut off, planed or chiseled square, a guide line must be marked across its surface. The guide line must be exactly at the required point and must be square with the edges. Unless the board is wide enough to require a carpenter's square, a try square is used for the purpose. The stock of the try square is pressed firmly against the edge of the board with the left hand and the guide line marked along the blade with a pencil.

To Square a Line Around a Board

Either a carpenter's framing square or a try square may be used, depending upon the width of the board. If the blade of the try square is not long enough to reach all the way across the board, a carpenter's square should be used.

Mark one edge and one face of the board with an X so that they can be distinguished readily as the working edge and the working face. Square a line from the working edge across the working face by holding the stock of the square firmly against the working edge and marking a line along the blade in one clean stroke.

The working edge must be perfectly flat so that the square will not rock. Lines are squared from the working face across both edges. Then holding the stock of the square against the working edge, square a line across the face on the side of the board opposite the working face.

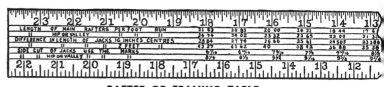

RAFTER OR FRAMING TABLE

This table appears on the body of the Square. It is used to determine the length of the common, valley, hip and jack rafters and the angles at which they must be cut to fit at the ridge and plate. Complete directions for reading and using are packed with each Square.

The various scales inscribed on a carpenter's square are shown at right along with an explanation of their many uses.

Carpenter's or framing square shown below is often used in figuring out angles and for solving of laying out problems.

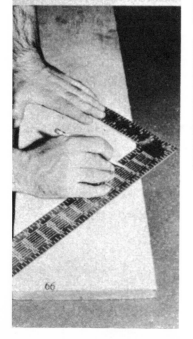

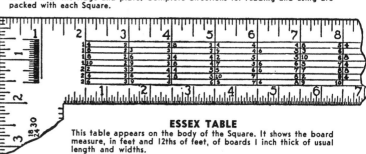

ESSEX TABLE

This table appears on the body of the Square. It shows the board measure, in feet and 12ths of feet, of boards 1 inch thick of usual length and widths.

OCTAGON SCALE

This Scale appears on the tongue of the Square. It is used to lay out a figure with eight equal sides on a square piece of timber, as for a pillar.

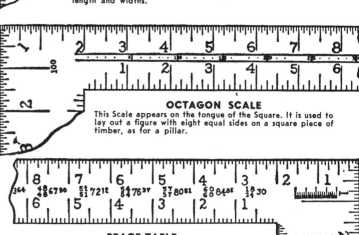

BRACE TABLE

This table appears on the tongue of the Square. It shows the length of the Common braces.

HUNDREDTHS SCALE

This scale appears on the tongue of the Square. With a pair of dividers, decimals of an inch can be quickly obtained.

Courtesy Stanley Tools

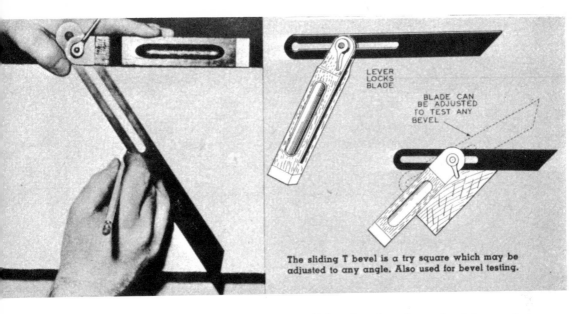

LEVER
LOCKS
BLADE

BLADE CAN
BE ADJUSTED
TO TEST ANY
BEVEL

The sliding T bevel is a try square which may be
adjusted to any angle. Also used for bevel testing.

Sliding T Bevel

This tool is a try square which can be adjusted to any angle. It is used for laying out angles other than right angles and for testing bevels. A bevel is any edge not at right angles to the face of a piece of wood. The hand tool used to produce a bevel is a plane. A sliding T bevel is used to lay out and test a bevel for a given angle.

Gauging

Gauging is a term used by woodworkers to mean the marking of guide lines parallel to an edge, end or surface of a piece of wood. A good example of gauging is the marking of guide lines for chamfers.

Gauging with a Pencil

When a not too accurate guide line is to be drawn less than 1″ from an edge, a pencil and the fingers may be substituted for the tool called a marking gauge.

Suppose a guide line for a chamfer is to be gauged on a board ⅜″ from the edge. First, make a locating mark ⅜″ from the edge. Then grasp the pencil near its point with the thumb and first and second fingers of the right hand and hold it at an angle of approximately 30 degrees to the surface to be marked. The third finger rests against the edge of the wood and acts as a guide in keeping the pencil mark parallel to the edge of the work.

The line may be gauged by pushing the pencil either away from the worker or toward him. In order to keep the line parallel to the edge, the angle of the pencil must be kept constant.

When accuracy is not an important consideration and a guide line is to be gauged more than 1″ from the edge, a pencil and a rule can be used. The point of the pencil is held against the end of the rule with the right hand. The rule is held between the thumb and forefinger of the left hand with the second finger against the edge of the wood as a guide. Both hands are moved in unison when the line is drawn.

The Marking Gauge

A marking gauge is used for gauging when accuracy is necessary. This tool, made of either wood or steel, consists of a beam about 8″ long on which a head slides. The head can be fastened at any point on the beam by means of a thumbscrew. The thumbscrew presses a brass shoe tightly against the beam and locks it firmly in position. When the gauge is used, a sharpened steel pin or spur cuts the gauge line on the wood. The spur is adjustable. It should project about $\frac{1}{16}$″ and be filed so that it scores the wood like the point of a penknife blade.

A marking gauge must be adjusted by setting the head the proper distance from the spur. Although the bar of a marking gauge is graduated in inches, the spur may work loose or bend, thus calibrating inaccurately. Consequently, the careful workman pays no attention to the calibrations but sets his gauge accurately by measuring between block and spur.

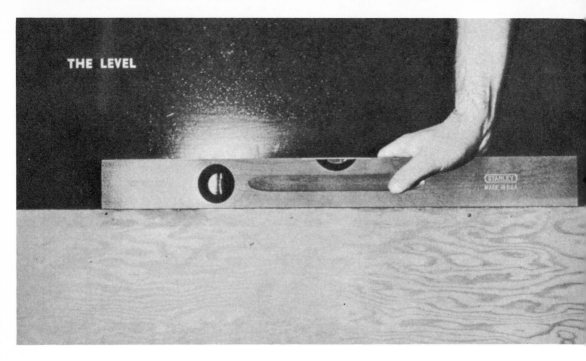

To draw a line after the gauge has been properly set, grasp the head with the palm and fingers of the right hand in much the same manner as you would a ball. Extend the thumb along the bar toward the pin. Press the head firmly against the edge of the piece to be marked and with a wrist motion tip it forward slightly until the spur just touches the wood. The line is made by pushing the gauge away from the worker while keeping the head firmly against the edge of the work at all times.

The spur must project no more than approximately $\frac{1}{16}''$ and must be kept sharp.

The Mortise Gauge

The mortise gauge is a marking gauge with two spurs. It is used chiefly for laying out mortises and tenons. The two spurs mark two parallel lines the distance between which can be changed by moving one of the spurs controlled by an adjusting screw in the end of the beam. The two spurs are set the proper distance apart first. Then the head is set the correct distance from them. The mortise gauge is then used much like a marking gauge.

Many mortise gauges are made with a single spur on the side of the bar opposite the one bearing the two spurs. This makes a dual purpose tool, for, turned over, the mortise gauge can be used as a marking gauge for making one line.

Using the Level

The level is a simple instrument which indicates a true vertical position or a true

Level shows true vertical or horizontal position by means of an air bubble sealed in tube of liquid.

Sketch shows marking gauge set for marking line parallel to an edge. Double check setting with rule.

LOCKING SCREW

HEAD

STOP SCREW

PIN

BEAM

HEAD

PIN SHOULD PROJECT ABOUT 1/16

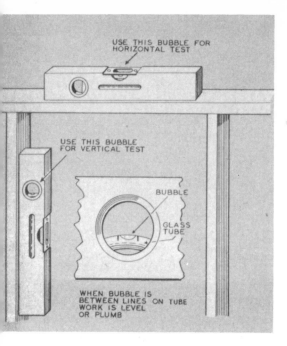

USE THIS BUBBLE FOR HORIZONTAL TEST

USE THIS BUBBLE FOR VERTICAL TEST

BUBBLE

GLASS TUBE

WHEN BUBBLE IS BETWEEN LINES ON TUBE WORK IS LEVEL OR PLUMB

Drawing shows how to place and read a level, which is used mostly for building construction.

level position by means of a liquid sealed in a glass tube. The tube is mounted in a frame which may be aluminum, iron or wood. Aluminum levels, light in weight, will not warp or rust. Wood levels are light and are not cold to the touch when used outdoors in cold weather.

Iron levels, which are heavier and which will rust, hold their shapes better and withstand more abuse than either wood or aluminum levels. However, do not drop a level on the ground or floor.

Carpenters and woodworkers generally use levels with either an aluminum or a wood frame, equipped with two, four or six glasses, as the tubes are called. One set of tubes is built in the frame at right angles to the other set. There is an air bubble in each tube.

When a level is laid on a flat surface or held against a vertical surface, the surface is true level or true vertical, as the case may be, if the air bubble in one of the tubes is *in the center*. If the bubble is at either end of the tube or not exactly centered, the surface being tested is not true level or not true vertical. •

Grasp marking gauge as illustrated, head firmly against board. Push away from you to score line.

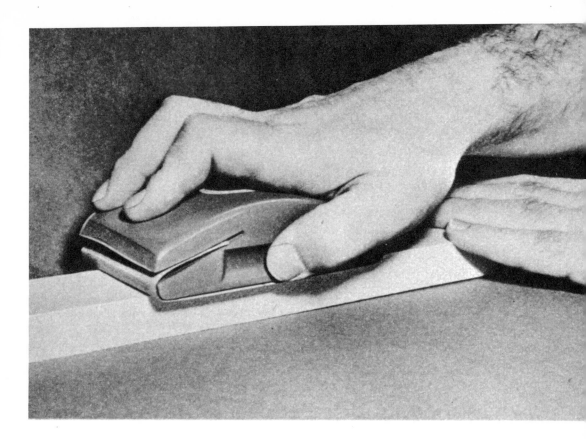

scraping and sanding

Wood should be flat and smooth before it's painted or finished.

WHEN a job of woodworking has been completed, it is usually given a finish, meaning a protective and decorative coating of paint, lacquer, wax, stain, varnish, oil or shellac. The coating gives the surface of the work color, texture and durability and prevents the wood from warping or shrinking because of the temperature

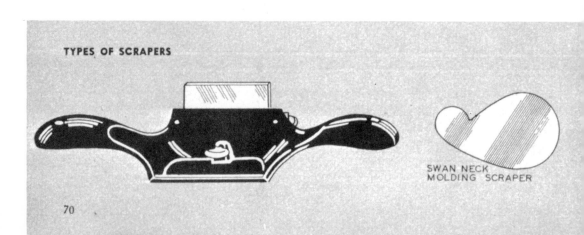

TYPES OF SCRAPERS

SWAN NECK MOLDING SCRAPER

changes and humidity of the atmosphere.

Before any finishing coat can be applied to woodwork to successfully accomplish these purposes, the surface of the work must be smooth. Final smoothing operations on fine woodwork are done by hand with scrapers and with sandpaper. Two types of scrapers for fine woodworking are the cabinet scraper and the hand scraper.

The Cabinet Scraper

The cabinet scraper has a beveled blade set in an iron frame with two handles. It resembles a spokeshave in appearance.

A cabinet scraper takes a much thinner shaving than a plane and it is used only on flat surfaces after they have been planed or on surfaces that are difficult to plane because of irregular grain. It will produce a smooth cut against the grain, making it indispensable for putting a smooth surface on cross-grained woods. The tool is held in both hands. Although it may be either pushed or pulled, it is probably pushed more often.

A sharp cabinet scraper takes off a thin even shaving, removing the slight ridges left by a plane. Dust instead of shavings indicates a dull blade. A scraper, no matter how sharp the blade is, will not work satisfactorily on soft wood.

A scraper blade dulls quickly. If you watch an experienced scraper at work you will see him occasionally renew the edge of his blade by rubbing it with a burnishing tool. This can be done several times before the edge must be reground.

The blade used in a cabinet scraper has a beveled edge which has been turned slightly by drawing a burnisher along it. The blade can be removed from the body of the scraper by loosening the adjusting and the clamp thumbscrews. A new blade is inserted from the bottom, between the body and the clamp with the bevel side toward the adjusting thumbscrew.

The blade is adjusted so that it is even with the bottom of the scraper body by placing the latter on a flat wood surface and pressing the blade down lightly against the wood. Then the clamp screws are tightened to hold it in this position. The adjusting screw is tightened until it just touches the blade and a trial cut is made.

If one corner of the blade projects farther than the other, draw it back in by tapping the side of the blade near the top. If the blade does not project far enough to make a thin shaving, tighten the adjusting screw a little at a time between trial cuts until a fine shaving is produced.

The Hand Scraper

The hand scraper produces finer shavings than a cabinet scraper and can be used on both flat and curved surfaces. Veneers or veneered surfaces generally cannot be planed but must be scraped. A scraper is almost the only tool that will give satisfactory results in refinishing furniture.

The common form of hand scraper is a rectangle of high-tempered hand saw sheet steel varying in width from 2″ to 3″ and in length from 4″ to 6″. Curved forms, called molding scrapers, are also made for scraping concave and convex curves in cabinetmaking, joinery and pattern work.

Some scrapers have square edges and others beveled edges. The edges of both are turned with a tool called a burnisher. A square-edge scraper makes a smoother surface but does not cut as fast as a scraper with a bevel-edge. The square-edge produces a flatter surface but dulls sooner than

Rectangular hand scraper removes fine shavings; and it may be pulled on wood or pushed as below.

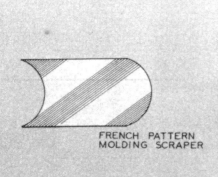

FRENCH PATTERN
MOLDING SCRAPER

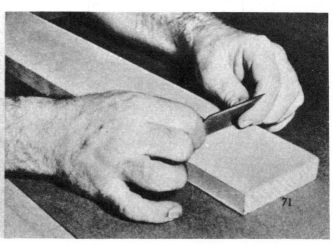

71

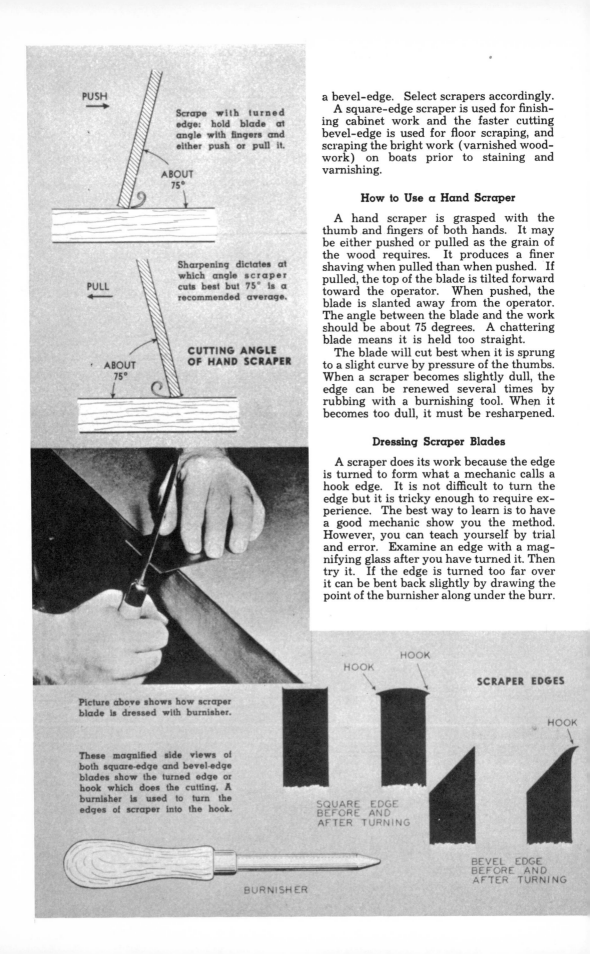

PUSH →

Scrape with turned edge: hold blade at angle with fingers and either push or pull it.

ABOUT 75°

PULL ←

Sharpening dictates at which angle scraper cuts best but 75° is a recommended average.

ABOUT 75°

CUTTING ANGLE OF HAND SCRAPER

Picture above shows how scraper blade is dressed with burnisher.

These magnified side views of both square-edge and bevel-edge blades show the turned edge or hook which does the cutting. A burnisher is used to turn the edges of scraper into the hook.

BURNISHER

HOOK   HOOK

HOOK

SCRAPER EDGES

HOOK

SQUARE EDGE BEFORE AND AFTER TURNING

BEVEL EDGE BEFORE AND AFTER TURNING

a bevel-edge. Select scrapers accordingly.

A square-edge scraper is used for finishing cabinet work and the faster cutting bevel-edge is used for floor scraping, and scraping the bright work (varnished woodwork) on boats prior to staining and varnishing.

How to Use a Hand Scraper

A hand scraper is grasped with the thumb and fingers of both hands. It may be either pushed or pulled as the grain of the wood requires. It produces a finer shaving when pulled than when pushed. If pulled, the top of the blade is tilted forward toward the operator. When pushed, the blade is slanted away from the operator. The angle between the blade and the work should be about 75 degrees. A chattering blade means it is held too straight.

The blade will cut best when it is sprung to a slight curve by pressure of the thumbs. When a scraper becomes slightly dull, the edge can be renewed several times by rubbing with a burnishing tool. When it becomes too dull, it must be resharpened.

Dressing Scraper Blades

A scraper does its work because the edge is turned to form what a mechanic calls a hook edge. It is not difficult to turn the edge but it is tricky enough to require experience. The best way to learn is to have a good mechanic show you the method. However, you can teach yourself by trial and error. Examine an edge with a magnifying glass after you have turned it. Then try it. If the edge is turned too far over it can be bent back slightly by drawing the point of the burnisher along under the burr.

Sharpening Square-Edge Scrapers

Some cabinet scrapers are supplied with plain edges which must be dressed before the scraper will cut. To dress a scraper:

1. Clamp the scraper in a vise and draw file the edges straight at right angles to the face of the scraper, using a smooth mill file. Round each corner very slightly. If the filing is properly done, it will produce perfectly square but rough edges which must be smoothed on an oilstone. The blade should not be hollow in the center.

2. Whet the edges of the scraper on an oilstone, holding the blade square to the surface of the stone. Do not allow the blade to rock from side to side or it will produce a rounded edge. A square edge is necessary. A rounded edge on a scraper is useless.

3. Lay the scraper flat on the oilstone and rub to remove any burr which was produced by previously filing and whetting the edges. The edges should be very smooth, square and sharp.

4. Lay the scraper flat on the bench and draw the edge with three or four firm strokes of a burnisher held flat against the scraper. A cabinet burnisher is a piece of highly polished steel rod set in a hardwood handle. The burnisher is so hardened that without scratching itself it will turn the edge of a cabinet scraper and other edge tools.

5. Clamp the scraper blade in a vise and turn the edge with a few strokes of the burnisher. Hold the handle of the burnisher in the right hand; hold the tip in the left and, after depositing a drop of oil on it, draw the burnisher toward you using a sliding stroke. Starting at the far corner of the blade, draw the burnisher the full

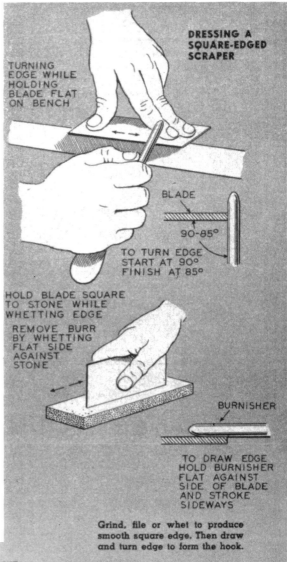

DRESSING A SQUARE-EDGED SCRAPER

TURNING EDGE WHILE HOLDING BLADE FLAT ON BENCH

BLADE

90-85°

TO TURN EDGE START AT 90° FINISH AT 85°

HOLD BLADE SQUARE TO STONE WHILE WHETTING EDGE

REMOVE BURR BY WHETTING FLAT SIDE AGAINST STONE

BURNISHER

TO DRAW EDGE HOLD BURNISHER FLAT AGAINST SIDE OF BLADE AND STROKE SIDEWAYS

Grind, file or whet to produce smooth square edge. Then draw and turn edge to form the hook.

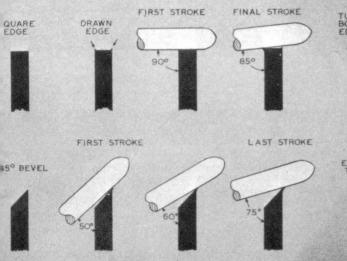

QUARE EDGE

DRAWN EDGE

FIRST STROKE

90°

FINAL STROKE

85°

TURN BOTH EDGES

TURNING A SCRAPER BLADE TO FORM HOOK

45° BEVEL

FIRST STROKE

50°

60°

LAST STROKE

75°

EDGE TURNED

A square-edge scraper is illustrated at top. The method of turning bevel-edge scraper is shown in the bottom illustration, left.

73

length of the blade. For the first stroke the burnisher should be held at 90 degrees to the face of the blade. Thereafter tilt the burnisher slightly and gradually until after five or six strokes it is at an angle of about 85 degrees. In this way the edge is pressed out and turned slightly to form a hook.

Sharpening Bevel-Edge Hand Scrapers

To dress a bevel-edge scraper:
1. File or grind the edge to a 30-degree bevel. If the former method is used, push the file forward and to one side with a sliding motion.
2. Whet the bevel side of the blade by the same method used to sharpen a chisel. Then, laying the face side of the scraper flat on the oilstone, rub it back and forth a few times to remove the wire edge.
3. Clamp the blade in a vise and run a burnisher along the keen edge to turn it. Make the first few strokes firm with the burnisher at an angle which is only a little greater than the bevel. Increase the angle until at the last stroke the burnisher is at an angle of about 75 degrees to the face of the blade. This produces a fast-cutting hook-edge.

Sharpening the Bevel-Edge Cabinet Blade

To resharpen the bevel-edge of a cabinet scraper blade:
1. Clamp the blade in a vise with the cutting edge up. Remove the old burr with a smooth mill file held against the flat side of the blade.
2. Restore the old bevel by filing or grinding it to an angle of 45 degrees. If the blade is filed, use a smooth mill file pushing it sideways at the same time it is pushed forward. This will produce a smooth edge when done with proper care.
3. Whet the bevel to a smooth edge on an oilstone. Maintain the 45-degree angle.
4. Whet the blade, flat side down, on an oilstone to remove the wire edge.
5. Lay the blade on the workbench bevel-side down with edge projecting slightly over the edge of the bench. Hold the burnisher flat against the flat side of the blade and rub it back and forth with a few firm strokes to draw the edge.
6. To turn the edge, place the blade, edge up, in a vise. Rub a drop of oil on the burnisher. Make the first stroke firm with the burnisher at an angle 3 or 4 degrees greater than the bevel. Then make several firm strokes with the burnisher at about 75 degrees to the face of the blade.

To Resharpen a Dressed Scraper

Oftentimes the cutting edge of a scraper blade can be renewed several times by a few strokes of the burnisher. After this it will be necessary to file and whet the edge. A square-edge blade must be filed square and whetted to a keen, smooth edge and then have its edge turned with the burnishing tool. All vestiges of the hook-edge must be filed or ground from the bevel-edge scraper, a new bevel formed and the edge turned in the manner already described.

Sandpaper and Sanding

Not always with good reason, everyone seems to think he knows how to use sandpaper. The general opinion is that you rub it back and forth, but there are many little tricks in its use.

Available in rolls and in sheets 9″ x 11″, sandpaper is made of tough paper which has been coated with glue and sprinkled

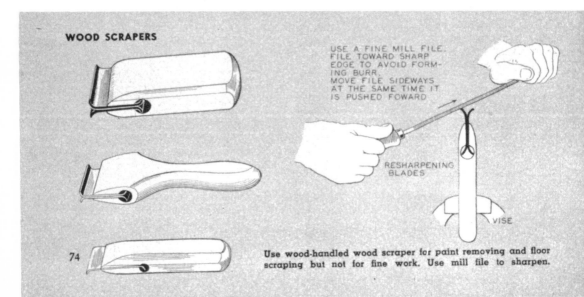

WOOD SCRAPERS

USE A FINE MILL FILE. FILE TOWARD SHARP EDGE TO AVOID FORMING BURR. MOVE FILE SIDEWAYS AT THE SAME TIME IT IS PUSHED FOWARD

RESHARPENING BLADES

VISE

74

Use wood-handled wood scraper for paint removing and floor scraping but not for fine work. Use mill file to sharpen.

with particles of quartz, garnet or flint. The variety known as garnet paper is red and is the best, not because of its color, but because it retains its sharpness longest.

Sandpaper is graded according to the fineness of its grit. No. 3 is the coarsest and No. 8/0 is the finest. Nos. 1½, 1, ½, 0 and 00 are the grades most commonly used. If the surface is rough and wavy it is either scraped or rubbed with No. 1½ sandpaper. This grade leaves fairly large scratches. After it No. 1, No. ½ and finally No. 0 must be used. Each finer grade makes the scratches smaller until finally they become invisible.

Sanding Wood

All work with planes, scrapers and other edge tools must be completed before sandpaper is used. When wood is rubbed with sandpaper, minute particles of grit become loosened from the paper and embedded in the wood surface. These dull edged tools.

A surface should usually be sanded *with the grain*. Sanding across the grain tears and roughens the surface fibers and produces scratches which show through the finish. When sandpaper is rubbed over the wood at a slight angle to the grain instead of exactly with the grain, the abrasive will cut faster. This is especially true of soft woods, such as white pine, and of old lumber.

Sanding at an angle cuts the fibers more easily. If the angle is not too great, a little rubbing with the grain will remove the scratches.

Unless a 9″ x 11″ sheet is folded, or divided, it is too large to use for hand sanding. The coarse grades can be folded more easily if the sheet is first flexed by grasping opposite edges and drawing the back over the edge of the workbench. A sheet is usually folded twice so that it is 4½″x5½″, or it is torn into halves or quarters.

Sanding must be done carefully to avoid rounding edges and corners which are not supposed to be rounded. In many instances it is just as necessary to sand an edge or corner squarely as it is to plane it squarely. If the sandpaper is wrapped around a rectangular block of wood, rounding edges and some of the other pitfalls of sanding can be more easily avoided.

A block of soft wood 4″ to 5″ long, 3″ wide and 1″ to 1½″ thick is a handy size. Much better than the block of wood is a block of cork of the same dimensions.

A piece of sandpaper 5½″ x 9″, obtained by tearing a full-sized piece in half, can conveniently be wrapped around the block. It is held in place with the thumb and fingers. More even pressure can be applied with a block and a better surface will be produced.

There are a number of handy, patented sandpaper holders on the market which are pushed by hand and which hold the paper tightly to give good sanding results.

Sandpaper soon fills up with fine wood particles. It will cut faster and longer if the dust is eliminated by slapping it against a hard surface once in a while.

Concave surfaces are sanded with sandpaper wrapped around a piece of dowel or round stick of proper diameter.

Most convex surfaces can be sanded with a piece of sandpaper held firmly in the hollow of the hand. •

Photograph shows full flat view of scrapers which are all used similarly in scraping wood surfaces.

Cutting edge angle ground at factory is maintained in resharpening. Don't turn edge to form a hook.

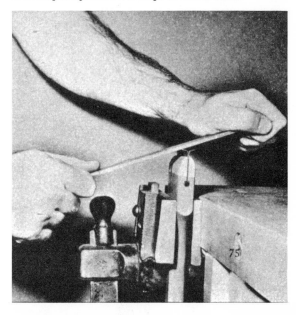

75

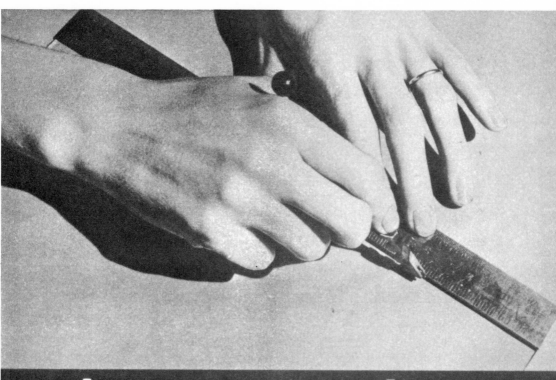

how to cut glass

To cut circular areas from glass, the sections are scored separately from the circle and then broken off separately from the whole. Keep wheel clean.

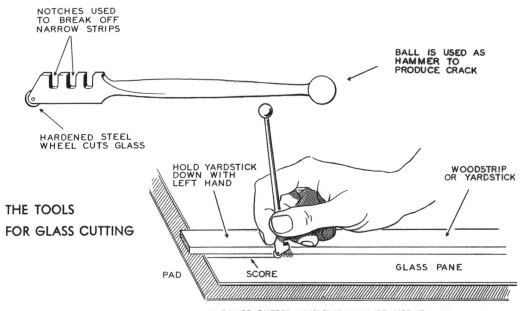

NOTCHES USED TO BREAK OFF NARROW STRIPS

BALL IS USED AS HAMMER TO PRODUCE CRACK

HARDENED STEEL WHEEL CUTS GLASS

THE TOOLS FOR GLASS CUTTING

HOLD YARDSTICK DOWN WITH LEFT HAND

WOODSTRIP OR YARDSTICK

PAD   SCORE   GLASS PANE

A GLASS CUTTER AND THE WAY TO USE IT

Glass can be cut smoothly and accurately in your home workshop once you learn how to use the steel wheel glass cutter correctly.

THE skill and confidence with which a glazier cuts a pane of glass makes it look easy. It *is* an easy art, but the novice cannot expect to cut glass like a professional until he develops the right touch.

The ordinary steel wheel glass cutter is the tool of the glazier. It will give good service if properly used and cared for. On the other hand, it can be ruined quickly by mistreatment.

Close examination of the cutter will reveal that its work is done by a small sharp-edged wheel. This wheel is made of extremely hard steel and it revolves when it is drawn over a pane of glass. It must be kept sharp and free to turn easily.

If it rusts, its sharp edge will be dulled and it may not turn. In that case throw the cutter away and buy a new one. The best way to prevent the wheel from rusting is to keep it wrapped in cotton or a small piece of rag saturated with sewing-machine oil or some other fine oil.

Accurately speaking, the wheel-type glass cutter does not cut glass to size, it *splits* it. If the wheel is sharp and it is drawn over the glass at the right speed and pressure, it makes a fine score or groove by slightly crushing or pulverizing the glass under the edge of the wheel. The

beveled sides of the wheel also act as wedges which push against the sides of the groove and pry the glass apart so that a crack is started.

Cutting Glass Panes

Ordinary window glass comes in two thicknesses, single light and double light. Single light is the thinner and easier to cut. Plate glass up to ¼″ in thickness can be cut in the same manner as ordinary window glass. Safety glass, which consists of two or more glass sheets cemented together by a transparent plastic requires special cutting equipment.

Place Glass on Level Surface

Unless the pane which is to be cut is placed on a firm level surface, it may crack in an unexpected place. Place a piece of carpet or several layers of newspaper on a table and lay the glass on top. This pad between the table and the glass equalizes the pressure and greatly decreases the danger of breakage during the cutting operation.

Make sure that the glass is thoroughly clean. Dirty glass does not cut well and also

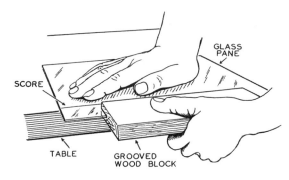

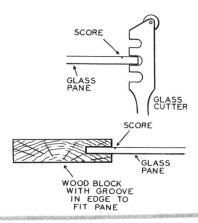

Narrow glass strip can be broken off with grooved board or by slipping notch in cutter head over edge to snap glass off.

dulls the cutter wheel. Wet a small brush with turpentine and run it along the line to be cut. This not only makes the cutter work better, it also keeps it sharp longer.

To make a straight cut it is necessary to use a straightedged guide strip to guide the cutter. A wooden strip is preferable because it does not slip as easily on a glass surface as metal. A wooden yardstick makes a good guide strip. The guide is held against the glass with the fingers of the left hand. The cutter is held in a vertical position in the right hand. The forefinger should be extended along the back of the cutter with the tip of the finger down near the wheel.

When placing the guide strip in position to cut a pane of glass to a specified size, bear in mind that the wheel does not cut exactly at the edge of the strip but makes the score or groove about $\frac{1}{16}''$ from it.

Start the score at the far end of the guide and draw the cutter toward you. Using the correct pressure in applying the wheel against the glass is one of the tricks of cutting glass. Too much pressure may crack the pane; too little may make an unsatisfactory score.

The Correct Pressure

The novice should practice on some old, *clean* pieces of window glass. Wipe a small

brush, wet with turpentine, over the surface along the line to be cut. If the correct pressure is applied and the cutter is drawn toward you at the right speed, the wheel will make a scratching sound as it cuts the score mark into the glass. If the wheel is dull, or too much pressure is applied, the sound will be more like crunching than scratching.

Draw the cutter over the line *once* only. If it becomes necessary to doctor an imperfect score, do not use a new cutter for the purpose. Use an old one. Drawing a sharp cutter over a score mark the second time dulls it.

To cut a pane of glass it is necessary to make a continuous score mark all the way across from one edge to the other. If the score is properly made, a slight crack will be visible all the way along the score. The crack may not extend through from one surface to the other. It can best be seen from the side opposite the score. If the crack is continuous or nearly so, the glass will easily split into two pieces with little pressure being required.

To part the glass along the score line, slide the pane over to the edge of the table so that the score line will be parallel to and projecting about $\frac{1}{8}''$ beyond the edge. Hold the portion resting on the table firmly under the palm of the left hand. Grasp the projecting portion between the fingertips

Before cutting, lubricate cutter wheel by applying drop of sewing machine oil to slot. Remove excess.

Brushing turpentine directly on glass with brush will keep it out of bearings, prevent gumming.

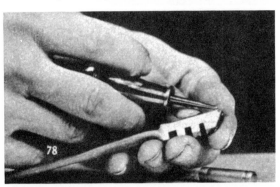

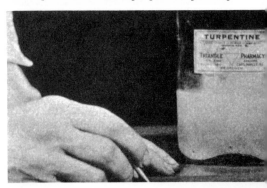

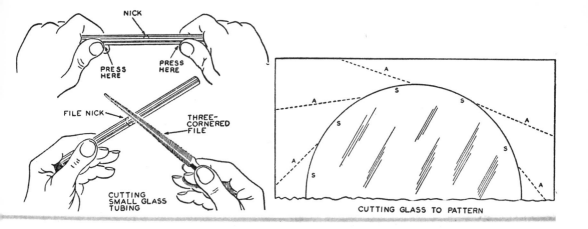

NICK

PRESS HERE   PRESS HERE

FILE NICK

THREE-CORNERED FILE

CUTTING SMALL GLASS TUBING

CUTTING GLASS TO PATTERN

and palm of the right hand. Apply light firm pressure to break the pane into two pieces along the score line.

The pane should lie on the table with the scored surface uppermost. The pressure which parts the glass is applied so as to open the crack which has been started by the cutter wheel. It can't be done the opposite way.

The novice may find it much easier to make a clean break along the score line by using a slotted wood strip. This device is especially useful when the piece to be broken off is narrow. A slot about ½" deep is made in the edge of a wood strip about ¾" thick. The slotted strip should be nearly as long as the strip of glass which is to be broken off. The slot can be cut in the wood strip with a hand saw but a power driven circular saw will certainly do the job better and with considerably less effort.

Tapping

A pane of plate or double light glass will part along the scored line most easily and accurately if a continuous crack is started along the bottom of the groove. A sharp cutter and the right pressure will usually start this crack when the groove is scored.

If the crack does not appear then, it can generally be started by turning the pane over and tapping against the unscored surface with the end of the cutter handle. Tap directly over the line scored on the opposite side. A crack which is not continuous can be extended all the way along the groove by tapping in this manner.

Cutting Glass to Pattern

A simple method for the novice to employ in cutting glass to a pattern of specified dimensions is to first lay out a full-size drawing on paper. Use a drawing pen or a soft pencil to make the outline so that it will be distinct. Place this drawing under the pane to be trimmed to size. Circles, ovals and curved shapes are cut by tracing them through the glass with the cutter wheel. Straight lines are cut best by using a guide strip placed so that the cutter wheel will score the glass directly over the lines seen through the glass.

Cutting Glass Tubing

Glass tubing is cut by nicking it with a three-cornered file. Hold the tubing in both hands and apply pressure as if the glass were to be bent with the nick on the outside of the curve. It will crack apart at the nick. Glass rods may be cut in the same manner. This method is used in chemical laboratories, where quick, accurate cuts in tubing are demanded all the time. •

Rub the working edge of yardstick or straightedge with tallow candle so the cutter will glide smoothly.

Assure keen, free-running wheel. Keep head, protected by cotton, in can of light oil and kerosene.

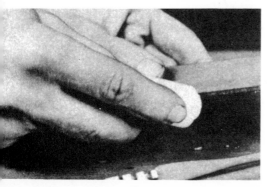

79

sharpening
woodworking tools

It takes sharp tools to do good woodworking so why not sharpen up and make your work more fun?

EXPERIENCED mechanics know the value of sharp tools. Tradition credits dull tools to the novice and less expert craftsman. A dull tool requires a lot more driving power than a sharp one; it does its work more slowly and less accurately. The time required to sharpen dull tools is regained many times in quality of workmanship and quicker operations.

All edged tools become dull with use and need to be resharpened. The proper sharpening of tools is one of the most important things for a mechanic to learn. To be in first class condition, edged tools such as chisels, gouges and planes should not only be ground to the correct angle but they should be honed until they are sharp enough to shave a hair off your arm.

Files are used to sharpen saws and auger bits. Oilstones are used to renew the cutting edges of planes, chisels, scrapers, gouges and knives. After the latter have been resharpened several times it may be necessary to restore the original bevel of the cutting edge by grinding. A badly nicked edge must be ground also.

To remove the wire edge which results from grinding it is necessary to whet the tool on an oilstone. The wire edge which is formed by grinding and also sometimes by whetting is a thin edge, so thin, in fact, that it bends back and forth like paper.

Types of Oilstones

Tools are whetted on fine, hard stones called oilstones. There are two types: Washita oilstones, cut from a natural stone found in the Ozark Mountains in Arkansas and the artificial stones such as Carborundum and Aloxite. Carborundum is silicon carbide and Aloxite is aluminum oxide. Both substances are made in electric furnaces at Niagara Falls.

A few mechanics still use natural stones which have disadvantages. They cut slowly and only one kind of grit is available in one stone. To sharpen tools properly it is necessary to have a coarse grit stone for fast cutting and a fine grit stone for putting on a finishing edge.

Combination artificial stones are obtainable having a coarse, fast cutting grit on one side and a fine, slower, smoother cutting grit on the other. A single combination artificial stone can therefore serve the purpose of two natural stones. Artificial stones cut faster than those that nature made.

Sharpening stones are called oilstones because when in use they are kept wet with oil. The pores of a dry stone become clogged with fine particles of steel sooner than the pores of a well-oiled stone. A clogged stone loses much of its cutting ability.

Never use water on a natural stone or a very fine grained artificial stone. Small particles of steel rapidly become imbedded in the surface of a stone wet with water. A black, shiny, glazed surface indicates this objectionable condition.

The oil used on an oilstone must be thin and it must not gum. Good oils for this purpose are Three-in-One and Pike Oil. A mixture of equal parts of light machine oil and kerosene works well on most stones.

Carborundum stones may be used either dry, with oil or with water, but lubricated it will produce a cleaner, smoother edge.

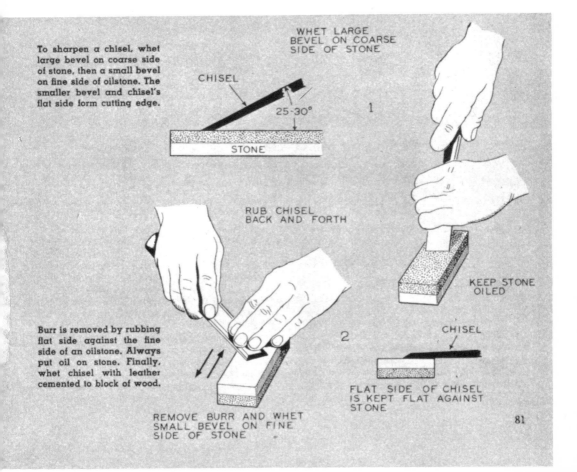

To sharpen a chisel, whet large bevel on coarse side of stone, then a small bevel on fine side of oilstone. The smaller bevel and chisel's flat side form cutting edge.

WHET LARGE BEVEL ON COARSE SIDE OF STONE

CHISEL

25-30°

1

STONE

RUB CHISEL BACK AND FORTH

KEEP STONE OILED

Burr is removed by rubbing flat side against the fine side of an oilstone. Always put oil on stone. Finally, whet chisel with leather cemented to block of wood.

2

CHISEL

FLAT SIDE OF CHISEL IS KEPT FLAT AGAINST STONE

REMOVE BURR AND WHET SMALL BEVEL ON FINE SIDE OF STONE

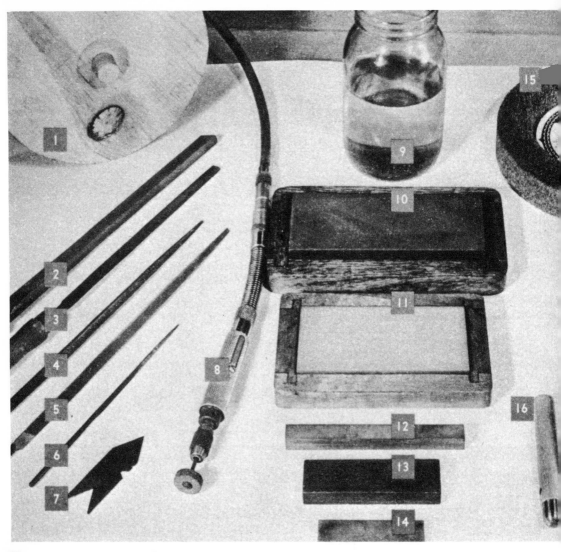

1 Circular saw blade clamps	**5** A 10 in. slim taper file	**9** Kerosene for oil stones	**13** Carborundum hand stone
2 Nicholson cross cut file	**6** Triangular Swiss pattern file	**10** Carborundum bench stone	**14** Hard Arkansas slip stone
3 An 8 in. pillar file	**7** A 60° gauge to shape bits	**11** Hard Arkansas bench stone	**15** Horiz. drill grinding wheel
4 A 10 in. round file	**8** Grinding wheel & flex. shaft	**12** Medium India stick	**16** Diamond point dressing tool

Keep Sharpening Stones in Condition

To prevent an oilstone from becoming gummy, keep it wrapped in a piece of cloth that is moistened with oil.

When a stone becomes gummy or clogged up it can be reconditioned by heating it in an oven. Place the stone in a shallow pan. Put two ten-penny finishing nails under the stone so that it is kept above the bottom of the pan thus avoiding contact with the oil and dirt which the heat will bring out. The oven should not be hot enough to evaporate the oil which oozes out. Wipe the stone dry while it is still fairly hot.

When a stone has been worn hollow by long use, it is difficult to bring chisels and plane irons to a true straight edge. The stone needs dressing which is a simple task. A flat cast iron plate having a smooth surface at least three or four times the area of the surface of the oilstone is necessary.

You will need about half an ounce of aluminum oxide powder of a grit size slightly coarser than that in the stone. Mix this with a little water until the consistency of the mixture is about that of thin mud. Smear this all over the surface of the plate and lay the worn sharpening stone on it face down. Use both hands, bear down with moderate pressure and scrub the stone around on the plate with a circular motion.

It will not take long to grind the stone perfectly flat. Examine the surface being dressed and as soon as the hollow has disappeared, the job is done. You have a stone which is as good as new.

How to Sharpen Chisels

Accurate work cannot be done with a dull chisel. It is very difficult to cut end grain on hard wood with a chisel which is even slightly dull. A chisel should always be kept sharp enough to shave the hair off the back of your hand.

Chisels are ground from time to time in order to restore the angle of the bevel. It is not usually necessary to grind the bevel each time the edge becomes dull. Grinding is essential when the cutting edge has become badly nicked and the nicks cannot be removed by whetting on a coarse oilstone, or when the bevel has become too short or rounded as a result of frequent whetting or of careless whetting.

A common oilstone of coarse grit on one side and a fine grit on the other is used to sharpen a chisel which does not require grinding. It is also used to whet a chisel after grinding.

The first "do not" in sharpening a chisel is *do not whet it on a dry stone.* Whetting tools on a dry stone will fill the pores of the stone with fine particles of steel. The surface will become black and glazed; its whetting qualities will be spoiled.

The second "do not" is *do not use water or saliva.* Water will not prevent the stone from filling with steel particles. *Use kerosene and light machine oil.* The kind of oil used in the crankcase of an automobile is suitable if mixed with sufficient kerosene. Keep a bottle of oil handy on your bench and keep the oilstone covered with it when whetting tools. The oil will float the fine particles of steel which are ground off the tools and prevent clogging the stone.

Whetting a Chisel

The oilstone should be clamped in the bench vise or otherwise firmly held so that it cannot slide easily. Hold the chisel in the right hand with the bevel flat against the coarse side of the oilstone. Then raise the hand to lift the back edge of the bevel slightly off the stone.

One of the important things to know when sharpening a chisel is that a chisel is like a plane iron in that it has *two bevels.* For ordinary work the large bevel which is ground with a wheel or the coarse side

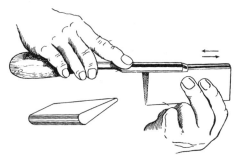

Sharpening a gouge: wire edge which remains after bevel is ground is whetted off with a slip stone.

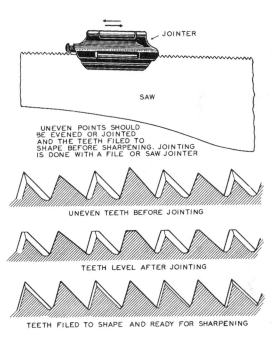

UNEVEN POINTS SHOULD BE EVENED OR JOINTED AND THE TEETH FILED TO SHAPE BEFORE SHARPENING. JOINTING IS DONE WITH A FILE OR SAW JOINTER

UNEVEN TEETH BEFORE JOINTING

TEETH LEVEL AFTER JOINTING

TEETH FILED TO SHAPE AND READY FOR SHARPENING

Jointing saw teeth, above, is done prior to the setting and filing if the points of teeth are uneven.

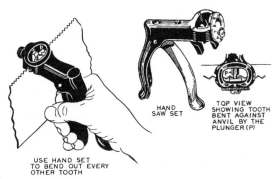

HAND SAW SET

TOP VIEW SHOWING TOOTH BENT AGAINST ANVIL BY THE PLUNGER (P)

USE HAND SET TO BEND OUT EVERY OTHER TOOTH

Drawing shows the pistol grip hand sawset. The handle moves plunger, bends one tooth at a time.

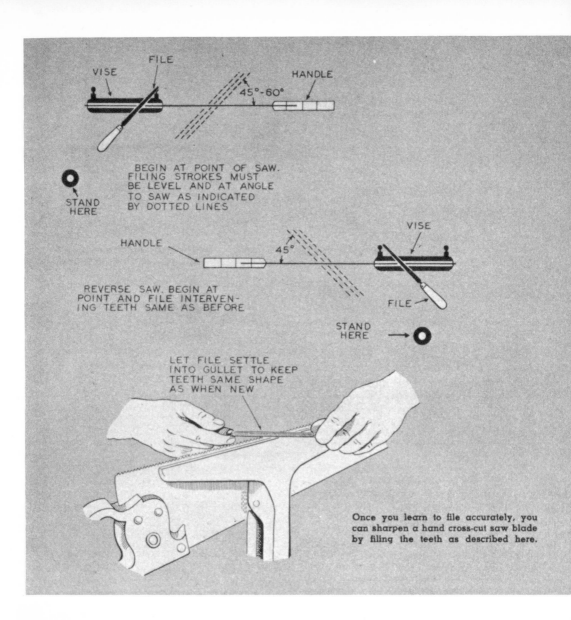

FILE

VISE

HANDLE

45°-60°

BEGIN AT POINT OF SAW.
FILING STROKES MUST
BE LEVEL AND AT ANGLE
TO SAW AS INDICATED
BY DOTTED LINES

STAND
HERE

HANDLE

VISE

45°

REVERSE SAW. BEGIN AT
POINT AND FILE INTERVEN-
ING TEETH SAME AS BEFORE

FILE

STAND
HERE

LET FILE SETTLE
INTO GULLET TO KEEP
TEETH SAME SHAPE
AS WHEN NEW

Once you learn to file accurately, you
can sharpen a hand cross-cut saw blade
by filing the teeth as described here.

of an oilstone is usually at an angle of 25 to 30 degrees. For fine cutting and paring, the angle may be slightly less. The small bevel is the whetting bevel and is put on by the fine side of the oilstone. It is usually at an angle of 30 to 35 degrees.

The proper angle for the whetting bevel is obtained by holding the chisel so that the whole of the large bevel is in contact with the flat surface of the stone, then raising the back edge of the ground bevel slightly off the oilstone.

It is only the whetting angle of the chisel that is ground against the face of the oilstone. Use the first and second fingers of the left hand to steady the chisel and hold it down against the face of the stone. With light pressure only, rub the chisel back and forth on the stone with smooth even strokes. Use the coarse side of the stone.

After a few strokes, a burr or wire edge is produced. You can see the burr if you have good eyesight. You can see it plainly with a magnifying glass. It can also be felt by rubbing the finger tip against it *very lightly*. It is flexible enough to be bent back and forth.

This part of the sharpening process requires a little skill and experience. The main trick is to keep the hand steady, moving it back and forth *parallel* to the surface of the stone at all times. Do not rock the blade. The angle of the blade with the stone must remain constant during the whetting process. The entire surface of the stone should be used to avoid wearing a hollow in the center. The edge must be whet so that it is square with the side of the chisel, not at a skew.

For whetting chisels and plane blades there is a very convenient gadget which holds them at a constant angle. This removes all the guesswork and gives the beginner a chance to do a whetting job equal to that of a skilled mechanic.

Removing the Burr

The burr, wire edge or feather edge (it is known by all three names) is removed by whetting it on the fine side of the oilstone or on a finer and harder separate stone. First, take a few strokes with the flat side of the chisel held *flat* on the stone. Be careful not to raise it even slightly. You must avoid putting the slightest bevel on the flat side, for then the chisel must be ground until the bevel is removed.

Next, turn the chisel over (bevel side down) and hold it at the same angle used when whetting on the coarse stone. Take two or three *light* strokes. These may be sufficient to remove the burr. On the other hand, it may be necessary to take one or two light strokes again with the flat side of the chisel flat against the surface of the stone in order to get rid of the burr.

Many mechanics give a finishing touch to the edge by stropping it a few times on leather or canvas. For this purpose a piece of leather cemented to a block of wood is a useful item in a tool kit.

Testing the Edge

Many craftsmen judge the sharpness of an edge by testing it on a thumbnail or by carefully feeling it with the ball of the thumb. If it is sharp, the edge will take hold on the nail; if not, it will slide. You can quickly learn to recognize a sharp edge by looking at it. A small magnifying glass or a watchmaker's glass will reveal whether or not the burr has been entirely removed and whether the edge is blunt or sharp.

Your eye, unaided by a magnifier, will also tell you whether or not you have produced a really sharp edge by whetting. Hold the chisel where a good light will shine on the cutting edge. A keen edge does not reflect light. If there are no shiny or white spots, it is a good edge.

Grinding a Chisel

The amateur craftsman who uses his chisels only occasionally will seldom need to grind them. They can be kept sharp by whetting them on an oilstone or on a combination Carborundum stone. If, in the course of time, the edges and bevels do become worn down and need grinding, it is usually possible to have this done in some neighboring shop. The grinding is done on a revolving stone. It is more difficult than whetting.

The grinding of chisels and other edged woodworking tools can be done on a variety of wheels, ranging from the old-fashioned

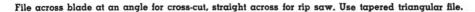

File across blade at an angle for cross-cut, straight across for rip saw. Use tapered triangular file.

CROSSCUT BEVEL

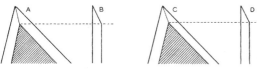

The bevel is important. Long bevel (A, B) is best for soft woods; shorter bevel (C, D) for medium-hard.

RIP AND CROSSCUT TEETH

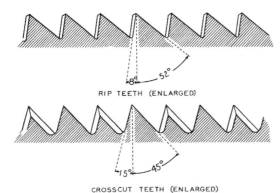

RIP TEETH (ENLARGED)

CROSSCUT TEETH (ENLARGED)

Diagram pictures the difference between rip and crosscut saw teeth. Note the variation of angles.

DRESSING THE TEETH

SMOOTH SIDE OF STONE DOWN

After filing and before setting, run fine oilstone on teeth to remove burr. Dress both sides lightly.

SHARPENING A CROSSCUT SAW

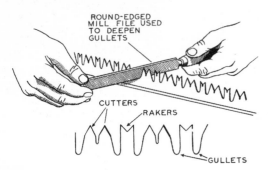

ROUND-EDGED MILL FILE USED TO DEEPEN GULLETS

CUTTERS

RAKERS

GULLETS

On a large crosscut saw, teeth can be sharpened with a mill file or a special crosscut saw file.

foot-driven grindstone to the modern power-driven oil grinder. Grinding woodworking tools on a dry emery or Carborundum wheel requires care and experience. The tool must be dipped in water frequently to keep it cool.

The hazard of using a dry grinder is the risk of burning the steel. The edge overheats; it turns a blue-black color, loses its temper and softens. Soft steel cannot be sharpened.

Burning must be avoided and can be by grinding very lightly, at the same time keeping kerosene or water dripping on the grinding wheel. An experienced mechanic can keep a tool cool during the grinding process by dipping it in water frequently. However, this is not as easy as it looks. It is difficult to repeatedly remove the tool from the wheel to cool it and then place it back on the wheel at the same angle each time.

An old-fashioned sandstone wheel, kept wet by water dripping on it, is really best for the novice at grinding woodworking tools, whether they are chisels, gouges, plane irons or spokeshave blades.

Modern plants where woodworking tools must be kept sharp are usually equipped with motor-driven oilstone grinders. The revolving wheel is in the form of a shallow cup. The outside edge is the grinding surface. Kerosene, fed through a tube from a small reservoir, drops on the inside of the cupped wheel and filters through to the surface. This grinder produces a smooth bevel with little danger of burning.

A small hand-driven grinder fitted with a Carborundum wheel of the right variety for woodworking tools can be used for plane iron, chisel, gouge and spokeshave grinding. The expert can turn the crank with one hand and hold the tool with the other. The beginner will find it much easier if he holds the tool with both hands while some one else turns the crank.

No matter which type of grinder is used, it should be one provided with an adjustable tool rest which can be set to produce the desired bevel. The face of the wheel should be smooth. If it is grooved or out of true it should be dressed or put into good shape with a Carborundum stick made for the purpose. The Carborundum stick, held on the revolving wheel, will cut the wheel.

Now let us return to chisel grinding. The wheel should turn toward the chisel. The bevel of the tool is held against the wheel lightly and moved from side to side evenly across its surface. The edge must be maintained at right angles to the sides of the chisel. A chisel which is off-square is said to be skewed and it is almost impossible to do accurate work with it. You can tell whether the chisel is against the wheel in such position to grind a bevel of the right angle by looking at it from the side when the wheel is not running.

The chisel blade should rest on the tool rest in front of the wheel. When the right position has been found, grasp the chisel blade so that the back of the forefinger of the left hand touches the tool rest. The finger acts as a stop and you do not shift its position on the blade until you are through grinding.

You can dip the tool in water from time to time or examine the bevel and always get the chisel back in the position on the wheel by using this finger as a guide. In grinding, the only motion of the chisel should be from side to side. If you move the chisel forward or back in relation to the wheel, you will change the bevel.

How to Sharpen a Gouge

Sharpening a gouge is much the same as sharpening a plane iron or chisel. After all, a gouge is simply a chisel with a concave blade. There are two operations: grinding and whetting. Grinding is not always necessary. Generally, the edge may be whetted several times before it becomes necessary to grind it again.

There are gouges with the bevel on the inside and those with their bevel on the outside of the tool.

An outside-bevel gouge is ground on an ordinary wet grindstone, a Carborundum wheel or an oilstone grinder. It is handled like a chisel. The tool rest on the grinder should be adjusted to suit the bevel required, and the gouge moved across the edge of the wheel with a rolling motion during the grinding operation. The inside-bevel gouge is ground on a cone-shaped emery wheel.

The same precautions necessary for grinding chisels and plane irons are also taken for grinding gouges. Use light, firm pressure. Do not risk burning the edge by letting the tool become overheated. If a wet grinder is not available, dip the gouge in water frequently during the grinding process. Keep the bevel uniform, either flat or concave. A convex bevel produces an edge which will not cut well.

After grinding, the edge must be whetted. Rather than ordinary flat oilstones for whetting, small wedge-shaped stones with rounded edges to fit into concave surfaces are employed. These, called slipstones, should be kept wet with a mixture of kerosene and machine oil while being used.

A gouge is whetted just as a chisel is to remove the wire edge and produce a keen edge. First the bevel is whetted, then the flat side of the edge. When whetting the concave side of the gouge, instead of moving the tool over the stone, hold it still and rub the stone over it. A slight rotary motion should be given the gouge when it is being whetted.

While whetting the flat side of either type of gouge *use every care not to produce the slightest bevel on it.*

How to Sharpen Hand Saws

The teeth of a hand saw do their cutting with their edges and points. Consequently these edges and points must be kept sharp for the saw to cut efficiently. Sharpening the teeth is done with a file. There are three operations: jointing and shaping, setting and filing.

The teeth of most saws are set alternately to the left and right so that the saw kerf or slot cut in the work is wider than the thickness of the saw blade. By thus reducing the friction between the saw and the work, it makes sawing easier. All saws need set. The teeth usually require setting if a saw is used considerably before sharpening.

However, it is not necessary to reset the teeth every time the saw is filed. In most instances a saw may be sharpened with a file four or five times before it needs setting. A hand saw should be treated like a knife or a chisel. As a knife or a chisel is whetted lightly every once in a while to keep its

Hand sawset tool sets teeth by bending them outward evenly and alternately to each side of blade.

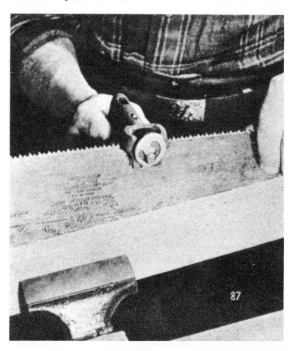

87

edge keen, so from time to time the teeth of a saw should be touched up with a file. If this is done, the saw will cut longer and better; its set will remain longer.

Setting and Filing Hand Saws

A mechanic can tell when a saw is dull or when it needs setting by its feel when he cuts wood with it. He can also tell by examining the teeth. If the teeth are uneven, if the points and edges are not sharp or if there is not enough set, he can see it. The edges and points are easier to see when they are dull. They reflect more light Sharp edges and points are almost invisible.

Study the teeth of a new saw or one which has just been sharpened by an expert. Then look carefully at the edge of a saw which has had a great deal of use without being sharpened. Feel the points of the teeth on a sharp saw and a dull saw. You can readily see and feel the difference.

Who Can Sharpen a Saw

Many fairly skillful woodworkers cannot sharpen a hand saw properly except with a saw-filing machine. The reason is that they cannot use a file well. If you can file accurately, you can file a saw after a little practice. It is advisable for the beginner to practice on an old saw with a new one before him as a guide.

The filing stroke must be kept level. Efficient saw filing demands a steady hand. If you cannot do a good job of hand filing, let someone who knows how sharpen your saws for you or else use a filing guide and clamp. This device is especially designed for those not experienced in filing hand saws. It holds the file at the proper angle and guides it. The operator merely pushes the file back and forth and moves it from tooth to tooth.

The Equipment Necessary

To file the teeth of most saws properly, the blade must be held rigidly in a vise. The best equipment for this purpose is a saw vise. This is an inexpensive device which can be purchased at hardware stores. The best substitute, when a saw vise is lacking, is a large machinist's vise and two smooth pieces of hardwood approximately 12"x2"x¾".

The saw blade is placed between the wood strips and clamped in the vise. The handle of the saw should be to the right and the toothed edge should not project far above the wood strips. The strips should be parallel to the toothed edge of the saw. The

saw teeth must be held firmly so that they do not vibrate when filed. Those directly over the vise jaws are held most firmly. The saw can be shifted from time to time as the filing proceeds.

When a saw vise is used, the blade is placed between the jaws with the handle to the right. The toothed edge should not project far above the jaws and should be parallel to them.

If the teeth of a saw are uneven, irregular in size or shape or incorrectly shaped due to misuse of the saw or improper sharpening, it is useless to file and set the saw without first performing the operation called jointing. This is done with a tool called a hand saw jointer or with an 8" or 10" mill bastard file and will be explained in detail in a later paragraph.

The file used for saw sharpening must be the right one for the job. It must be of the correct design, cut and size for the kind of saw and the kind of teeth to be filed. Saws are of many types and the files required for saw sharpening must necessarily be of considerable variety.

The files used for sharpening the teeth of a hand saw have a triangular section. They are single cut files, are made in lengths from 3" to 12" and are called slim taper files.

The proper size of file to use for any particular saw is determined by the point of the saw, or, in plainer words the number of tooth *points* to the inch of length. This number is usually stamped on the blade near the handle. If it is not stamped on the blade, count the number of tooth points to the inch, measuring one inch from the point of any tooth including both the first and last points.

When counting the tooth points on a rip saw, bear in mind that the teeth at the point of the blade are closer together than elsewhere on the blade. To determine the point of a rip saw, count the tooth *points* per inch at the *center* or *butt* of the blade. If seven points are counted, the saw is said to be a "seven point" saw. Five points indicate a "five point" saw, etc.

When you know the point of the saw to be sharpened, select the proper file by using the following table as your guide:

For 4½, 5, 6 point saws use a 7" slim taper file

For 7, 8 point saws use a 6" slim taper or a 7" extra slim taper file

For 9, 10 point saws use a 5" slim taper file

For 11, 12, 13, 14, 15 point saws use a 4" to 4½" slim taper file

For 16 point saws and finer use a 4½" to 5" No. 2 cut slim taper file.

The First Step

Setting, when it is required, must be done *before* the filing is begun. Before the teeth are set, the first step is to inspect them carefully and make sure their points are even. This is the operation already mentioned called jointing and can be done with a saw jointer or with an 8″ or 10″ mill bastard file. When a file is to be used for jointing, a special holder can be obtained but is not necessary.

The saw jointer opens and closes like a hinge so that it can be slipped over the toothed edge of the saw blade and run back and forth over the teeth. It is fitted with a file. The jointer eliminates any chance of tipping the file so that the points of the teeth are rounded at the sides. Anyone can use a jointer. Skill is required to use a file for jointing.

If a mill file is used, place the saw in the vise and lay the file lengthwise on the teeth. Pass the file lightly lengthwise along the tops of the teeth the full length of the blade until the file touches the top of every tooth. Careful examination of the teeth will show that some have been flattened on top while others were barely touched.

Before the saw can be sharpened each one of the flattened teeth must be restored to its original size and shape by filing. To be done properly, this operation requires considerable skill. The novice should practice on an old saw with a new one before him as a model.

Clamp the saw in the vise with the handle to the right and use the same file which will be used later in beveling the teeth. A 6″ slim taper fine is suitable for the average handsaw. Filing should be begun in the gullet nearest the handle. Hold the file at right angles to the blade and file straight across. Do not bevel the teeth when filing them to shape. Continue until all teeth have been filed to shape.

If the teeth are very uneven, do not attempt to make them all the same height in one jointing. Joint only the highest teeth and file these flattened teeth into shape before proceeding. Then joint the teeth a second time. This time the file can be passed over the teeth until it touches them all.

Remember to hold the file flat when jointing. Do not allow the file to tip or rock from one side to the other. Remember also that if you joint the teeth more than necessary, you are making extra work for yourself in filing them back to shape.

A hand saw does not need jointing every time the teeth are sharpened. And as already mentioned, the teeth of a first grade hand saw do not need setting every time

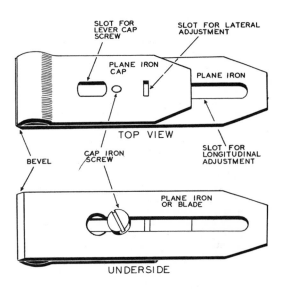

Double plane iron is shown above. Plane iron cap must be removed before a plane iron is sharpened.

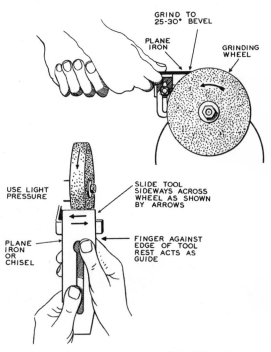

In grinding plane iron, control it with both hands; dip tool in water often to keep edge from burning.

that they require a light sharpening. In general, a well-tempered hand saw may be lightly filed four or five times before it requires setting. It is always necessary to set the teeth after they have been jointed and shaped.

The only satisfactory way to set saw teeth is to use the tool made expressly for the purpose—the sawset. There are two types of sawsets made for the average user. One type resembles a pair of pliers and is operated by squeezing the handles together. Squeezing the handles moves a plunger working against a cylindrical drum of uneven thickness. The edge of the drum is marked to show the proper adjustment. The numbers correspond with the numbers indicating the points to the inch.

The pistol grip or hand sawset is not an expensive tool. Better obtain one if you do much of your own saw sharpening.

The bench type of sawset attaches to the workbench or table and can be operated by striking the plunger with a mallet or working the plunger by foot power. Both types accomplish the same result—they bend the teeth slightly so that the width of the cut made by the saw will be greater than the thickness of the blade.

A sawset must be adjusted to suit the point or number of teeth per inch on the saw to be set. No matter whether the teeth are coarse or fine, the alternate teeth are set in opposite directions on both a cross-cut and a rip saw to a distance of about *half the thickness of the teeth* and the set *should not go lower than half the tooth.* If too much of a tooth is bent it may crack or break off.

Set the teeth in the same direction in which they were previously bent.

When the hand type of sawset is used, the saw should be clamped in a vise. The teeth which were originally bent away from the worker, that is, every other tooth, are all set first. The saw is then reversed in the vise and the remaining teeth are set in the same way, namely, away from the person setting them.

Soft woods and wet woods are cut most easily with a saw which has coarser teeth and more set than the saw which is preferable for dry, hard woods. A saw with a great deal of set does not leave a surface which is as smooth as that produced by a saw with fine teeth and not so much set. The latter type of saw is best for fine work on dry, hard woods.

The blade of a taper-ground saw tapers in thickness from the toothed edge to the back edge. It also tapers slightly from butt to point along the back. The taper provides part of the clearance necessary for easy running and consequently the teeth require very little set.

In setting a saw blade, it is essential to give every tooth the same amount of bend. The toothed edge must be the same width from point to butt and the teeth must pro-

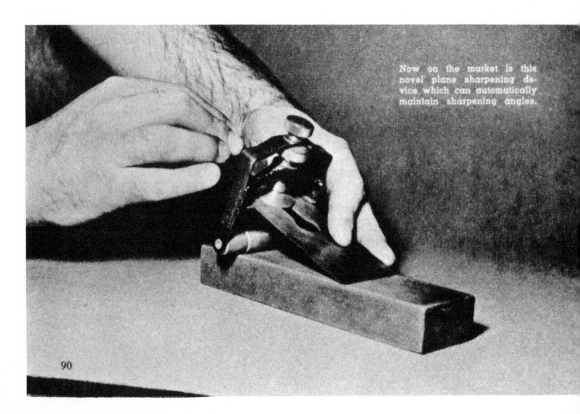

Now on the market is this novel plane sharpening device which can automatically maintain sharpening angles.

ject the same distance on both sides of the blade. Otherwise the saw will run out of line and fail to cut true.

Filing the Crosscut Saw

This saw should be clamped in the vise with the *handle to the right*. Since the filing is begun at the point of the saw and progresses toward the handle, the point should be clamped in the jaw when starting. As the filing progresses the saw is moved toward the left in the vise.

The V-shaped space between two teeth is called the gullet. The saw should be placed in the vise so that the bottoms of the gullets of the teeth are ⅛″ above the jaws of the vise or the wood strips used in the vise. If the blade is any higher than this, it will vibrate and chatter when filed.

Chattering quickly dulls the file. A very keen edge cannot be produced on a chattering saw.

Included here is an enlarged sketch of the teeth on a hand cross-cut saw as they were when new and as they should be when you have filed them back to shape and a keen cutting edge. Notice the angles. Also included is an enlarged sketch of the teeth on a hand rip saw as they are when new. Observe the differences.

Stand in front and slightly to the left of the saw vise. Select the *first tooth that is set toward you* and place the file in the gullet to the *left* of this tooth. Hold the file perfectly level with the file handle swung toward the left so that the file is at an angle of approximately 60 degrees in relationship to the blade.

The handle of the file should be held in the right hand. The thumb and forefinger of the left hand grasp the tip of the file to steady it. At the correct angle with the blade, the file should rest firmly in the gullet and touch evenly on the bevels of two teeth. It should cut on the push stroke only and file the back of the tooth to the left and the front of the tooth to the right at the same time. It will help the beginner to find the correct angle for the file if he places it in the gullet between two of the unused teeth that can usually be found at the handle end or butt end of the saw.

Let the file find its own bearing against the teeth it touches. Observe the shape and bevel of these unused teeth and the angle of the file. Try to reproduce these at the point of the saw.

The file must be kept level throughout the file stroke. Be sure the file sets down well in the gullet, finds its own bearing against the teeth and is not allowed to tip

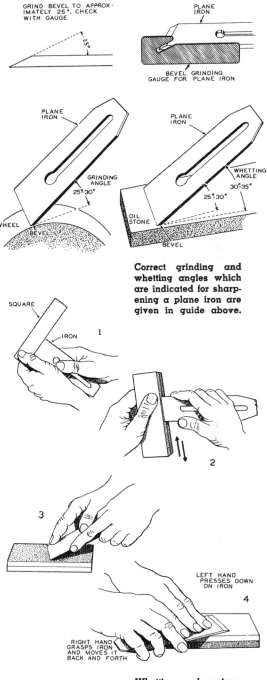

Correct grinding and whetting angles which are indicated for sharpening a plane iron are given in guide above.

Whetting a plane iron: 1. Test for squareness. 2. Square by rubbing on oilstone edge. 3. Whet bevel side, 4. flat side.

91

upward or downward during the forward cutting stroke.

If jointing the teeth has left flat tops, at this time such teeth should be filed only until *one-half* the flat top is cut away. Lift the file from the gullet and, skipping the next gullet to the right, place the file at the same angle in the second gullet to the right.

Follow the same procedure until every other gullet has been filed and you reach the handle-end of the saw. Be careful to keep the file level and always file at the same angle.

Now reverse the saw in the vise so that the handle is to the left. The point of the saw should be in the vise jaws and the bottoms of the gullets should be ⅛" above the jaws of the vise as before. Stand in front and slightly to the right of the vise.

Beginning again at the point of the saw, place the file in the gullet to the *right* of the first tooth set *toward* you. This is the first gullet skipped when you were filing the other side of the saw. Hold the file level and swing the handle to the *right* to form the desired angle to the right instead of to the left as when the first side was filed.

File every other gullet all the way to the handle. File until the remaining half of the flat tops have been cut away and the teeth are sharpened to a point.

Sharpening Mitre Saws

Mitre saws, back saws and dovetail saws are crosscut saws and are therefore filed as such. Because of their fine teeth, they are filed with 4½" extra-slim taper file.

Filing Hand Rip Saws

The teeth of a hand rip saw are set and jointed in the same manner as those of a hand crosscut saw. Follow the same procedure. Select the same file that you would use if the saw were a crosscut having the same number of teeth per inch.

Place the saw in the vise with the handle to the right and the bottom of the gullets about ⅛" above the vise jaws. Notice from the illustration or from the saw itself that the teeth of a rip saw are so shaped that they act like a row of miniature chisels, one following along after the other. The teeth are filed so that the tooth *points,* not the tooth edges, do the cutting.

Rip saws are filed with the file level and *straight across* the saw at right angles to the blade. Also notice from the illustration that the angle on the front of each tooth is 8 degrees and not 15 degrees as in the case of a crosscut saw, and that the angle at the back is 52 degrees and not 45 degrees. The

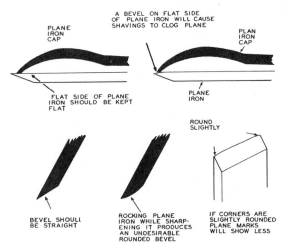

A BEVEL ON FLAT SIDE OF PLANE IRON WILL CAUSE SHAVINGS TO CLOG PLANE

PLANE IRON CAP

PLAN IRON CAP

FLAT SIDE OF PLANE IRON SHOULD BE KEPT FLAT

PLANE IRON

ROUND SLIGHTLY

BEVEL SHOULD BE STRAIGHT

ROCKING PLANE IRON WHILE SHARPENING IT PRODUCES AN UNDESIRABLE ROUNDED BEVEL

IF CORNERS ARE SLIGHTLY ROUNDED PLANE MARKS WILL SHOW LESS

file must be so held as to hold these angles.

Place the file in the gullet to the left of the first tooth set toward you and start filing. Continue to file in every second gullet so as to bring every other tooth to a square edge. Then reverse the saw in the vise end for end so that the handle is at the left. Start filing at the point again. Place the file in the first gullet skipped when filing from the other side. Continue to file in every second gullet until the remaining teeth have been brought to a square edge.

Shape and Angle of Teeth Are Important

Filing a hand saw properly is more of an art than the procedure described would indicate. The skilled saw filer pays a great deal of attention to the angle of the teeth and also to the bevel of the teeth on a crosscut saw.

Angles of 15 degrees at the front and 45 degrees at the back for crosscut saws and 8 degrees at the front and 52 degrees at the back for rip saws are the most satisfactory for general use. If the front angle is made smaller, the teeth will have too much hook or pitch. This causes the saw to grab in the slot. The quick stop may bend the blade.

Experience is the best guide to the amount of bevel on the front and back of a crosscut saw. The first illustration at the top of page 86 should be helpful to the beginner. Two different teeth are illustrated. Notice that both have the same amount of bevel at the front edge.

Teeth like that shown at A with the same amount of bevel front and back have a long bevel at the point (as shown in the end view at B) which best suits them to soft woods where rapid cutting rather than fine work is desirable.

Teeth like that shown at C with less

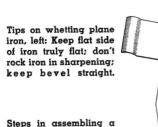

Tips on whetting plane iron, left: Keep flat side of iron truly flat; don't rock iron in sharpening; keep bevel straight.

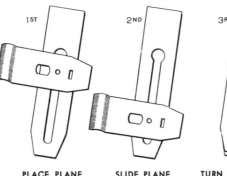

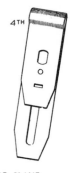

1ST   2ND   3RD   4TH

Steps in assembling a double plane iron are given in sequence, right. Handle iron with care to avoid nicking edge.

PLACE PLANE IRON CAP ON FLAT SIDE OF PLANE IRON WITH SCREW IN SLOT

SLIDE PLANE IRON CAP BACK AS SHOWN

TURN PLANE IRON CAP STRAIGHT WITH PLANE IRON

SLIDE PLANE IRON CAP FOR-WARD UNTIL EDGE IS 1/16" BACK OF CUT-TING EDGE. TIGHTEN SCREW

bevel on the back than at the front have a shorter bevel on the point (as shown in the end view at D) which best suits them to medium hard woods.

Filing a Crosscut Saw

The common type of crosscut saw used for hand sawing large timbers and logs has two sets of teeth, called cutters and rakers. The cutters, slightly longer than the rakers, do the cutting. The rakers clear out the cut. There are usually more cutter teeth than raker teeth.

The points of the teeth should be jointed if they are not of uniform height. The tops of raker teeth should be from 1/100" to 1/64" below the tops of the cutter teeth.

A mill file or a special crosscut saw file is used to file all cutting teeth to a sharp point. If the saw blade is clamped in a saw vise tilted away from the filer at an angle of about 45 degrees, it will be easier to file the cutters than if the blade is vertical.

The raker teeth are best sharpened with the blade in a vertical position. They are filed straight across with a mill file or a special crosscut saw file. A cant saw file may be used to finish both sides of the raker teeth at the same time.

If the saw has been sharpened so many times that the teeth have been shortened making the gullets too shallow, deepen them with a round edge file.

Don't be lazy and try to save time and trouble by filing all teeth from the same side of the blade. Never do this. It will cause the saw to run to one side.

How to Sharpen Plane Irons

Sharpening a plane iron is like sharpening a chisel. There are two operations:

grinding and whetting. Grinding is not always necessary. Ordinarily the edge may be whetted several times before it is necessary to grind it.

When the cutting edge of a plane iron has been nicked or been whetted on an oil-stone so often that its bevel has become short, it must be ground on an emery wheel or grindstone.

The first thing to do after the plane iron has been removed from the plane (if it is a double plane iron) is to separate the iron from the cap. This is done by loosening the screw and sliding it along to the end of the slot where the head will pass through the hole. You cannot sharpen a double plane iron with the plane iron cap in place. An examination of the plane iron will reveal if it needs grinding prior to whetting.

Grinding a Plane Iron

A plane iron is more difficult to grind than a chisel or a gouge. The hazards which confront the novice in grinding a plane iron are: burning the edge and the difficulty of forming the correct bevel at *90 degrees to the sides of the iron.*

Grinding wheels for wood-working tools have already been discussed in the section on grinding a chisel. Read this carefully before attempting to grind a plane iron. No matter which type of grinder is used, it should be one which is provided with an adjustable tool rest. The wheel should turn toward the tool. The edge must be dressed smooth for easy sharpening.

The right bevel or grinding angle is 25 to 30 degrees. To get this angle, the length of the bevel ground should be equal to fully twice the thickness of the tool. The wheel should turn toward the tool and the latter should be moved from side to side across the edge of the wheel. Only a light pressure against the wheel is used. Too much pressure causes overheating, spoiling the tool.

The edge should be straight and at right angles to the sides of the plane iron. Test it for squareness with a small try square. If out of square, it can be corrected by rubbing the cutting edge on the edge of a medium fine oilstone. The edge of the stone is used because, unless the stone is new, the flat surfaces are seldom true.

Avoid forming a bevel which is much outside the 25 to 30 degree angle recommended. A short thick bevel of more than 30 degrees will not enter the wood easily. A long thin bevel of less than 25 degrees is weak enough to nick easily.

If you have a protractor, you can measure the bevel in degrees and grind it to the desired angle. A bevel of 25 degrees makes the plane slightly easier to push than one of 30 degrees. The 30 degree angle is best for hard wood full of knots. The finished bevel should be flat or slightly concave. A rounded or convex bevel produces an edge which cuts poorly.

The plane iron is ground until a fine burr or wire edge appears. Then comes the next step in the sharpening process.

Whetting a Plane Iron

After grinding, a plane iron is whetted on an oilstone to produce the final keen cutting edge.

The oilstone should be clamped in a vise so that it cannot move. The whetting process is begun by holding the plane iron, bevel side down, on the flat surface of the oilstone. Hold the plane iron in the right hand. Use two or three fingers of the left hand to help hold the iron against the stone. At first the whole bevel should be in contact with the stone. Then the back edge is raised very slightly and the plane iron moved back and forth over the stone.

The whetting bevel is at a slightly greater angle than the grinding bevel, usually 30 to 35 degrees. The bevel must be kept straight. Rocking the iron even slightly as it is moved back and forth produces a rounded bevel which will not cut efficiently. Hold the iron firmly, keep an even moderate pressure against the stone, and move the hands parallel to the stone. Keep the surface of the stone moist with oil.

Move the iron sideways slightly over the surface of the stone as well as to and fro to wear the stone evenly, making certain that all parts of the cutting edge come into contact with the stone. The main pressure should be on the forward stroke and the angle between the iron and the stone *must be kept constant*. Usually from six to a dozen strokes will be enough.

The plane iron is then reversed and its flat side placed in contact with the oilstone. Rubbing it back and forth a few times will remove the wire or feather edge. Keep both hands on top of the cutter so as to avoid any possibility of lifting it, thereby producing a bevel on the flat side of the iron. If this should happen, the cap iron will not fit tightly, causing shavings to clog the plane. If the slightest bevel is produced on the flat side, the plane iron must be reground.

If the wire edge is not removed after a few strokes with the *flat* side of the plane

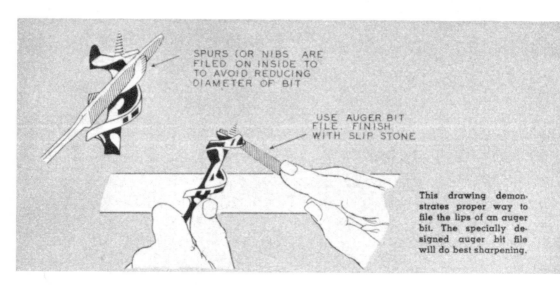

SPURS (OR NIBS) ARE FILED ON INSIDE TO TO AVOID REDUCING DIAMETER OF BIT

USE AUGER BIT FILE. FINISH WITH SLIP STONE

This drawing demonstrates proper way to file the lips of an auger bit. The specially designed auger bit file will do best sharpening.

iron held *flat* on the stone, reverse the iron and whet the bevel side again. Usually the feather edge drops off quickly and is found on the oilstone in the form of a silvery thread.

The whetting is finished by drawing the edge over a smooth wood block or a leather strop. A sharp plane edge is invisible. If it is dull, the edge will appear as a fine white line. If the shiny edge of bluntness or a nick can be seen, repeat whetting processes.

The thumbnail test can be applied to plane irons as well as chisels. If the edge is allowed to rest on the thumbnail by its own weight and it takes hold in the nail, it is sharp. If it slides over nail, it's not sharp.

Plane marks will show less on a surface which has been planed if the corners of the cutting edge are very slightly rounded. For this reason the cutting edge of the plane iron in a jack plane is often given a slight curve during the whetting operation.

How to Assemble a Double Plane Iron

A newly sharpened plane iron must be handled with care to avoid nicking its keen edge. To put a plane iron and the plane iron cap together, lay the plane iron cap across the flat side of the plane iron with the screw in the slot. Then pull it down and away from the cutting edge. When it is almost to the end of the slot turn the cap parallel to the iron.

Holding cap and iron together, slide the cap forward toward the cutting edge of the iron until the edge of the cap is just back of the cutting edge. The cap must not be moved or dragged across the cutting edge

for it will nick and dull it before it's used.

For general work the edge of the plane iron cap should be about $\frac{1}{16}''$ back of the cutting edge. It should be set as near to the cutting edge as possible when the plane is to be used on cross grain and curly wood. When the cap is in its proper position hold the cap and iron firmly together and tighten the screw which keeps them together.

How to Sharpen an Auger Bit

An auger bit becomes dull if it is frequently used to bore holes in hard wood. It can easily be resharpened by filing with a specially designed auger bit file. These files are small, double-ended and tapered.

One end of the file is made with its sides safe or uncut while the other end has cut edges. In sharpening a bit both the lips and the nibs or spurs are filed. The safe portions of an auger bit file make it easy to file either the lips or nibs without damaging adjacent surfaces in the process.

When filed, the bit may be held in a vise or firmly held down against the top of the workbench. The lips should be filed on the top surface of the cutting edge. Remove sufficient metal to take any bruises out of the edge. Remove an equal amount from both lips. Follow the original bevel. The lips are filed on the *top surface only* to maintain the clearance on the under side.

The nibs or spurs are filed on the *inside only* in order to maintain the diameter of the bit. For an extra keen edge on both lips and nibs, after filing, use a slipstone. •

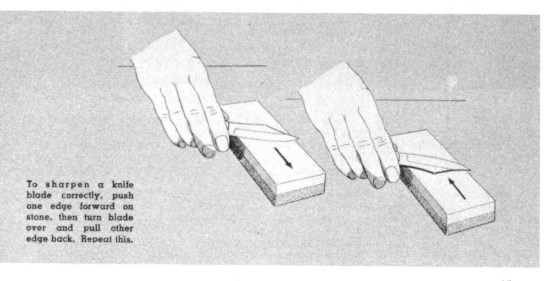

To sharpen a knife blade correctly, push one edge forward on stone, then turn blade over and pull other edge back. Repeat this.

preparing and using glues

To glue successfully, plan your work with care and use the correct glue.

GLUING is frequently the most satis-factory method of fastening woodwork together. It is used almost to the exclusion of nails and screws in fine cabinet, furniture and pattern work. Glued joints between side and edge grain can be made stronger than the wood itself. Glue does not hold well on end grain, however, for it is drawn into the wood by the open cells of end grain before it has a chance to set.

The process of gluing consists essentially of applying liquid glue to the surfaces to be fastened together and then applying a clamping pressure which holds them to-gether until the glue has set. It requires several hours for glue to set.

Glue does not act as a cement and filler between two surfaces. Its holding power depends upon its bonding action. While in a liquid state, the glue penetrates the wood by passing into the tiny pores or spaces between the fibers. When the glue hardens, thousands of tiny filaments of glue reach-ing out between the wood fibers and clinging there join the two pieces of wood firmly.

There is much more involved in the use of glue than spreading it on a joint and pressing the parts together. To make a strong joint requires knowledge and experience. Most of the necessary knowledge can be obtained by careful study of this chapter. Experience is acquired by practice.

In mass production woodworking plants part or all of the gluing process is done by machinery. The glue is applied to the wood by glue-spreading machines and the parts are clamped together in special fixtures.

In small shops and schools and in the household, gluing is a hand operation. The glue is spread on the wood with a brush or small wooden paddle and the joints are pressed together with hand screws and clamps of various types.

There are several kinds of glue, the common ones being fish, vegetable, animal, casein and plastic resin glues. Each of these has special properties and no one kind meets all requirements. It is necessary to choose the glue best suited to the job.

Fish and vegetable glues are usually liquid glues used cold and can generally be ignored by the woodworker. The most useful glues in woodworking are the animal, casein and plastic resin glues.

Prepared Liquid Glue

The glues which make the strongest and most enduring joints in wood are not sold in liquid form and must be prepared when needed. There are many brands of prepared liquid glues on the market which are convenient to use and satisfactory for some purposes. Because they are ready to use immediately, they are good household glues, handy when making minor quick repairs. Their disadvantages are that they are not moistureproof and they deteriorate considerably with age.

Animal Glue

Animal glue was long the favorite glue of cabinetmakers but casein glue is gradually replacing it. Animal glue is strong, sets quickly, flows into joints well and is stainless. Its disadvantages are that it requires time and care in its preparation, must be used while hot and applied quickly. It is satisfactory only for indoor work which is not exposed to extreme moisture or mold-producing conditions.

Animal glue is made from hides, bones and other parts of animals obtained from tanneries and slaughterhouses. It reaches the retail market in sheet or flake form. Sheet glue is very hard and brittle. The

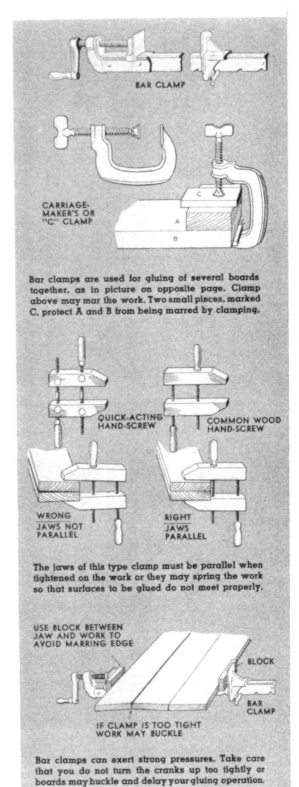

BAR CLAMP

CARRIAGE-MAKER'S OR "C" CLAMP

Bar clamps are used for gluing of several boards together, as in picture on opposite page. Clamp above may mar the work. Two small pieces, marked C, protect A and B from being marred by clamping.

QUICK-ACTING HAND-SCREW

COMMON WOOD HAND-SCREW

WRONG JAWS NOT PARALLEL

RIGHT JAWS PARALLEL

The jaws of this type clamp must be parallel when tightened on the work or they may spring the work so that surfaces to be glued do not meet properly.

USE BLOCK BETWEEN JAW AND WORK TO AVOID MARRING EDGE

BLOCK

BAR CLAMP

IF CLAMP IS TOO TIGHT WORK MAY BUCKLE

Bar clamps can exert strong pressures. Take care that you do not turn the cranks up too tightly or boards may buckle and delay your gluing operation.

97

Here is a workman's eye view of bar clamps used to hold glued boards together. Note that pieces of scrap wood protect edges of work from damage.

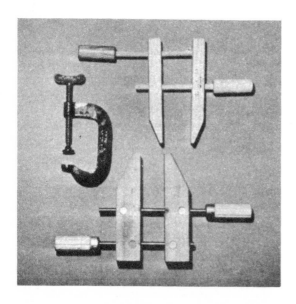

Every woodworker can use a set of these clamps: top, wooden thread hand-screw clamp; left, metal C clamp; bottom, a metal thread hand-screw clamp.

first step in preparing it for use is to place it in a cloth or bag and break it into small pieces with a hammer or mallet. The cloth will prevent the pieces from scattering.

A suitable glue pot is necessary for heating and melting animal glue. A glue pot is always provided with a water jacket so that the glue cannot be heated above 150 degrees F. Use care not to boil glue. Heating above 150 degrees F. weakens it.

There are various glue pots on the market. An electric glue pot is perhaps best but an ordinary double boiler is satisfactory. Agateware is preferable to aluminum for this purpose. When only a small quantity of glue is needed, a tin can set in a pan of water may be used as a glue pot.

Flake glue or small pieces of sheet glue are put in the pot, covered with water and allowed to soak 12 to 16 hours. Good grade glue is transparent and brittle before soaking. After sufficient soaking the pieces will have swollen to several times their original size, will become soft and jelly-like and will have absorbed most or all of the water. Then melt the glue by heating the double boiler on a gas stove or on an electric hot plate.

The proper amount of water in preparing animal glue varies with the glue and the kind of wood to be joined. It is usually

Glue—1 part   Water—1½ to 2 parts

by weight. The "rough" rule is usually 2 parts of water for hardwoods and 1½ parts of water for softwoods. Continued or repeated heating of glue evaporates some of the water it contains, decreases its strength.

Inexperienced workmen usually make glue too thick. Thick glue prevents the parts of a joint from making the close contact which is necessary to secure strength. Hot animal glue should be thin enough to run freely from the brush. If it is too thick, add water.

Casein Glue

This glue is in wide use in woodworking plants. The amateur craftsman will find it superior to liquid and animal glues for home repairs and many other purposes. While not waterproof, casein glue is much more resistant to moisture and heat than animal glue. The latter must be applied quickly while it is hot. It sets rapidly. Not much speed is necessary in using casein glue, because it is used cold and does not begin to set until 10 to 15 minutes after it is applied.

Casein glue is not satisfactory for work exposed to extreme moisture or mold-producing conditions. Under such circumstances a plastic resin glue should be used. Ordinary casein glue will stain certain kinds of wood, especially mahogany, oak and redwood. In fine cabinet work where glue stains would be objectionable, a special non-stain casein glue is used.

Directions for mixing casein glue should be followed carefully. Put the required amount of *cold* water (50 to 70 degrees F.) in any convenient mixing cup or jar. Water below 50 degrees F. will make too thick a glue. Water above 70 degrees F. forms a glue which is too thin and sets too quickly. Add the dry casein glue powder to the water and stir rapidly for several seconds. The mixture will thicken and become pasty but do not add more water.

The correct proportions of powder and water to use in making a mix are:

1 part glue powder by volume (measure loosely filled)
1 part water by volume
or
1 part glue powder by weight
2 parts cold water by weight

In other words mix one tablespoonful of glue powder with one tablespoonful of cold water or one ounce of dry powder with two ounces of water. Four ounces of dry glue mixed with 8 ounces of cold water will make from ¾ to 1 pint of liquid glue.

When mixing the powder with water stir only until the powder has absorbed the water. Then let the mixture stand for 10 to 15 minutes. Stir again for a few seconds until smooth. It is then ready to use.

The liquid life of casein glue mixed with water is not over 6 to 8 hours at 70 degrees F. Before the glue hardens, brushes and utensils which were used in gluing should be washed clean.

Plastic Resin Glues

These completely waterproof glues are sold under various trade names of which Cascamite and Weldwood are examples.

Plastic resin glues are used for making wood joints which are to be exposed to water, weather and excessive dampness. They can be employed in boat-building. In most instances plastic resin glues set up hard enough to work in 4 to 8 hours but require 2 to 7 days to develop full strength and become waterproof.

Plastic resin glues reach the market in the form of dry powder and must be mixed with cold water before use. Directions for mixing are given on the container and it is essential to follow them closely.

In general, the mixture of glue and water should have the consistency of heavy cream but should be applied to surfaces in a very *thin* spread only. The manufacturers of plastic resin glues supply pamphlets giving complete directions for mixing and using their product. It is advisable to obtain one from a hardware dealer or manufacturer.

Mix only as much resin glue as you need immediately. It will not remain a liquid for more than a few hours. Stir until all the water is absorbed and the mixture is smooth. It is then ready to use. Wash out brushes, spoons and utensils in water soon after use before the glue has set.

The resin powder and the water for a mix may be measured by weight or by volume. The weight method is more satisfactory because it is more accurate. When measuring by volume do not pack or shake the powder down in the measure. Measure it loosely packed, just as it comes from the original container.

When measuring by volume use 2 parts of powder (loosely filled) to 1 part of cold water. The proper proportions by weight are 1½ parts of powder and 1 part of cold water.

Pour one half the measured water into a convenient mixing container. Add the measured glue powder and stir rapidly until the mixture is smooth. The glue is now ready to use. The remaining water can be discarded or all or part of it added to the mix. The amount of water controls the setting time of the glue.

If you can work fast, use only one half the water. This will make a stronger, faster-setting glue than if the whole amount were used.

The receptacle in which a plastic resin glue is mixed should be glass, china or enameled ware free from all traces of alkali. Soda, soap and the residue of casein glues are alkaline and the presence of a slight trace in the mixing vessel will greatly retard the setting of a plastic resin glue.

General Directions for Gluing

The conditions required for using the different glues vary. But there are two basic requirements which apply to all glues:

1. The joint must fit perfectly before glue is applied.
2. The glued surfaces must be pressed together and kept under pressure for several hours. This pressure time varies slightly with temperature, glue and type of wood. In general, soft woods should be kept under pressure for a minimum of 6 hours at 70 degrees F. and hardwoods for at least 8 hours or more at 70 degrees F.

All surfaces which are to be joined by glue *must fit together tightly.* When put under pressure they must touch at all points. Glue is not a space filler. It is true that if glue is thick enough, it will fill up a space in a joint, but *when it hardens it will crack* and the joint will not be strong. The adhesive strength which holds glue to wood is much greater than the cohesive strength which holds glue together. In other words, a thin film of glue between two pieces of wood makes a stronger job than a thick film.

It is advisable to test the fit of all pieces by clamping them together under pressure before applying any glue. If they do not fit perfectly, make them do so.

Types of Clamps

Bar clamps, C clamps, handscrews, vises, heavy weights, rubber bands, wedges and cords are used to hold work together under pressure until the glue has set. Several clamps may be necessary to hold a job properly. It is sometimes necessary to make a special fixture to clamp irregular shapes and mitered joints. These are explained in a later paragraph.

Plan Gluing Operations

To make a strong, permanent glued joint it is necessary to plan the whole operation. If it is a large job, it should be studied and divided into small units. This will make it easier to get the clamps in place quickly and true the joints.

For example, it would be difficult to glue together the back, front, side rails, legs and stretchers of a chair in one operation.

In addition to testing the fit of the parts to be glued, it is well to plan and test the method of clamping which is to be used. After the glue has been applied is the wrong time to discover that the handscrews or clamps slip or pull the work out of line. It may be necessary to prepare some small softwood blocks or strips which can be slipped between the clamps and finished surfaces to prevent the latter from being marred.

If a test proves the method of clamping to be satisfactory, all clamps and handscrews needed for the job should be adjusted so that they can be put back in place and tightened quickly and conveniently.

Near at hand on the workbench should be a square, straightedge, rule, mallet, chisel, scraper and a damp cloth. The square, straightedge and rule may be needed to check the alignment and squareness of the job when the clamping pressure is applied. Sometimes a tap with the mallet will help force the joint together or align the parts properly. The chisel, scraper and damp cloth are used for removing surplus glue before it hardens.

Directions for Using Animal Glue

Animal glue must be used hot. When chilled it does not penetrate into the pores of the wood and does not adhere satisfactorily. Also, chilled glue does not squeeze out of a joint properly when pressure is applied. Consequently the wood surfaces cannot come together.

A weak joint results from the use of cold glue or glue which is too thick. It will come apart when the glue hardens and shrinks.

Speed is essential when using animal glue. Have everything ready so that no time is lost in applying the glue and the clamping pressure. The room temperature should not be less than 70 degrees F. It is well to warm the parts to be glued.

The glue should be applied generously and quickly with a brush to the surfaces which are to be joined. The pieces are then immediately pressed together with sufficient pressure to squeeze all surplus glue out of the joint and bring the parts into close contact. With the clamps still in place the job should be checked for alignment, squareness, flatness, etc. Any necessary correction can then be made by shifting the position of the clamps and screws or adjusting the pressure. The joint must then remain clamped under pressure for several hours without disturbance.

Surplus glue which has been smeared on the work or squeezed out of the joint can be removed with a chisel or scraper as soon as it chills and thickens. If glue is removed while it is still warm, it will smear the surface. After it has thoroughly hardened, it is very difficult to cut off.

Directions for Using Casein Glue

Casein glue is used in much the same manner as animal glue. However, since casein glue is used cold and does not begin to set until 10 or 15 minutes after its application, room temperature and speed are not of quite as much importance.

The correct mixture of casein glue is much thicker than hot animal glue of the proper consistency. It should be applied in an even spread, preferably with a brush with very stiff bristles. Special brushes for applying casein glue can be purchased.

Enough glue should be used so that it oozes out along the edges of the joint when

100

the clamping pressure is applied. This surplus glue should be wiped off with a damp cloth immediately after the joint is clamped.

A job with casein glue should be planned so that the glue can be spread, pressure applied and the alignment of the parts checked (and corrected if necessary) within fifteen minutes. If too much time is taken, the glue may start to set and the excess will not squeeze out, preventing the parts from making proper contact.

The room temperature preferably should not be below 70 degrees F. Softwood joints made with casein glue should be kept under strong pressure for at least 2 hours. Hardwood joints should be kept under pressure for a minimum of 4 hours and preferably 12 to 16 hours. Casein glue requires nearly a week to develop its full strength and water resistance. Do not strain or test casein joints until they have set for 7 days.

Some woods, among them teak, yellow pine, osage orange, lemonwood and yew are oily. Glue does not adhere to them as well as to other woods. Casein glue is the best glue to use for joining these materials. They can be improved for gluing by washing the surface with a strong solution of any alkaline household cleaning compound.

Using Plastic Resin Glue

When using plastic resin glues, the workroom and the material to be glued should be 70 degrees F. or warmer. The liquid life of a mix using three quarters of the measure of water is 3 to 4 hours at 70 degrees F. Less water will shorten the liquid life, more water will lengthen it.

The joints to be glued must fit perfectly with no rough surfaces. Use a stiff brush to spread the glue and apply a film only about half as thick as is used with casein glue. Apply glue to *one surface only*. In other words, use much less plastic resin glue than casein or animal glues. There should be practically no oozing of glue from the joint when pressure is applied.

Clamping pressure should be applied as soon as possible and continued for 5 hours at 70 degrees F. in the case of soft woods. Hard woods should be kept under pressure for 6 hours.

Plastic glues require nearly one week to develop full strength and water resistance. Joints made with this type of glue should not be strained until they have had full time to season.

Glue stains on exposed surfaces are objectionable in fine cabinet work. Even though the glue which is squeezed out of a joint when the clamps are applied is care-

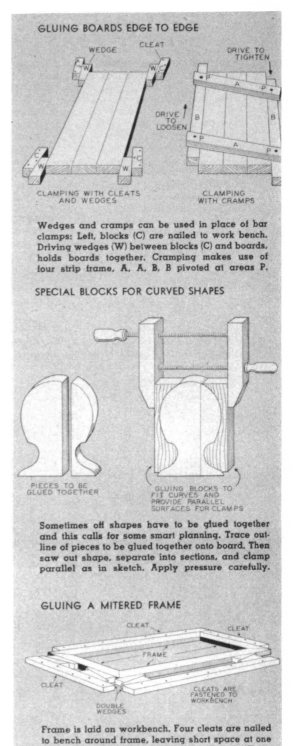

GLUING BOARDS EDGE TO EDGE

CLAMPING WITH CLEATS AND WEDGES

CLAMPING WITH CRAMPS

Wedges and cramps can be used in place of bar clamps: Left, blocks (C) are nailed to work bench. Driving wedges (W) between blocks (C) and boards, holds boards together. Cramping makes use of four strip frame, A, A, B, B pivoted at areas P.

SPECIAL BLOCKS FOR CURVED SHAPES

PIECES TO BE GLUED TOGETHER

GLUING BLOCKS TO FIT CURVES AND PROVIDE PARALLEL SURFACES FOR CLAMPS

Sometimes off shapes have to be glued together and this calls for some smart planning. Trace outline of pieces to be glued together onto board. Then saw out shape, separate into sections, and clamp parallel as in sketch. Apply pressure carefully.

GLUING A MITERED FRAME

CLEAT

CLEAT

FRAME

CLEAT

CLEATS ARE FASTENED TO WORKBENCH

DOUBLE WEDGES

Frame is laid on workbench. Four cleats are nailed to bench around frame, leaving short space at one side and one end between frame and cleats. Drive double wedges of wood into space between cleats and frame to clamp latter while glue is setting.

fully wiped off it may leave stains. One of the tricks of cabinetmaking is to use a colored glue which will match the finish of the wood. Any glue which is prepared by mixing with water can be colored. All of the dry animal, casein or plastic resin glues can be colored.

In the case of animal and casein glues this is done by dissolving water-soluble dye or alkali-proof dry earth color, obtainable at paint and hardware stores, in the water used for preparing the glue. The dye should be dissolved in the water before the glue powder is added.

Plastic resin glues should be colored only with a soluble, *acid-fast* dye. No directions can be given as to how much dye should be used to produce any certain color. That must be ascertained by mixing some test samples. Very little dye is required. The tendency of the novice usually is to use too much.

Gluing Boards Edge to Edge

Butt joints between the edges of two boards can be made stronger and more permanent by gluing than by nailing or screwing together. Adjoining edges should be planed their entire length and fitted so

Gluing boards together for desk top. Use old brush and paint glue on both edges of wood. Allow about ten minutes for glue to get tacky before clamping.

that no cracks show on either side before the glue is spread. If the pieces have been matched for figure and grain and carefully fitted, the glued joints will be practically invisible to the eye.

Some experienced craftsmen, after applying the glue, press the edges together and rub them back and forth several times before applying the clamps. There are many ways of clamping and holding boards together until the glue has set. Cabinetmakers' clamps, wedges, cleats and cramps may be used. Several of these are illustrated in this section.

The amateur craftsman who does not possess the equipment of a professional woodworker will find the cramping or cleat method most convenient. Regardless of the method of clamping, there is a tendency for long glued joints between edges to spring apart at the ends. Greater clamping pressure should be applied at the ends than in the center.

To glue two or more wide boards edge to edge, employ three clamps if cabinetmakers' or bar clamps are used. Place two of the clamps on the under side of the boards near opposite ends and the third clamp on the top side near the center. The center clamp should be tightened first, then the two end clamps. Avoid too much clamping pressure or the board may bulge in the center.

Before applying the final pressure and putting the job away to set, test it for flatness with a straightedge or framing square. The surfaces of the boards can be brought to the same level by holding a block of wood near the glue joint and tapping it with a mallet.

In order for the finished work to form a perfectly flat surface as, for example, when boards are glued together to form a table top, it may be necessary to clamp a straightedged board or plank *across* each end.

Gluing Doweled Joints

Cut a small V groove the full length of each dowel so that air and excess glue may escape when the dowel is forced into its hole. Point the end of each dowel slightly so that it will enter its hole more easily. In order to make a strong joint, all dowels must fit snugly into their corresponding holes. A simple method of building an under-sized dowel is described in the paragraph on gluing rickety chairs.

To Glue a Panel

If a panel is formed of more than one piece, the pieces should be glued together as described under section on gluing boards edge to edge. However, no glue should be used to fasten the panel into the frame into which it fits. The panel itself should be free to expand and contract in accordance with changes in the weather and in the moisture of the atmosphere.

To Glue Irregular Shapes

Clamps cannot be applied directly to some irregular shapes and curved surfaces. It is necessary to make special gluing blocks for them. The blocks are made to fit the curves and at the same time provide parallel surfaces for the jaws of the clamp so that the joint may be drawn up tightly.

To Glue Miters

Picture frames, mirrors and small paneled cabinet doors mitered at the corners cannot be drawn together with ordinary clamps. It is necessary to make a special fixture consisting of a board to which four cleats are fastened at right angles to each other. The mitered frame can be clamped together and the corners kept under pressure by driving double wedges between two of the cleats and the frame.

A piece of paper should be placed between each corner and the base of the fixture to prevent the glue squeezed out of the joints from fastening the frame to the fixture. Any paper which sticks to the frame can be removed with a sharp chisel and fine sandpaper.

How to Make Crack Filler

Woodworkers have long used a mixture of fine sawdust and animal glue as a filler for small holes and cracks in wood. It is customary to use mahogany sawdust for making filler for mahogany, pine sawdust for pine, etc. If woodwork is to be painted it makes no difference what kind of sawdust is used. Sufficient sawdust should be thoroughly mixed with glue to produce a filler having the consistency of thick paste. The filler must be freshly prepared when needed. It soon hardens.

Since a filler of this type shrinks upon drying, fill cracks and holes high enough to allow for shrinkage. Any excess can be removed with fine sandpaper when it has dried completely.

A waterproof, stain-free, crack filler which is almost non-shrinking can be made with plastic resin glue. Use the following formula and be very careful to measure the ingredients by their volume only:

Dry plastic resin glue powder ... 1 part

White wheat or rye flour .... 1 part

Wood flour or very fine saw-
    dust .... 1 part

Water .... 1 to 1½ parts

Do not shake any of the dry ingredients down in the measure; use them loosely packed. Use only common wheat or rye flour—not the self-raising kind. Self-raising flours contain chemicals which are injurious to plastic resin glues.

To prepare this type of filler, first mix all the dry ingredients together. Then add part of the water and stir until it is completely absorbed. Add more water slowly and stir. Use only enough water to make a mixture having the consistency of a very stiff paste.

Press the filler firmly into any cracks or holes to be filled. Fill slightly higher than the level of the surrounding wood. Remove excess filler by sanding after it has dried overnight. This filler is very hard when dry. It can be stained to match the surrounding wood. Use only acid-fast dyes to color a filler for best results. •

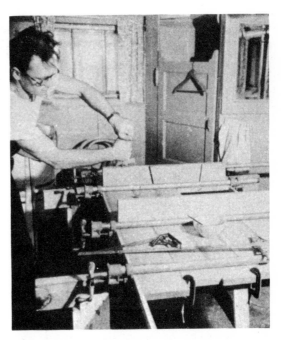

While desk top is still held by bar clamps after glue has set, screw the cross pieces to bottom of desk top and you'll have a strong, smooth surface.

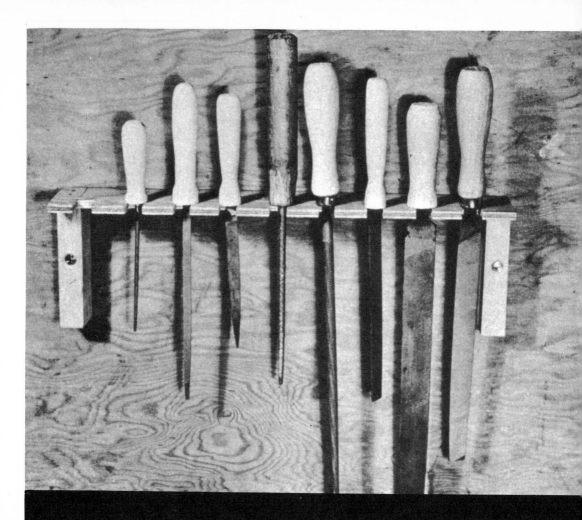

files and filing

THE file is the most widely used hand metal-working tool. In the shaping and finishing of all metals and in the sharpening and maintenance of other tools, it has an unusually important place.

Probably more than any other tool, the file can be made an extension of the hand. The tricks in filing are in selecting the right file for the work to be done, in holding it in the right position and in employing the proper stroke for accurate results.

A tool kit would not be complete without an assortment of files. It is not necessary to be a professional mechanic to find a certain amount of skill of inestimable value in using a file. With files, saws and axes can be kept sharp and fast-cutting, hoes and garden tools can be sharpened, work to be soldered can be cleaned and fitted, ignition points can be cleaned and evened. These

are only a few of the uses for many files.

A file consists of a blade or body with a tapered end called a tang which fits into a wooden handle. The part where the tang begins is called the heel. The size of a file is not its over-all length but is the distance measured in inches from the point or tip of the blade to the heel. Teeth are cut into the faces and sometimes the edges of the file body. The teeth do the cutting.

Files are named by their shape and sectional form, by type or cut of the teeth and by the tooth spacing. Each variety of file is made in different lengths. Sizes for each variety may range from 3″ to 18″.

There are more than 3,000 kinds, sizes and cuts. Only the standard types which are likely to be required for ordinary work are discussed here. Learn to use these and you'll be able to do skillful filing.

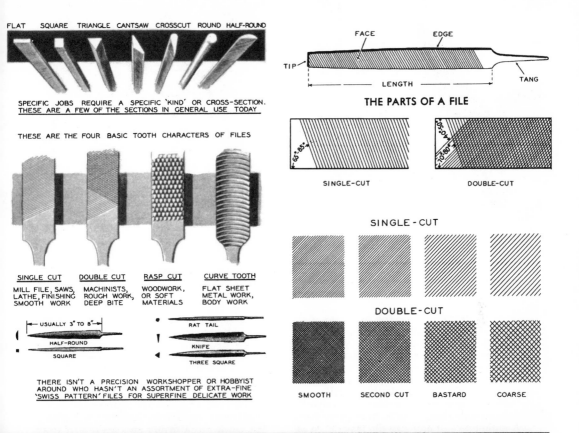

FLAT SQUARE TRIANGLE CANTSAW CROSSCUT ROUND HALF-ROUND

SPECIFIC JOBS REQUIRE A SPECIFIC 'KIND' OR CROSS-SECTION.
THESE ARE A FEW OF THE SECTIONS IN GENERAL USE TODAY

THESE ARE THE FOUR BASIC TOOTH CHARACTERS OF FILES

SINGLE CUT	DOUBLE CUT	RASP CUT	CURVE TOOTH
MILL FILE, SAWS, LATHE, FINISHING SMOOTH WORK	MACHINISTS, ROUGH WORK, DEEP BITE	WOODWORK, OR SOFT MATERIALS	FLAT SHEET METAL WORK, BODY WORK

← USUALLY 3" TO 8" →

HALF-ROUND

SQUARE

RAT TAIL

KNIFE

THREE SQUARE

THERE ISN'T A PRECISION WORKSHOPPER OR HOBBYIST
AROUND WHO HASN'T AN ASSORTMENT OF EXTRA-FINE
'SWISS PATTERN' FILES FOR SUPERFINE DELICATE WORK

THE PARTS OF A FILE

FACE   EDGE

TIP   TANG

LENGTH

SINGLE-CUT   DOUBLE-CUT

SINGLE - CUT

DOUBLE - CUT

SMOOTH   SECOND CUT   BASTARD   COARSE

An assortment of files is a must for the tool kit of anyone who considers himself a craftsman. Learn how to use files correctly.

Cut of the Teeth

The teeth cut into the face of a file are set at an angle. A file with a single row of parallel teeth is called a *single-cut* file. Files which have a row of teeth criss-crossing another row are called *double-cut* files. The double cut produces a very large number of small pointed teeth like the end of a diamond pointed cold chisel.

Single-cut files are used when a smooth finish is desired. Single-cut mill files are used for lathe work, draw filing and for finishing various compositions of brass and bronze. Double-cut files cut faster than single-cut but leave a rough finish which usually must be smoothed down later.

Teeth are sometimes cut into one or both edges of a file of flat or rectangular section. When an edge has no teeth, it is called a

safe edge. An edge having teeth can be made safe by grinding all of them off.

There are many different shapes of files but the several types pictured here are the most satisfactory for ordinary work. The cross-section of each file is also illustrated.

The cross-section of a file makes it especially adapted to some particular work. For example, a round file can be used for enlarging holes and also for filing concave surfaces; a triangular file is useful for cleaning up burred or damaged threads or for filing small notches and square or cornered holes.

The Importance of a Handle

It is dangerous to use a file without a handle. Usually the tang is sharp. If a file used without a handle meets an obstruction

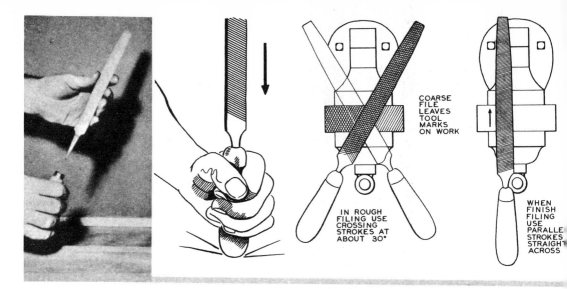

COARSE FILE LEAVES TOOL MARKS ON WORK

IN ROUGH FILING USE CROSSING STROKES AT ABOUT 30°

WHEN FINISH FILING USE PARALLEL STROKES STRAIGHT ACROSS

Without a handle, any file is dangerous. Strike handles solidly, as shown above, to wedge tang in.

This diagram illustrates the proper way to use both coarse and fine files. Work must be tight in vise.

on the forward stroke, the pressure of the hand against the tang may result in a bad wound. A file without a handle lying on the workbench is dangerous. Wooden file handles are cheap. They are easier to hold than the tang. They eliminate hazards. Before using any file, equip it with a handle.

Four or five different sizes of wooden file handles are obtainable in hardware stores. A handle to suit any size file from 3″ to 14″ can be selected. Make sure the hole in the ferrule end of the handle is large for the tang. Insert the tang into the hole. Grasp the handle and hold it, handle down and file up. While holding it in this position, strike the end of the handle against the workbench or something solid such as the flat surface on a vise. This will drive the file tang down into the handle. See the illustrations at the top of this page which show how the file tang is inserted.

Do not drive it too far or the handle will split. The ferrule or metal sleeve on the handle keeps the wood from splitting when the tang is forced into the hole but it is not able to prevent it if the tang is driven too far into the wood.

To remove a file from its handle, hold it in the right hand and tap the ferrule end sharply against the edge of the workbench.

The Work Must Be Held Rigidly

Accurate filing can be done only when the work is held firmly. Since both hands are used to manage the file, whenever possible, the piece to be filed should be clamped rigidly in a vise.

When using large files and consequently filing heavy work, the filer stands at the vise. The top of the vise should be at about elbow height. If the work is small or to be filed with great precision, the filer usually sits on a stool or a chair of proper height to bring the work in the vise practically level with his eyes.

The jaws of a vise are often made with a roughened surface so that they will clamp the work more firmly and prevent it from slipping. The pressure of the roughened steel jaws may damage finished surfaces.

For example, it would not be advisable to clamp the smoothly ground bearing surface of a steel shaft in the jaws of a vise, without protecting the shaft. If the smooth surface of the shaft were marred, it would cut and score its bearing when put back in service.

To prevent vise jaws from damaging finished surfaces, cover them with caps made of copper, brass, zinc, lead or some other soft material.

How to Hold a File

Filing is one of the most difficult of the hand metal-working operations to master. To hold a file properly is the first step in learning to file. The instructions given here are for the right-handed individual. The position of the hands is reversed for the left-handed worker.

The position of the right hand on the file handle is always the same, but the position of the left hand on the tip of the file varies according to the type of file being used. The end of the file handle rests in the palm of the right hand; the thumb and index finger are extended along the

106

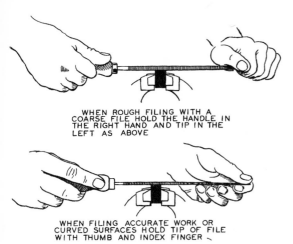

WHEN ROUGH FILING WITH A COARSE FILE HOLD THE HANDLE IN THE RIGHT HAND AND TIP IN THE LEFT AS ABOVE

WHEN FILING ACCURATE WORK OR CURVED SURFACES HOLD TIP OF FILE WITH THUMB AND INDEX FINGER

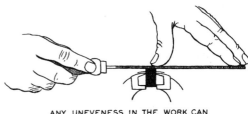

ANY UNEVENNESS IN THE WORK CAN BE DETECTED BY HOLDING FILE AS SHOWN ABOVE

The correct way to hold a file while working is shown here. Note grips for fine and rough work.

Improperly finished areas can be felt through the fingers held lightly on file moved over the metal.

top and side of the handle for control.

When a large file is used and a large quantity of metal is to be removed quickly the tip of the file is grasped in the left hand so that the file is under the palm of the hand and the fingers are against the underside of the file. This grip enables considerable downward pressure to be applied.

When a small file is used or accurate filing is essential, the tip of the file is held between the thumb and index finger of the left hand.

Another method of holding a file, frequently used by skilled mechanics, consists of holding the handle of the file in the right hand as usual and in pressing it down against the work with the fingertips of the left hand.

The thumb and fingers are stretched as far as possible and pressed evenly against the upper face of the file. Thus the downward pressure is more evenly distributed over the whole length of the file and there is more tendency for it to run perfectly horizontally on the forward cutting stroke. This is a good way to hold the file in order to feel for any unevenness in the work.

Filing Methods

A file cuts on the forward stroke only. Consequently, downward pressure should be applied only on the forward stroke. Except when filing aluminum, lead and any soft alloys which tend to clog the teeth, the file should be lifted lightly from the work on the return stroke.

The forward motion of the file must be parallel to a flat surface. This requires practice. Beginners allow the file to rock or see-saw, producing a convex, not a flat surface. If the work is to be filed true, it will have to be tested frequently with a straightedge or square. Hollow spots are revealed by light shining under the straightedge. Angles are tested with a bevel square for trueness.

The reason a file is raised on the return stroke when filing steel, iron and other hard metals is that allowing it to rub against the work on the return wears away the back of the teeth destroying their cutting edges. This is not true of soft metals. They do not easily wear the teeth. They do, however, have a tendency to clog the teeth. Drawing the file back along the work on the return stroke tends to loosen the soft filings thereby cleaning the teeth.

Draw Filing

When a piece of metal has been filed to the size and shape desired, it is often finished by draw filing which produces a smooth, true surface. A smooth file is used. It is held in both hands with the thumbs on the edge toward the worker and the fingers on the rear edge. The work is placed in a vise and, parallel to the longest edges, the file is drawn and pushed back and forth over the surface to be finished. The pressure should be even. The file marks running across the work are removed and replaced with relatively few fine lines running lengthwise.

Draw filing produces sharp wire edges but these are easily removed by running a smooth file over the edges of the work at an angle and using only very light strokes.

A file with a short-angle cut should not be used for draw filing because such files are made to cut on a longitudinal stroke. When used sideways they will score or scratch rather than shave or shear.

A file surface can be finished further by rubbing it with fine emery or crocus cloth.

Clogging of a File

The teeth of a file often become clogged with fine pieces of metal called pins, especially when the file is used on brass, aluminum, copper and other non-ferrous metals. A clogged file will scratch the surface of the work. A clean file cuts faster and more accurately than one which has become filled with dirt or pins.

Never tap a file to clear its teeth. Tapping may break the points. Files should be cleaned with a stiff wire brush called a file card. Chalk may be rubbed on a file to prevent it from clogging or pinning.

Lead, aluminum and copper all clog files badly. When a file is used to work these metals, rubbing it with paraffin or turpentine helps to prevent clogging. However, the general rule is to keep files clean by frequent brushings. Sometimes it may be necessary to use the point of a scriber to remove pinning when brushing does not clean particles out well.

Beginners' Faults

The best advice to the beginner at filing is to practice on some scrap metal whenever he has spare time. Endeavor to do an accurate job. Practice filing one edge of a piece of soft steel straight and at right angles to a face. Test the work frequently with a try square.

The most common mistake a beginner makes is to rock the file. This produces a convex instead of a flat surface. The ability to push the file forward so that it cuts on an even plane is attained by careful practice.

By filing, testing and trying, the mechanic learns to feel the work through the medium of the file. He can feel whether his file is cutting close to an edge, in the center or all the way across a flat surface. He learns to detect through the run of the file any unevenness in the surface.

There is also a tendency for a beginner who is filing a long edge to bear down harder when the file is in the center thus producing a hollow. This fault can be discovered by checking the work with a straightedge. The hollow spot can, of course, be corrected by a few additional strokes at the ends.

Care of Files

More files wear out through abuse than by use. They should not be thrown together in a drawer or laid with other tools unless each file is individually wrapped in paper. Otherwise the teeth will be damaged and dulled. The best places to keep files are vertical racks or shallow drawers with partitions between the files. They can also be kept separated by standing them in a row of holes or by hanging them by their handles.

A file used on steel will not cut brass, copper, aluminum and other soft metals efficiently. The order in which a new file is used on metals is therefore of consequence. If it is used on brass, copper, aluminum, zinc, die-castings, *soft* steel, etc., only during the first part of its life, its teeth will not usually be sufficiently dulled to spoil it for cutting harder metals.

If not kept in firm contact with the work on the forward stroke, the toothpoints of a file are damaged and the file wears out

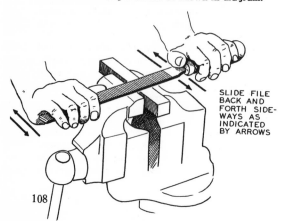

To produce a smooth finish on edges and narrow surfaces, use a single-cut file as shown in diagram.

SLIDE FILE BACK AND FORTH SIDE-WAYS AS INDICATED BY ARROWS

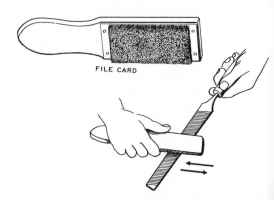

A wire brush, called a file card, is used to clean files. Use the motion as indicated by arrows below.

FILE CARD

quickly. Keep a file pressed firmly to the work on the forward stroke to keep it cutting smoothly.

Strangely, a file will often cut faster after it has been used a short time than when it is brand new. There is a good reason for this. When a file has never been used, all of the teeth are not of the same height so that only a few of the teeth cut at first. As these extra long teeth wear down, more teeth come into contact with the work allowing the file to cut off more metal at each stroke.

Files should be kept in a dry place to avoid rust which would dull the teeth.

Filing the Different Metals

All the more than 3,000 different files which are manufactured have a reason for their existence. The various combinations of size, cuts, and shape give each file characteristics which make it more suitable for some particular job.

The first rule in the selection of files is to use deep-biting double-cut flat or hand files for removing metal quickly and single-cut mill files for smooth finishing and sharpening tools.

The fast-moving industrial progress of recent years has brought forth a number of special purpose files which are more efficient than the older types for cutting stainless steel, aluminum, die castings and other alloys. The mechanic should become familiar with these new types. They save time and energy.

Here is a list of metals and the proper file to use for each hardness:

Cast Iron. The ordinary flat, a double-cut file, is the most satisfactory for general removal of stock from an iron-casting. The mill, which is a single-cut file, is best for securing a smooth finish on cast iron.

Copper. A special purpose brass file is recommended for filing copper.

Brass. Although brass is a soft metal, it is tough and ductile. It requires a file with very sharp teeth which are cut at an angle that will prevent grooving the work. The special purpose brass file fulfills these requirements. In addition, it does not clog as easily as an ordinary file.

Bronze. A special purpose brass file is recommended for filing bronze.

Stainless Steels. The chromium and nickel content of stainless steels makes them sufficiently abrasive to quickly dull the teeth of an ordinary file. Special purpose stainless steel files have much longer life if properly used with light pressure and a slow cutting stroke.

Soft Steel. The ordinary flat, a double-cut file, is most satisfactory for general removal of soft steel stock. The mill, which is a single-cut file, is best for securing a smooth finish on soft steel.

Aluminum. This soft, malleable metal soon clogs the teeth of a general purpose file. The special purpose aluminum rasp is more satisfactory for fast metal removal. For cutting rapidly, yet leaving a good finish, a special purpose aluminum file is recommended. It does not clog and if it is used with a slight shearing stroke to the left, it will produce a good finish.

Lead. This metal, pure copper and babbitt are extra soft and present a clogging problem when a general purpose file is used on them. Special purpose lead float files will cut them rapidly without clogging.

Die Castings. When die castings consist of zinc, aluminum or magnesium alloys they clog general purpose files. A special purpose die cast file is manufactured for filing these metals. It cuts rapidly and smoothly and does not clog easily. •

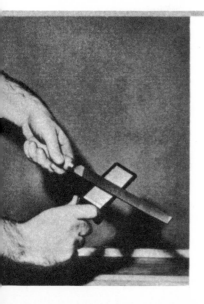
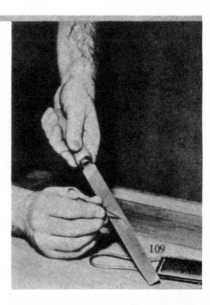

109

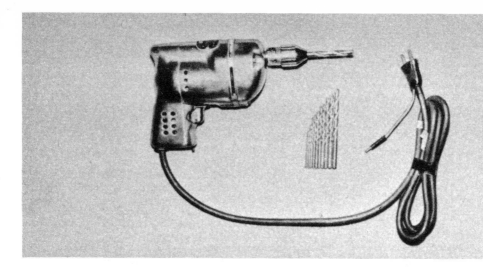

drilling holes
in metal

**Whether you use an electric power drill or
a hand drill, drilling metals is a science.**

DRILLING is one of several methods of
producing holes in metal and other
hard materials. The Morse twist drill, designed for this purpose, is the most widely
used of all metal cutting tools, and is probably also the most efficient mechanic's tool
in existence. The use of special steels
and manufacturing methods improved the
quality of this type of drill from time to
time but no one has ever been able to
improve its basic principle.

1. Square shank twist drill for brace. 2. Small
straight shank fractional size drill. 3. Large
straight shank drill. 4. Taper shank twist drill.

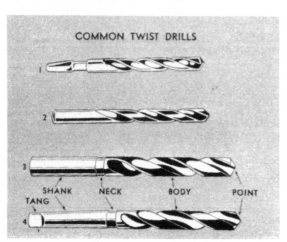

COMMON TWIST DRILLS

SHANK   NECK   BODY   POINT
TANG

The Morse Twist Drill

This tool is a cylindrical piece of steel in
which two equal and diametrically opposite
helical grooves, called *flutes,* are milled.
The flutes form a cutting edge at the cone-
shaped end of the drill and at the same time
provide channels for the escape of chips
when the drill is working in a hole. For
some materials it is necessary to keep the
drill well lubricated to cool the cutting
edges and assist the escape of chips. The
flutes provide a channel for the lubricant
to flow to the cutting edges.

Although a twist drill is essentially a
roughing tool (accurate holes are produced by first drilling and then grinding
or reaming) when *properly* sharpened, the
cutting edges will produce a hole which is
reasonably round, straight and of the same
diameter as that of the drill.

The three principal parts of a twist drill
are the *shank, body* and the *point.* The
fluted and pointed end is the "business end"
—it does the cutting. The opposite end is
the shank. It has no flutes. To it the driving
power is applied.

There are several types of shanks. The
average mechanic and the home craftsman
need concern himself with three only: the
straight, taper and square shanks.

The Square Shank Drill

This is designed to fit into the chuck of a carpenter's ratchet brace and is tempered to make holes in both wood and soft metal. It is useful in repair and jobbing work where hidden nails or unexpected metal may be encountered when wood is being drilled. A brace is not very satisfactory for driving a twist drill except when no other means is available. It turns too slowly to be efficient. Square shank twist drills are available in diameters ranging from 1/16" to 3/4" by 1/32".

Straight Shank Twist Drills

These are of two types: those with a neck and those without. The neck is a ring-shaped groove in the shank. The number sizes and the small fractional sizes have no neck. Straight shank twist drills (up to 1/2" diameter) are intended for use in hand drills, breast drills, small power drills and drill presses fitted with either a 2-jaw or a 3-jaw chuck. The shank of the drill is gripped in the chuck.

Usually turning the sleeve outside the chuck opens and closes the jaws of small hand drills and small breast drills intended for driving the fractional sizes of twist drills up to 1/4" diameter. Chucks for larger drills are opened and closed by means of a wrench called a key.

Taper Shank Drills

Drills of more than 1/2" diameter require more driving power than a hand drill or a breast drill can supply. They ordinarily have tapered shanks. The small end of the tapered shank is machined flat to form a tang which fits in a slot in the end of a tapered socket in the spindle of a drill press, or in a tapered sleeve or socket which is held in the spindle of a drill press, or in a tapered sleeve or socket which is held in the spindle. The tang helps to drive the drill. No chuck is used with a tapered shank drill. The end of the drill shank is machined at an angle which conforms to the angle of a wedge-shaped tool called a *drift*. When the drift is driven into a slot in the socket in which the drill is held, it forces the drill out.

Carbon and High Speed Drills

Twist drills are made of both carbon tool steel and high speed steel. Carbon tool steel drills are the least expensive. They are used in hand drills and breast drills and for low speed drilling in drill presses. High speed steel drills, although more costly in the beginning, are more economical in the long run for production work where time is a factor. They may be operated at much higher cutting speeds, will run hot without damage and are longer lived. High speed steel drills are recommended whenever power drive is employed for drilling.

Morse Twist Drill Sizes

Twist drills are arranged according to size in four different groups: Numerical, Alphabetical, Fractional or Machinist's and Metric.

The Numerical Sizes

These are numbered from 1 to 80 and range in diameter from 0.0135" to 0.228". The number is stamped upon the shank of the larger sized numerical drill. The smaller sizes which bear no numbers can be identified by measuring them with drill gauge or micrometer. A drill gauge for numerical sized drills is a flat piece of steel in which, usually, 60 marked holes have been drilled. There is a hole to correspond to the diameter of each of the numerical drills from 1 to 60. Sizes 61 to 80 are seldom used and are too small to gauge accurately except with a micrometer caliper. The number beside the hole into which a drill fits snugly is the number size of that particular drill. If the diameter in decimal parts of an inch is not also marked on the gauge, this can be ascertained by referring to a table of drill sizes.

The handiest way to keep twist drills is in a drill stand. There is a numbered space for each size so that when one is wanted, it can be identified quickly.

Drilling with a Hand or Breast Drill

The 3"-jaw chuck with which the average hand drill is fitted will usually take straight shank drills up to 1/4" in diameter. It is necessary to employ care and patience when drilling with small sizes for they bend and break easily.

Only the shank of a drill should be gripped. Never put a drill in so far that any of the fluted portion is within the chuck. Because the shank is softer than the fluted body of the drill, the jaws will grip it more tightly and it will bend farther than the fluted portion without breaking. Not all of the shank should be gripped in the chuck. Leave a portion outside to take up some of the strain. If you set it all the way in, there is much greater chance that it will break.

When a drill has been properly gripped in the chuck, check to see that it runs true before using it. If it runs out of true, examine for a bent shank or for a burr on the shank causing it to wobble. A drill which is out of true will not bore a hole to exact size and is likely to break.

The work in which a hole is to be drilled must be so well secured by clamps or in a vise that it cannot move. Work which moves under the drill will cause the drill to break and may cause an accident.

An attempt to force a small drill will usually break it, especially when the point of the drill is cutting through at the end of the hole.

It is necessary to hold a hand drill or a breast drill very steady and in line with the twist drill. If the hand drill or breast drill is not kept in line, the twist drill may be bent or broken.

When drilling deep, small-diameter holes, the twist drill must be withdrawn frequently from the hole to clear the flutes of chips. Small drills do not clear themselves of chips as readily as the large ones do.

It is difficult for any one except a skilled mechanic to drill holes smaller than 1/16" in diameter with a hand drill without bending or breaking drills. Drills of such small diameter should run at high speed and should be driven by power in a sensitive drill press solidly mounted.

Speeds and Feeds

The speed and feed depend upon the size of the drill and the kind of material being drilled. For example, a 1/16" diameter drill working in brass or bronze can be operated at a speed of 9000 revolutions per minute. But a 2" diameter drill working in the same material should turn only about 280 rpm. The same drills drilling into cast iron or mild steel should turn at about one fifth the speed used for brass or bronze. The general rules for drill speeds and feeds are:

Small drills should turn faster and be fed into the work more rapidly than large drills.

When making a hole in soft steel, a drill should run slowly and should be fed slowly. Hardened steel cannot be readily drilled with a twist drill.

In drilling cast iron, the speed of the drill must be greater than when drilling soft steel.

A drill cutting its way into brass, bronze, copper and aluminum should turn faster than for iron or steel.

If a drill squeaks when it is working in a hole, the probable reasons are: it is being fed too fast, the flutes are clogged with chips or the drill is dull. It should be checked and the correction which will remedy the trouble should be made. A squeaking drill soon becomes overheated and may lose its temper. Feeding a drill will dull its cutting edge quickly and a dull drill overheats. Clogged flutes will also cause a drill to heat. A hot drill will lose its sharp cutting edge more quickly than a cool drill.

Drilling Thin Sheet Metal Stock

When a twist drill cuts through thin sheet brass or any thin stock, the stock is likely to ride up on the drill. To prevent this, the work must be securely clamped and a narrow bevel should be ground or stoned on the cutting edges of the drill.

Altering the cutting edge in this manner does away with the tendency of the work to ride up. Clamping the work gives the drill a better opportunity to make a clean hole at the edges where it breaks through.

Laying Out a Hole

Locating and marking the exact spot where a hole is to be drilled is called laying out the hole.

The exact spot where the center of the hole is to be must be marked by scratching an X with a sharp-pointed tool called a scriber. The crossing point of the two lines which form the X should correspond to the center of the hole. If the surface of the metal is rubbed with chalk before scribing, the lines will show more plainly. Then an indentation is made with a center punch and hammer at the exact center of the planned hole. A center punch is used to mark the location of a hole which is to be drilled in metal.

When a great many parts exactly alike are produced in a factory, each hole is not individually laid out. The holes are located by the use of a drilling jig or template. The work is clamped in the jig, the drill passes through properly located holes in the jig and drills into the work at exactly the right spots. Thus, the time and labor of laying out the holes on each piece are eliminated.

If you try to drill a hole in metal with a

twist drill without a jig and before locating it with a center punch mark, you will not be able to control the exact location of the hole. The drill point will walk around before the drill takes hold. But when the point of a revolving drill is placed in a center punch mark, it does not usually walk. It drills a hole exactly at that spot, using the punch mark as its center.

A Center Punch

This is a pointed tool, generally made from round or octagonal steel rod. The point is ground to a true taper point which is central with the shank. There are two types. One, called a prick or dot punch, has a point in which the included angle is 60 degrees. The other has a point with an angle of 90 degrees. The 60 degree prick or dot punch has the sharper point and does not hide the spot where the scratch-marks cross. It is used to make a small indentation which will locate the center of the hole. This indentation is then widened and deepened with the 90 degree punch.

One of the things which a metal worker must learn is to hold a center punch exactly on the desired spot to make the punch mark exactly where it belongs. The right method is to hold the punch at a slight angle while the point is placed at the exact spot where the center of the hole is to be. Then it is straightened up until it is perpendicular to the surface. The shank of the punch is held between the thumb and the first and second fingers. The tip of the third finger is held against the bottom of the punch in order to steady the point and prevent it from sliding off the spot. The blow of the hammer on the upper end of the punch must be a quick firm tap in line with the punch so that it is not knocked off the mark.

The amateur or novice mechanic who does not have this skill should practice laying out and punching marking holes on scrap metal. A center punch should not be used on metal which is so hard that it will dull the point. It requires considerable skill to regrind the point of a center punch by hand to the proper degree of accuracy.

Precision Work

A very accurate center punch mark exactly where it should be is not easy to make. For precision work center punches are ground to a fine tapered point. A very light hammer is used to strike the punch. The punch is placed exactly at the right spot with the aid of a loupe or some other magnifying glass. A light blow of the hammer is given the punch to make a locating indentation. This is examined under the glass and if correctly located, the point of the punch is replaced in the indentation and it is deepened by one or two additional hammer blows. If the original shallow locating punch mark is not exactly where it should be, it is possible to shift its center slightly by holding the punch at an angle and striking one or two light blows with the hammer.

Automatic Center Punch

For laying out fine work, such as tool and instrument work, an automatic center punch is useful. This convenient tool has a spring-actuated hammer in the handle. The point is placed in position on the exact spot where the indentation is desired. A steady downward pressure is then applied

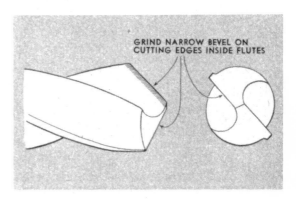

GRIND NARROW BEVEL ON CUTTING EDGES INSIDE FLUTES

Drawing shows how to grind twist drills to prevent work riding up in drilling thin sheet metal.

Correct way to hold center punch is illustrated below. Make fine center mark with 60° dot punch.

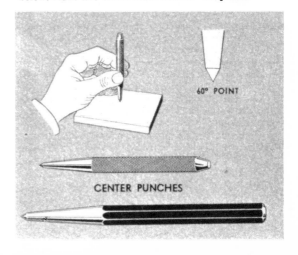

60° POINT

CENTER PUNCHES

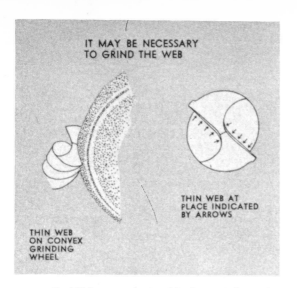

IT MAY BE NECESSARY
TO GRIND THE WEB

THIN WEB AT
PLACE INDICATED
BY ARROWS

THIN WEB
ON CONVEX
GRINDING
WHEEL

As drill becomes shortened by frequent sharpening the web becomes thicker at the point and should be ground thin. Be careful to cool drill properly.

to the handle. This compresses the spring within. The force of the hammer blow which is adjustable is applied to the point.

The Bell Punch or Self-Centering Punch

This is a center punch arranged to slide in a cone-shaped casing. When placed square over the end of a bar it will locate the center.

Sharpening Twist Drills

It is not easy to sharpen a twist drill. Some otherwise skillful mechanics never learn to hold a two-fluted twist drill against a grinding wheel so as to produce the same point angle and lip clearance on both sides. A twist drill can be either held in the hand or clamped in a drill sharpener while it is ground. Practice is required to become skillful at grinding the point of a twist drill while holding it in the hands. It is not possible to explain the trick in the pages of a book. A good mechanic can show it to you. With a drill sharpener, sharpening twist drills is much easier. To anyone who uses twist drills frequently, it is well worth its small cost.

A sharp twist drill cuts faster and cleaner and keeps cooler than a dull drill. A great deal of pressure is required in order for a drill to cut its way into steel. If the lips are dull it may be necessary to increase the pressure 50 to 100 per cent. The lips of a dull twist drill appear and feel dull to the touch. If put to work it will bore a rough hole and will heat quickly.

How a Morse Twist Drill Cuts

To sharpen a drill intelligently it is necessary to know how this tool performs its duty. A twist drill is guided principally by its lips and the full diameter edges or margins. That portion of the body immediately behind the margins is reduced in diameter or relieved so as to reduce the friction between the drill and the walls of the hole. The margins do no cutting, they guide only.

The central section of a twist drill, the part that connects the two other portions bearing the margins, is called the *web*. In drilling, the point of the drill is forced against the work so that the material beneath the web is slightly crushed and the sharp edges of the lips are enabled to bite into the material. The lips do the actual cutting. They are ground to an angle to provide the clearance or relief necessary for the edges to bite into the work. The flutes provide rake at the cutting edges which causes the chips to curl.

A two-lipped twist drill will not bore a true cylindrical hole unless both lips are of the *same length* and at the *same angle with the axis* of the drill. Also, in order to bore a true cylindrical hole, *the axis of the drill* and its *axis of rotation must coincide*. In simpler words, a drill must not be sharpened so that it is lop-sided and it must revolve around its center if you wish it to cut true and smoothly.

Grinding a Drill

Small carbon tool steel twist drills should be ground on a dry grinding wheel of medium or fine grain and soft grade. The wheel must run true and the face must be absolutely flat. It is impossible to make a good job of sharpening a drill on a wheel which is chipped, hollowed out or rounded off. If the wheel surface is not flat, it should be dressed with a grinding wheel dresser. The drill point should be examined frequently during the grinding. Use care not to overheat it thus spoiling its temper. Keep the point cool by frequently dipping it into water.

High speed steel twist drills should be ground on a true-running dry wheel of medium grain and soft grade. They should not be cooled by dipping them into water as this will cause them to crack.

When any cutting tool (a category including twist drills) is sharpened on a grinding wheel, a slight burr or wire edge remains. A tool used in this condition will lose its edge quickly and will leave tool marks on the work. The wire edge should be removed by rubbing it with a small oilstone or Carborundum stone. The novice at sharpening drills should examine the edge both before and during stoning with a magnifying glass or a watchmaker's loupe. In stoning the edge smooth do not change the lip clearance angle or the rake produced at the edge by the flute.

Angles and Clearances

The ordinary twist drill is ground at the factory so that the angles and clearances of its point and lips are most suitable for average work. The point is ground to an included angle of 118 degrees and the lips are ground to have a clearance angle of 12 to 15 degrees. This angle and clearance is nearly standard for drilling cast iron and steel and is the best for average work. It is the angle and clearance to which the amateur craftsman should sharpen his twist drills unless he wishes to use them at their highest efficiency on some very soft or very hard material.

In drilling steel or ordinary cast iron if the included angle of the point is more than 118 degrees, the drill will have a tendency to center improperly. If the angle is more than 118 degrees when drilling cast iron or steel, more power will be required to drive the drill and it will cut less rapidly.

The angle of the drill point is increased for drilling hard materials and decreased for drilling soft materials.

For production work on hard material, the included angle of the drill point is increased to approximately 150 degrees.

A good included angle for heat treated steel is 125 degrees.

For plastics and for soft grade cast iron the included angle may be much sharper than 118 degrees. It may be between 60 and 90 degrees.

A drill point without any lip clearance or with insufficient clearance really has no cutting edges. There is an edge on each of the lips but it cannot bite into the work.

If a drill is ground so that it has too much lip clearance, it will grab into the work and since the edges of the cutting lips have very little support when the clearance angle is too great, they are likely to break or chip.

The lip clearance angle of a two-fluted twist drill should not be less than 8 degrees nor more than 18 degrees. The correct amount depends upon the quality of hard-

ness or softness of the material to be drilled: 12 to 15 degrees is a good angle for average work and for ordinary cast iron and steel. For drilling harder materials, the clearance angle should be decreased to 8 to 10 degrees and for drilling softer materials it can be increased to 15 to 18 degrees.

The best point and clearance angle to use when drilling various materials can be ascertained quickly from the following table.

POINT AND CLEARANCE ANGLES

Material	Included Point Angle	Clearance Angle
Average	118°	12 to 15°
Brass	118°	" " "
Soft cast iron	90°	" " "
Copper	100°	" " "
Manganese steel and hard material	150°	10 to 15°
Heat treated steels, drop forgings, auto connecting rods (Brinell hardness 250)	125°	12 to 15°
Wood, hard rubber, Bakelite and fiber	60°	" " "

Thinning the Web

The Web thickness of a twist drill increases as the flutes approach the shank.

Below are shown tools for cutting large holes in sheet metal. The metal should be anchored well and backed up with waste wood. Make cut slowly.

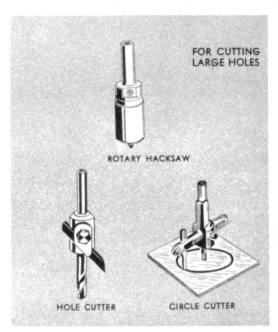

FOR CUTTING LARGE HOLES

ROTARY HACKSAW

HOLE CUTTER

CIRCLE CUTTER

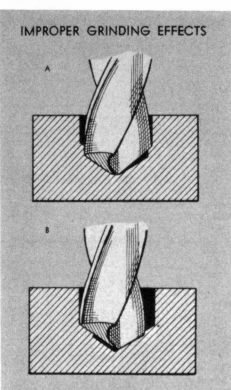

IMPROPER GRINDING EFFECTS

Sketch A shows drill with point ground on center but with cutting edges ground at different angles. Drill binds on one side, only one lip does work: hole becomes larger than drill. Sketch at B shows result if cutting edge angles are equal but lips are of different lengths. Hole is larger than drill, and great strain is placed on drill.

The drill is manufactured in this manner to give it what a college professor calls "additional torsional rigidity." In plain language this means more strength to resist twisting. When a twist drill is frequently sharpened and consequently shortened, the thicker portion of the web comes in contact with the work, making penetration into the work more difficult and causing greater wear.

This may be overcome by thinning the web on both sides at the point by grinding it on a convex-edged grinding wheel.

Rotary Hacksaws

These are ideal tools for quickly cutting large diameter holes in thin wood, metal, Bakelite, etc. The cutting is done by a thin-walled circular piece of steel having teeth along the lower end like those on a hacksaw. The round shank can be gripped in a chuck and driven in a breast drill, portable electric drill or small drill press.

Rotary hacksaws come in many sizes. Because they are not adjustable, each will drill only a one-size hole. The center of the hole to be cut is marked with a center punch. Place the center of the pilot drill in the punch mark and feed slowly until the work is pierced and the cutting teeth bite into the work. Lubricating compound will help when steel is cut.

Circle and Hole Cutters

It is difficult to drill a hole of more than ½″ diameter in thin sheet metal with a twist drill. The drill grabs the metal when it cuts through and deforms the sheet by bending it. Even though securely fastened,

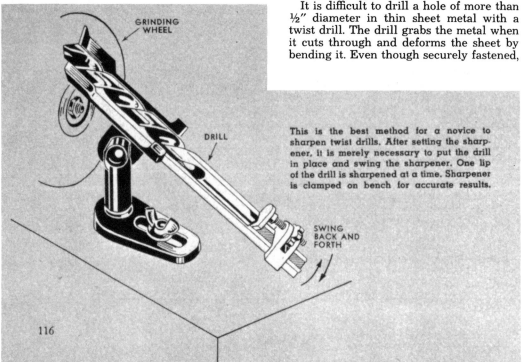

This is the best method for a novice to sharpen twist drills. After setting the sharpener, it is merely necessary to put the drill in place and swing the sharpener. One lip of the drill is sharpened at a time. Sharpener is clamped on bench for accurate results.

the work may be torn loose from its clamps.

Many shops formerly made for their own use a tool called a fly cutter for cutting large diameter holes in sheet metal. These are now produced commercially under the name of general purpose circle cutters and also as hole cutters. They provide an easy means of cutting accurate, clean circular holes in wood, Bakelite, hard rubber, sheet brass, aluminum and steel. Dealers in radio parts and electronic equipment carry them in stock. They are widely used to cut holes for sockets and plugs in sheet steel radio chassis. The cutters are made in several sizes and each one has considerable range. The smallest size will cut holes from 5/8" to 2½" in diameter. The largest size will cut holes from 1¼" to 8" in diameter.

Circle cutters and hole cutters may be driven by hand power when cutting holes up to 1½" diameter. Their round shanks will fit the chuck on a breast drill or on a drill press. It is easy to cut any size hole in a drill press with power. When the diameter is more than 1½", cutting in a breast drill with hand power is tedious.

The center of the hole to be cut should be marked plainly with a center punch and the work secured to the bench or the worktable of a drill press. Metal sheets should be laid on a flat piece of hardwood so that when the cutter breaks through, it will score the wood and not the worktable. The work must be well secured. You will get into trouble if it can move. The cutters are equipped with a pilot drill which bores a pilot hole. After placing the point of the pilot drill in the center punch mark, feed until the metal is pierced by the drill and the cutter can take hold. Feed very slowly. The hole cannot be made in a hurry. The plane of the work must be at right angles to the axis of the cutter on all sides so that the tool cuts evenly and not more on one side than the other.

When you cut steel, use a cutting compound.

To produce a satisfactory hole in wood it is essential to cut part way through, then turn the work over and finish from the other side.

It is much better to drive the cutter slowly taking a longer time to cut the hole than it is to turn and feed the cutter too fast.

The average safe maximum speeds are approximately:

Material	Surface Feet Per Minute
Steel	60 to 70
Aluminum	150 to 300
Wood	1000
Brass	120 to 200

Surface feet per minute means the number of feet per minute travelled by the cutting edge. For example, to cut a hole 1" in diameter the cutting point travels 1"x3.1416 or exactly 3.1416" each revolution. If it is cutting into steel the speed should be 60 surface feet per minute. 60 feet equal 720 inches. Divide 720" by 3.1416" to find the number of revolutions per minute the cutter should turn. For a 1" hole in steel it is 229. It need not turn at this exact speed. 250 rpm would be about right.

Since hole and circle cutters are not balanced tools, they must be securely gripped in the chuck in order to prevent an accident. Always double-check the chucks. •

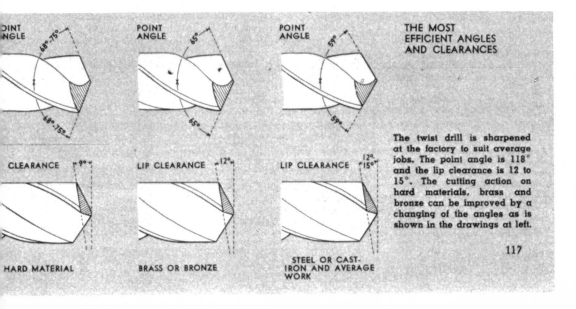

POINT ANGLE 68°-75°

POINT ANGLE 65°

POINT ANGLE 59°

THE MOST EFFICIENT ANGLES AND CLEARANCES

CLEARANCE 9°

LIP CLEARANCE 12°

LIP CLEARANCE 12°-15°

The twist drill is sharpened at the factory to suit average jobs. The point angle is 118° and the lip clearance is 12 to 15°. The cutting action on hard materials, brass and bronze can be improved by a changing of the angles as is shown in the drawings at left.

HARD MATERIAL

BRASS OR BRONZE

STEEL OR CAST-IRON AND AVERAGE WORK

117

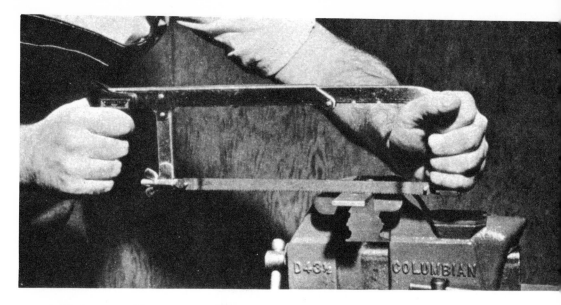

the hacksaw

Metal sawing is not difficult

if you select the right blade.

Hacksaws are used to cut metals of all kinds except hardened steel. They will also cut hard rubber, horn, Bakelite and other plastics which would spoil the cutting edge of the teeth of a wood saw.

A hand hacksaw consists of a toothed cutting blade and a frame to hold the blade. Since the blade is used to cut tough materials it dulls more quickly than that of a saw used to cut wood. Since the blade is tempered too hard to be resharpened by filing, it is discarded when dull. It is easily removed from the frame and replaced by a new sharp blade.

The Hacksaw Frame

The best frames are those equipped with a pistol-grip handle or a handle similar to those on carpenters' saws. These handles allow the maximum control, greatly reducing the muscular effort required to guide and drive the saw. Several manufacturers produce a frame with the handle in an inverted position so that the push on the forward stroke is applied in a direct line with the blade.

The frame of practically all hacksaws is adjustable to take blades of 8″, 10″ or 12″. The blade can be installed in the frame in either a vertical or a horizontal position so that the saw can be used where there would not otherwise be sufficient clearance.

Care of Hacksaw

When not in use, a hacksaw should be hung on a hook or a nail where it will be impossible for anyone to drop a heavy object on it. The blades are brittle enough to break if mistreated. If a hacksaw is kept in a drawer with other tools or carried in a tool kit, it should be placed so that other tools will not rub against the teeth.

A strip of cloth, wrapped around the blade, is a good protection for the teeth. Rubbing oil on the blade will prevent rust.

How to Place Blade in Frame

The frame must be adjusted to fit the length of the blade. There is a hole in each end of the blade fitting over pins in the stretchers at each end of the frame. The teeth on the blade should point *away* from the handle. The wing nut should be tightened until the blade is under strong tension which is necessary for sawing.

How to Use a Hacksaw Correctly

Few tools get as much misuse in the hands of the unskilled as does the hacksaw. Cutting off a piece of metal with a hacksaw is not half as hard a job as some mechanics make it.

First and always, the material which is to be cut must be securely fastened. If it moves while being sawed, teeth will be strained and perhaps broken from the blade. The blade itself may snap.

Second, a cut should not be started on a

sharp angle or a sharp edge. This violates the *three tooth rule* and risks breaking teeth or the blade itself. The teeth on the blade must be fine enough so that at least three consecutive teeth are in contact with the work at all times.

Blades for hacksaws are made with 14, 18, 24 and 32 teeth per inch. The blade selected for the job must have enough teeth per inch so that at all times at least three consecutive teeth are in contact with the point where the blade is cutting.

It is important to select a blade having the number of teeth per inch best suited to cutting the particular material to be sawed.

Starting a Cut

In starting a cut, it is a good plan to guide the blade with the thumb of the left hand until the kerf is established. It is not necessary to lift the blade off the work on the return stroke while the cut is being started.

The Technique of Sawing

When the cut has been well started, grasp the frame with both hands. One hand should be on the handle and the other on the far end of the frame. Like the file, a hacksaw cuts only on the forward stroke. Use a little downward pressure on the forward stroke but none on the return. After the cut is started, lift the saw *slightly* on the return so that the teeth scarcely touch the material being cut.

The stroke should be long and steady so that practically all the teeth on the blade are used. The most natural and least tiring stroke is made at a slight slant forward and downward.

Correct Pressure Is Important

Experience will teach the proper amount of pressure to use on the forward stroke. Lighter pressure should be used on soft metals and on thin sections than is used on hard metals and heavier sections. Insufficient pressure on the forward stroke will dull the teeth by rubbing them against the metal without cutting it.

The Right Speed

Lack of speed is important in hacksawing. "Take it easy" should be the guiding words for the use of a hacksaw. Most beginners saw too rapidly. Sixty strokes per minute is the top limit. Watch a good mechanic use his hacksaw. You will find

that he uses 40 to 50 strokes per minute. He actually cuts faster, his blade lasts longer and he is not as tired as he would be if he worked faster.

Keep the blade moving in a *straight* line. Avoid any twisting or wobbling and use enough pressure to keep the blade from becoming pinched or jammed, which might break the teeth or blades.

If the Blade Breaks

The set of the teeth can be seen plainly on a new hacksaw blade. The teeth are alternately pushed out in opposite directions from the sides of the blade like the teeth of a carpenter's saw. This set is necessary so that the kerf or slot cut by the teeth will be slightly wider than the blade, thus providing the clearance necessary to prevent it from sticking.

When a saw blade is used, the points of

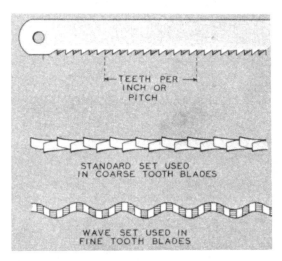

Number of teeth per inch is important factor in choosing correct blade to saw a specific metal.

Magnified view of blades. Fine toothed blade is for thin metal, coarse blade is for heavy sawing.

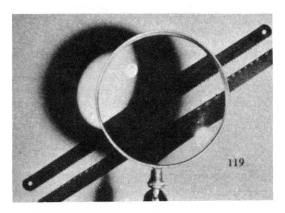

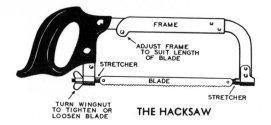

TURN WINGNUT
TO TIGHTEN OR
LOOSEN BLADE — **THE HACKSAW**

the teeth wear down gradually and become dull. As the teeth become dull and straighten slightly, the kerf or slot cut by the blade becomes narrower. A dull blade has a tendency to stick more than a new blade.

Since the slot cut by an even slightly dull blade is narrower than the slot cut by a new blade, a new blade will stick in the slot cut by a worn blade. If a blade breaks while a cut is in process and it is necessary to finish the operation with a new blade, it is always advisable to start a new cut in line with the first one, if possible.

In case a piece of round or square stock is being cut, rotate it 90 or 180 degrees and start a new cut in line with the first one. If the piece is flat, turn it over and start a new cut from the opposite edge.

When it becomes necessary to use a new blade before a cut is finished, do so with extreme care. *Work the blade into the slot gradually to maintain even cut.*

You Cannot Saw Tempered Steel

Tempered steel and chilled cast iron cannot be sawed with a hacksaw. There is a decided limit to the hardness of the metal that can be cut with this tool. To avoid ruining a hacksaw blade on hard steel or iron, first make a test with a file. If the metal cannot be filed, it cannot be cut with a hacksaw, so save your blades.

Cutting Bolts

A hacksaw is frequently used to cut bolts which must be shortened. Screw the nut all the way up on the threads before cutting off the bolt. Removal of the nut after the bolt has been cut will straighten out any threads burred or damaged by the saw. Use a wrench if necessary.

Use the Right Hacksaw Blade

Blades for hacksaws are made with 14, 18, 24 and 32 teeth per inch. Those with 24 and 32 teeth per inch are made flexible. They will bend or flex more than a hard blade without breaking. The 14- and 18-tooth-per-inch blades are made all hard. There is no such thing as an all-purpose hacksaw blade.

No matter how skillful a mechanic may be, he cannot do a first-class job with a hacksaw unless he uses the correct blade for the job. It is better to take a few minutes to change blades to suit the job than to waste the time and energy required by use of the wrong blade.

The Three Tooth Rule

The teeth on the blade used for a specific job of hacksawing should be fine enough so that at least three consecutive teeth are in contact at all times with the stock being cut. This is the three tooth rule referred to previously. Coarse-toothed blades cut faster than fine-toothed blades but with greater risk of breakage. Fine-toothed blades cut slowly but with less risk of tooth and blade breakage.

When it is not possible to change blades to fit each individual job, the 18-tooth-per-inch blade is the safest. However, it will not cut sheet metal or tubing. A 32-tooth-per-inch blade is needed for this purpose.

With very thin-walled tubes or thin sheet stock it is not possible to obey the three tooth rule even with a 32-tooth-per-inch blade. Thin sheet metal can be sawed successfully with a hacksaw if it is clamped in a vise between two pieces of wood. Saw through the metal and wood at the same time.

When cutting metal which is too thin to allow three teeth to make contact, use an extremely light steady stroke.

Three Rules for Hacksawing

Three important rules to follow when using a hacksaw are:

1. On tubing and thin sections use a fine-tooth blade and light steady pressure.
2. On thick stock use coarse-tooth blades and heavy even pressure.
3. Avoid sharp corners in starting a cut. Start the cut at a slight angle with a flat surface and guide the blade with the left thumb until the kerf is deep enough so that you can use both hands on the saw frame for accurate sawing.

Choosing the Right Blade

The nature of the material—brass, aluminum, steel, etc.—to be cut is a factor in choosing the proper blade.

To cut aluminum, brass, soft steel, and copper, except for very thin sections, use a 14-tooth-per-inch all hard blade.

Use an all hard 18-tooth-per-inch blade for tool steel and drill rod.

A 24-tooth-per-inch flexible blade is the best to cut electrical conduit, steel pipe and wrought iron pipe.

Light angle pieces should be cut with an 18-tooth-per-inch all hard blade.

Metal trim should be cut with a 24-tooth-per-inch flexible blade.

Thin tubing and thin metals require a 32-tooth-per-inch flexible blade.

Cause and Cure of Hacksaw Troubles

Broken blades are caused by:

1. Not enough tension on blade.
2. Too much tension on blade.
3. Use of new blade in kerf cut by an old blade.
4. Teeth on blade too coarse for hard stock.
5. Too much pressure on blade.
6. Frame being twisted as it saws.

Remedy:

1. If the blade showed a tendency to twist or bend before it broke, use more tension next time.
2. If the blade broke without twisting or bending or broke at the holes at the ends, there was too much tension. Use less force when you tighten the thumbscrew.
3. If you were using a new blade in a slot started by an old blade, turn the work around and start a new cut which will meet the old one.
4. Use a finer blade if the stock is hard.
5. Do not bear down so hard.
6. Make sure you push the saw back and forth in a straight line avoiding wobbling or twisting.

Breaking and stripping of teeth are caused by:

1. Too much downward pressure.
2. Cut started at corner.
3. Teeth too coarse for cutting soft stock or thin-walled sections.

Remedy:

1. Do not bear down so hard.

Correct way to start cutting. Note saw is nearly flat and several teeth hit surface at one time.

2. Start cut at slight angle with surface. Keep off sharp corners.
3. Use a finer toothed blade.

When teeth are dull the points are rounded. Dull teeth are caused by:

1. The blade becoming dull and worn by normal use.
2. Cutting speed being too high.
3. The saw frame not being lifted slightly on the back stroke.
4. Improper blade.
5. Teeth pointing in the wrong direction.
6. Pressure too light.

Remedy:

1. Nothing can be done to prevent a blade from becoming dull gradually through normal use.
2. Use a slower stroke.
3. Apply a slight lift to the hacksaw frame on the return stroke.
4. Use the proper blade to suit the material and type of stock.
5. Turn the blade in the frame so that the teeth point forward.
6. Use a firmer pressure.

Crooked cut is caused by:

1. The blade being dull and the set having been worn off the teeth.
2. The blade requiring tightening.
3. The frame being out of alignment.
4. Crooked sawing.

Remedy:

1. Use a new blade.
2. Check the tension of the blade. Tighten it if necessary. Do not bear down so hard.
3. Use a stiffer blade that will not bend.
4. Work easily. The first mistake a beginner makes is to saw too fast. He also bears down too hard. Avoid jerky, wobbly strokes and work slowly for accuracy. •

Wrong way. Sawing at angle lets only one or two teeth at a time meet metal and teeth break off.

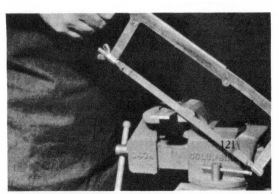

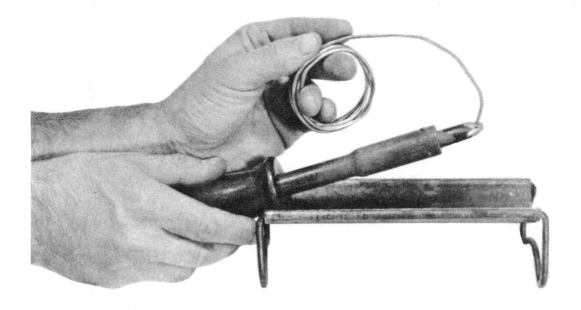

how to solder

Soldering skill has many applications around the home. You can save numerous repair bills by doing your own soldering work according to these rules.

ANYONE can learn to solder. Skill in soldering is useful to both amateur and professional craftsmen. The man or woman who does a little tinkering at home can, by soldering, salvage many broken fixtures, toys, electrical devices, kitchen utensils, etc.

There are two varieties of soldering, known respectively as *soft* and *hard*. Soft soldering employs solders which melt at temperatures under 700 degrees F. Soft solders are alloys. Lead or tin or both are usually among their ingredients. Hard solders melt at higher temperatures and are mechanically stronger than soft solders. Silver is the most often used hard solder.

Soft soldering is a simple process. As in most things, you can do a first-class job of soft soldering after a little practice—*if you follow the rules*. It is necessary to know the proper iron, solder and flux to use for a particular job.

Metals Which Can Be Soldered

Copper, brass, German silver, zinc, lead, tin, pewter, aluminum, magnesium, nickel, galvanized iron, wrought and cast iron, steel, stainless steel, silver, gold and tin and objects plated with these metals can be strongly joined together by soldering.

What Soldering Is

A solder is an alloy of two or more metals used for joining other metals by surface adhesion. Soldering differs from the process of welding. When two pieces of metal are *welded,* they are *fused* or *melted together.* When two pieces of metal are *soldered,* the *solder is melted* but the parts to be joined are not. They are heated and coated with solder and held together by *adhesion* not by fusion.

A necessary quality of a solder is that its

melting point must be lower than the melting point of the metals being joined. The most common solder is an alloy of approximately equal parts of tin and lead called "half and half." Although the melting point of tin is 449 degrees F. and that of lead, 621 degrees F., this alloy of the two metals melts at 370 degrees F.

Soft Solders and Hard Solders

This section gives specific information on how to handle soft solders and soft soldering equipment only. Soft solders are comparatively soft alloys. They contain lead and have low melting points. Soft soldering can be done either with a soldering iron or the flame of a blowtorch. Hard solders contain silver. Hard soldering can be done only with a flame.

Tools and Materials for Soft Soldering

The tools and materials needed for soldering are:

1. *A source of heat* for melting the solder and heating the parts to be joined to the proper temperature. This is usually a soldering iron which may be either electrically heated or fire-heated, but some work requires the flame of a blowtorch or blowpipe.

2. *A fusible solder* whose melting point is below that of the metal to be soldered. There are several varieties of solder. These are described later.

3. *A flux.* A soldering flux is a cleaning agent which permits the molten solder to alloy with the metals to be joined and form a solid metallic union. It is impossible to solder without a flux. There are several types of soldering fluxes. None of them is suited to all types of soldering. The fluxes most commonly used are rosin and zinc chloride.

Soldering Irons

The essential parts of a soldering iron are the handle and tip. Soldering "iron" is a misnomer, for the tip or portion of the iron which does the soldering is not iron but copper. An iron tip would be unsatisfactory. There is good reason for a soldering iron to be made of copper. Copper is a better conductor of heat than iron and can more easily be tinned or covered with a coating of solder. Tinning the copper tip is necessary in the soldering process.

As already stated, the two general types of iron are the old-fashioned kind which must be heated in a fire and the type which is heated by electricity. An electrically heated iron is far more satisfactory in every way than the fire-heated type. When connected to a 115-volt lighting or power circuit, an electric iron automatically raises itself to the proper temperature and remains hot until the current is shut off.

Soldering Iron Sizes

Like screw drivers, chisels and many other tools, soldering irons are made in different sizes. A small iron is used for light work and a large iron is used for heavy work. An iron must be large enough to store sufficient heat to raise the joint to be soldered to the temperature at which the solder will melt and run or sweat into

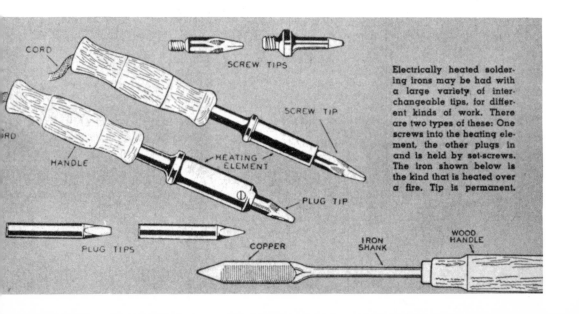

Electrically heated soldering irons may be had with a large variety of interchangeable tips, for different kinds of work. There are two types of these: One screws into the heating element, the other plugs in and is held by set-screws. The iron shown below is the kind that is heated over a fire. Tip is permanent.

In most cases, a flux must be used when soldering. There are three basic types of flux: Powder, paste and liquid. Tallow wax may also be used, when soldering copper or lead. It and rosin are the only non-corrosive fluxes. Rosin may be dissolved in alcohol or used as powder. Never use acid fluxes on electrical connections.

the joint. This is extremely important.

Fire-heated irons are sized according to their weight. The commonly used sizes are the ¼, ½, 1, 1½ and 2 lb. irons. The 3, 4 and 5 lb. sizes are not used in ordinary work.

Electric soldering irons are not sized according to their weight but are rated according to the number of watts they consume when operated at the voltage stamped on the iron. Thus an electric iron may be a 50-watt, a 60-watt, or a 100-watt.

The heat in an electric iron is produced by electric current flowing through a coil of resistance wire called the heating element. The heat is transmitted from the heating element to the copper tip.

The inexpensive, cheaply made electric soldering irons are satisfactory for use in the home workshop where they receive only occasional use. But they do not last long when used constantly.

The electric soldering irons used in factories and repair shops and by professional mechanics in various trades are industrial irons. They are ruggedly constructed to stand up well under continuous use. But since even the best and most rugged irons do not last forever, make sure that the important parts are interchangeable and replaceable.

There are two types of tips on electric irons. Plug tips which slip into the heater head are held in place by a set screw. Screw tips, which are threaded, screw into the heater head.

The common sizes of industrial electric soldering irons range from 50 to 500 watts.

50-watt Iron. This size is equal to a ½ lb. fire-heated iron. It is used for soldering small wires, fine instrument making

and repairing and general light soldering.

60- or 65-watt Iron. Equal to a ¾ to 1 lb. fire-heated iron and used for medium soldering on toys, radios, telephones, electrical appliances, fuses, delicate instruments, etc.

100-watt Iron. Equal to a 1 to 1½ lb. fire-heated iron and used for fast soldering on radio and electrical appliances. This is a practical size for light manufacturing and medium repair jobs in home and shop.

125- or 150-watt Irons. Equal to a 2 lb. fire-heated iron and used for high-speed soldering on radios and electrical appliances, automobile repairs, light tinsmithing, plumbing, wiring, small metal patterns, etc.

175-, 200- or 225-watt Irons. Equal to 2½ to 3 lb. fire-heated irons. Used for soldering medium sheet metal work, roofing, gutters, automobile repairs, small metal patterns and general shop work.

300-watt Iron. This is a heavy industrial iron equal to a 4 lb. fire-heated iron. It is the size used for heavy sheet metal work. vats, tanks, automobile radiators, refrigerators, large metal patterns, etc.

450- or 500-watt Iron. Equal to a 5 lb. fire-heated iron. Used for very heavy soldering on large tanks, heavy cans and large objects.

Tip of Soldering Iron Must Be Tinned

The heat of the copper tip, which is transferred to the solder and the parts, is responsible for adhesion of the parts to be soldered. Before any soldering iron, either the fire-heated or the electric type, can be used, the faces of the tip must be filed smooth and tinned or coated with solder.

Molten tinning is the medium by which the heat is conveyed from the iron to the object to be soldered. An untinned copper tip will not heat the work. Solder touched to a hot tinned face will melt instantly.

Unless the tip is kept tinned, a non-heat-conducting crust of metallic oxides forms, preventing the flow of heat to the work. If the coating is uneven or missing in places, the tip will have to be retinned.

For ordinary work, a soldering iron is tinned on all four faces. But for any work where the iron is held under the object to be soldered, as in the case of soldering splices in wire, only one face is tinned.

Molten solder on a tip with all faces tinned will not remain on the upper face but will run to the bottom, forming a drop. When one face only is tinned and that face is turned up, solder melted upon it will remain where it is wanted.

To Tin an Electric Soldering Iron

File the tip surfaces bright while the iron is cold. Turn the current on and as the iron heats up rub flux core solder over the tip surfaces every fifteen or twenty seconds. At first the iron will not be hot enough to melt the solder. As soon as the temperature has risen sufficiently, the solder will spread smoothly and evenly over the surface. The purpose of this procedure is to do the tinning as soon as the copper is hot enough to melt solder and before it has had a chance to oxidize.

If the iron is large, either acid core or rosin core solder may be used. Small irons used for soldering fine wires, radio parts, instruments, electrical devices, etc., should be tinned only with rosin core solder or solid solder and rosin.

When the tinning has been completed, wipe it with a rag while it is hot and molten. This will expose an even, almost mirror-like layer of molten solder on the tip surfaces.

An Iron Must Be Kept Well-Tinned

If an iron is properly tinned but not overheated, it will remain in good working order for a long time. Overheating will burn or oxidize the tinning and give it a yellow, flaky appearance. An iron in this condition is not in good working order.

If the tip is not badly overheated, it can be restored to good condition by rubbing it against the rough surface of a brick and applying flux and solder. If the tip has been so badly overheated that the tinned surfaces are pitted, it will be necessary to file and re-tin the faces.

Regulating Temperature of Electric Iron

Industrial electric soldering irons are designed for continuous use. Once connected they develop heat so rapidly that the tip becomes overheated if the iron is not used constantly.

It is often convenient to have a hot iron ready to use without waiting to heat it. This can be done by connecting the iron in series with a light bulb and a switch. The resistance of the lamp reduces the amount of current flowing through the iron thereby preventing it from developing its maximum temperature. When the switch is open so that the current flows through both the iron and the lamp, the iron may be left connected to the power line with no danger of overheating.

When the iron is to be used, close the switch to short circuit the lamp. This increases the current flowing through the iron, permitting it to develop its maximum heat. The size of the light bulb will

Three sizes of electrically heated irons are shown here. The smallest, left, is a 50-watt iron, used for fine work. The other two are 60- and 100-watt irons.

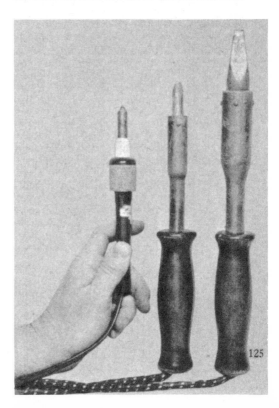

125

Proper way to solder a joint: Place iron against fluxed metal, heating it thoroughly. Then hold solder over tip, allowing it to flow evenly into joint.

depend upon the size of the iron and will have to be determined by experiment. It should be of such size (number of watts consumed) to permit the flow of that amount of current to keep the iron just hot enough to melt solder.

Care of an Electric Soldering Iron

The copper tip must be kept securely fastened in the frame of the iron so that it will heat properly. Some tips are constructed to screw in; others are held by a set screw. In either case it is important to keep the tip tight.

When heated, the surface of the copper tip of both the fire-heated and electric soldering iron becomes oxidized and covered with a red scale which ultimately becomes black. The red and black scales, both oxides of copper, do not conduct heat nearly as well as metallic copper.

Not only the exposed part of the copper tip on an electric iron becomes oxidized but the portion which fits into the frame or into the heating element also is affected. If this happens, the tip may stick in place. Therefore it should be removed occasionally to be cleaned by scraping off the scale.

If kept clean, the tip will not only receive more heat from the element but it can be removed easily when the time comes to adjust it or replace it with a new tip.

Kinds of Solders

All of the common soft solders are alloys of lead and tin. They are made in bar, ribbon and wire form. Wire solders may be either solid or cored. Cored solder is hollow like a tube and contains a core of flux. The flux is usually either rosin or an acid substance.

Ribbon and wire solder are used with small irons on small work. Bar solder is used with large work and large irons.

The standard soft solder alloy for all around work contains 48% tin and 52% lead. It melts at 360 degrees F. Some solders contain only 25% tin and 75% lead and melt at about 545 degrees F. These do not flow freely, and do not adhere as well as solders with a greater percentage of tin.

The common commercial plumber's solder which comes in bar form, frequently referred to as "half and half," is seldom made up of equal parts of tin and lead. Usually the tin content is from 30% to 40%. From 2% to 3% antimony is included and the remainder is lead. The antimony hardens and strengthens the solder.

The tin-lead solder with the lowest melting point, called slicker solder, contains 34% lead and 66% tin. It melts at 356 degrees F.

Solders containing tin, lead and cadmium came into wide use because of the shortage of tin during the war. They are hard, have low melting points, and in general have the same uses as tin-lead solders but are not as suitable for electrical work because they corrode more easily.

Tin-lead-cadmium solder, containing 80% lead, 10% tin and 10% cadmium, has about the same strength as the ordinary half and half tin-lead solder.

Soldering Fluxes

It is almost impossible to solder without a flux. Metal surfaces, at the point where they are to be joined together, must be absolutely clean and bright so that the solder will adhere to them. Even when scraped clean only a few seconds previously they become covered with a thin layer of oxide as soon as they are heated by the soldering iron.

Fluxes, which are chemicals that remove the oxide coating from metal surfaces, are applied at the point where metals are to be soldered together. The most frequently used fluxes are rosin and zinc chloride. The latter is an acid flux.

Rosin Flux

Rosin flux comes in lump or powdered form. It may be purchased at a hardware store or plumbing shop and sometimes at a drugstore. It is non-corrosive and non-

126

conductive. It is the best flux to use when soldering tinned metals, bright copper, tinware, lead, electrical connections, radios, telephones, fine instruments and small parts.

Use only rosin for electrical connections, radios and fine instruments. An acid, a paste flux, and sal ammoniac are taboo because they are *corrosive*. Even the so-called "non-corrosive" soldering pastes are usually slightly corrosive. Corrosive fluxes cause electrical connections to deteriorate rapidly. Since they are also usually electrically conductive, they cause short circuits and current leaks in electrical apparatus.

A non-conductive, non-corrosive soldering fluid can be made by dissolving rosin in alcohol. Use a small brush to spread the fluid on the surfaces to be soldered.

Practically the only disadvantage of rosin core solder and of rosin as a flux is that rosin is adhesive. Consequently a joint which may appear to be well soldered may actually be held together by the adhesive properties of the rosin and not by the solder. To prevent this, the soldering iron must be hot enough to cause volatization of the rosin and must be held against the joint until it smokes.

Zinc Chloride Flux

This is sometimes called killed acid. It is commonly used on untinned copper, brass, bronze, Monel metal, nickle-plated parts, galvanized iron, zinc, steel and German silver. Since it is corrosive, all traces of it should be washed off the work after soldering. It is never used in electrical work. Zinc chloride flux is probably the most generally useful soldering flux. It will give good results in soldering steel.

Zinc chloride flux can be made at home by cutting hydrochloric acid with zinc. Commercial hydrochloric acid (28%) is mixed with an equal quantity of water in a wide-mouthed glass jar. The drugstore name for hydrochloric acid is muriatic acid. When this flux is used only occasionally on small jobs, from two to four fluid ounces of the acid and an equal amount of water will be sufficient.

A few small pieces of sheet zinc are dropped into the acid. Granulated zinc obtained from a chemical supply house may be used or zinc taken from the outsides of old dry cells. The acid will begin to dissolve the zinc immediately. Bubbling and fuming will take place.

Too much zinc must not be dropped in at one time or the mixture may boil over. Since the fumes are unpleasant, the flux should be prepared in the open air. Because the bubbles are hydrogen gas, which is inflammable, keep cigarettes, matches, and flames away. When the zinc is completely dissolved, add more. When the addition of zinc causes no further bubbling, the flux is ready for use.

Zinc chloride flux will destroy an ordinary brush. A good brush for applying this

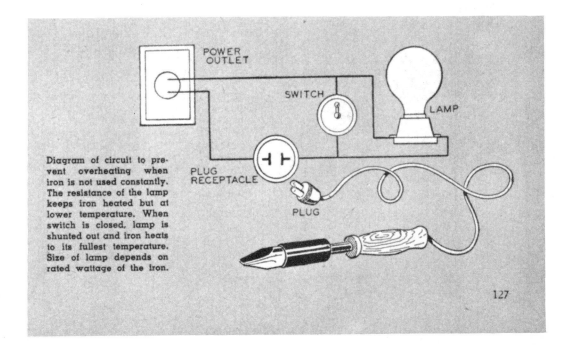

Diagram of circuit to prevent overheating when iron is not used constantly. The resistance of the lamp keeps iron heated but at lower temperature. When switch is closed, lamp is shunted out and iron heats to its fullest temperature. Size of lamp depends on rated wattage of the iron.

POWER OUTLET

SWITCH

LAMP

PLUG RECEPTACLE

PLUG

flux can be made of a piece of copper tubing having an inside diameter of ¼″ to ⅜″ and 5″ or 6″ long. The bristles consist either of sheet rubber cut into narrow strips or rubber bands. These are inserted into one end of the tube, about ½″ extending. About ½″ of that end of the tube is then flattened by squeezing it in a vise. This clamps the bristles firmly in their copper handle.

Zinc chloride will corrode a cork or metal bottle cap. It should be stored in a bottle having a plastic cap or glass stopper.

Soldering Salts

Soldering salts are usually a crystalline form of zinc chloride dissolved in water to make a fluid soldering flux. They are sold under various brand names. Instructions for using them are usually printed on the package labels. Since this type of flux is corrosive, it should be washed off after the soldering has been completed.

Soldering Paste

The common soldering pastes are usually zinc chloride mixed with Vaseline, ceresine wax, or palm oil. They are all corrosive, should not be used on electrical work, and must be wiped off after the soldering has been completed.

Tallow and Stearine

Tallow candles, like those used by plumbers, as distinguished from ordinary paraffin candles, make an excellent non-corrosive flux for soldering copper and lead.

The iron shown here has its heating element crooked at sharp angle to handle for soldering joints that are ordinarily very difficult to reach.

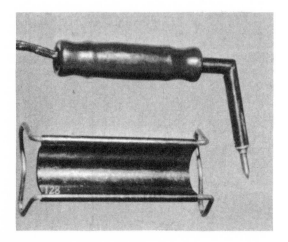

Muriatic Acid

Muriatic acid can be used full strength as a flux for soldering zinc, galvanized iron and steel. It also produces good results with cast iron and stainless steel. However, neither this nor any other flux is as satisfactory for iron and steel as for the non-ferrous metals such as brass, copper and tin.

All traces of muriatic acid flux must be washed off the work after soldering because it is highly corrosive. It will attack the skin and eat holes in clothing.

Stainless Steel Flux

There are several special stainless steel fluxes sold under various trade names. They are usually a highly corrosive mixture of acids. They will attack the skin and eat holes in woodwork and clothing. This type of flux must be handled carefully and all traces must promptly be removed from the soldered work by washing it with soap and water. A little washing soda dissolved in water is effective in neutralizing the acids.

Six Rules for Soldering

There are many rules to follow in order to do a successful soldering job but the six most important are:

1. The work which is to be soldered must be as clean as it is possible to make it.

2. The proper flux must be used; it must wet the entire surface to which the solder is to adhere.

3. The work must be properly and rigidly supported so that it does not move while the solder is setting.

4. The iron must be the right size for the job and must have the proper temperature.

5. The iron must be kept well tinned and clean.

6. The work must be heated so that the solder flows or sweats into the joint.

All oxide, corrosion, paint, grease, dust and foreign matter must be scraped off the work where it is to be soldered or the solder will not stick. It is necessary to scrape, scratch or grind the spot to be soldered until the metal is bright and shining at that point.

A steel scratch brush, emery paper, steel wool, file, knife, emery wheel or scraper, whichever works best for the particular job, may be used to clean the work and produce the required bright surface.

When the work is clean apply a small amount of flux.

Too much flux will interfere with soldering. By constant experimentation you can learn to apply the right amount. Rosin flux may be applied in the form of a powder which is sprinkled on or may be dissolved in alcohol and applied with a brush. In soldering brass, copper and tin-plated articles, rosin core wire solder can be used. In such cases it is unnecessary to apply flux separately.

When tallow is used as the flux, a few shavings cut from a tallow candle can be sprinkled on the spot to be soldered. The hot soldering iron will melt the tallow and cause it to spread over the surface.

Zinc chloride, or any of the fluid soldering fluxes, should be swabbed on to wet the entire surface to which the solder is to adhere. After the soldering has been completed, all traces of acid and zinc chloride fluxes should be removed by washing with a solution of soap and washing soda in water.

It is essential, in order to make a strong soldered joint, that the parts to be joined be rigidly fixed so that they cannot move. If a joint is moved while the solder is cooling and setting, the solder will be weakened by crystallization.

Sometimes the work can be held firmly in a vise or a clamp. If the point to be soldered is close to the jaws of the clamp or the vise, the latter may conduct the heat away so rapidly that the joint cannot be raised to the proper temperature. In that case, several layers of newspaper placed between the jaws and the work will usually provide an effective insulator which will prevent the escape of the heat.

A piece of fine copper wire may sometimes be used to bind parts together at the joint; this wire can be covered with the solder.

The best method of securing the work so that it cannot move will vary with each job and must be left to the ingenuity of the mechanic. The skilled craftsman can usually manipulate the iron with his right hand and hold the work with his left hand. Whenever possible the beginner should secure the work so that his left hand is free.

Small parts and sheet metal which can be laid on a bench for soldering should be placed on a piece of asbestos paper. Several layers of newspaper may be used as a substitute. Asbestos and paper act as insulators to prevent the heat from getting to the bench. Without such insulation it will be harder to heat the work to a proper soldering temperature.

Using the Iron

An iron must be large enough and hot enough to bring the parts to be soldered up to the temperature required for the solder to flow into the joint. When an iron is melting solder and heating the work, it loses its heat very rapidly. If an electric iron becomes too cool to solder, it is too small and a larger iron should be used.

Soldering small light objects does not draw a great deal of heat from the iron, but large lugs, pipe fittings, castings, and such will sometimes cool an iron so rapidly that a torch or flame must be used to preheat the work before the iron is applied. An alcohol or gasoline torch is very useful for this.

All areas to be soldered should be cleaned and the flux applied before the flame is used. Soldering can often be done with a torch alone, eliminating the iron.

Remember to work with an iron which is properly tinned and wiped each time it is removed from the fire, or, in the case of an electric iron, each time it is used. A piece of rag should be kept on the bench for that purpose.

Preheating and Soldering with a Blowtorch

Soldering wires, sheet metal, light tubing and other small objects do not draw much heat from a soldering iron. But when large pieces are to be tinned or sweated together they require so much heat they will cool a soldering iron before they become hot enough to melt solder.

Therefore a torch or flame is often used to preheat large pieces of metal before the iron is used. In some instances the job can be completed by heating the work directly with a blowtorch or blowpipe without using an iron.

If the work is done on a bench where gas is available, a Bunsen burner can provide the source of heat. Where gas is not available, an alcohol or gasoline blowtorch can be used. It is sometimes more practical to take the torch to the work than vice versa.

For soldering splices in wires, an electrician's alcohol torch is especially useful. It is small yet throws a very hot blue flame which will furnish more heat than a large soldering iron. Some electricians' torches generate their own pressure. Others are fitted with a small blowpipe attached to a rubber tube. Blowing into the tube will produce a small hot blue flame which can be pointed in any direction.

The general rules for soldering with a flame are: clean the work, apply flux and heat the joint until it will just melt solder. Then apply more flux and heat again until solder will run freely into the joint. Wire solder is the most convenient form to use. The solder should *not* be applied while the flame is on the work. It is imperative for the work to become hot enough for the solder to flow into the joint, for only the solder that flows in between the parts is of much effect in joining them.

The copper pipes used in modern plumbing systems are connected by sweating instead of the threads used with brass and galvanized iron piping (except the connections coupling the copper pipe to fixtures for which there are threaded brass fittings soldered to the copper pipe which fit threads on the fixture).

A blowtorch can be used satisfactorily to solder the joints in copper plumbing but an iron cannot.

How to Identify and Solder Various Metals

Before a metal can be soldered with any certainty of success, it must be identified. Knowing its composition, you can decide what is the best flux, solder and technique to use.

For example, you cannot solder the handle on a pewter sugar bowl with the same solder and heat used to fasten the handle on a galvanized iron watering pot. You must know that the sugar bowl is pewter and act accordingly if you wish to do a successful job. This is one of the fundamentals of soldering.

Aluminum. This bluish-white metal is used in the manufacture of countless articles where light weight and resistance to corrosion are important. The familiar "aluminum" pots and pans, vacuum cleaners and other household articles are not pure aluminum. They are generally an aluminum alloy containing a small percentage of copper which increases the strength as well as the weight of the utensils.

Commercially pure aluminum finds many uses, especially in extruded shapes and rolled sheets which are fabricated into countless articles.

Aluminum cannot be soldered with ordinary solder and ordinary fluxes such as zinc chloride or rosin. Here is the reason. If you scrape a piece of aluminum and obtain a fresh bright surface, it may re-main bright to your eye, but in the split part of a second it becomes covered with a thin, invisible layer of oxide. Ordinary fluxes do not remove this oxide. As long as it remains you cannot make solder adhere to the aluminum.

It is necessary to use a flux which will dissolve aluminum oxide. There are several such fluxes which may be purchased in hardware stores and automobile supply houses.

A good aluminum solder can be made by melting together equal weights of pure tin and pure zinc. Even with a slight excess of tin the solder will be effective, but a greater proportion of zinc will spoil the mixture. Although the commercial aluminum solders work well, not all of them melt as quickly or flow as easily as the mixture of tin and zinc.

It is imperative that aluminum to be soldered should be free from grease and dirt. The area to be tinned must be scraped and scratched to remove the entire surface film of oxide. Immediately after it is scraped, the special aluminum soldering flux is sprinkled over the cleaned surface.

If the article to be soldered is small, a soldering iron can be used. If it is large, a torch flame will be required.

If the job is one which can be done with an iron, the iron must be large and very hot (at least 500 degrees F.) The ordinary electric iron is seldom large enough or hot enough for soldering aluminum.

If an electric iron is used, a flat surface of the iron should be placed and held on the area to be tinned. The flux will melt, bubble and finally smoke. At this point, and not until then, without removing the iron, apply the special aluminum solder to the iron. This will melt and spread over the fluxed surface of the aluminum. Any additional solder required for a good joint can be applied with the tip of the iron in the usual manner.

When a blowtorch instead of an iron is used to melt the solder, the work is thoroughly cleaned and the special aluminum flux sprinkled on as already described. The torch flame is used to warm the parts to be soldered and then applied directly to the fluxed area. The flux will melt and then smoke. At this point, without removing the flame, feed solder into the area. If the cleaning, fluxing and heating have been done properly, the solder will instantly flow over the fluxed area.

Special aluminum solders will make a stronger joint than ordinary solders. Since a blowtorch furnishes considerable heat, the flame must be applied with caution to avoid melting the aluminum.

In soldering other metals to aluminum, generally, the procedure is to tin both metals first, using aluminum flux and solder on the aluminum. If possible, the heat should be applied to the underside of the aluminum.

Brass. This is an alloy of copper and zinc although some special brasses may contain a small amount of tin, lead, iron or manganese. The most common brass is about 65% copper and 35% zinc.

Since brass tins readily, it is easy to solder. Either zinc chloride or rosin can be used as a flux. Zinc chloride is usually most satisfactory. Any of the tin-lead solders can be used.

When a flame is used for soldering brass, take care not to overheat the job. Too much heat makes the brass more difficult to tin. If this trouble is experienced, let the work cool a little, scrape it clean and apply flux again. Then try tinning it with less heat. Because zinc chloride corrodes brass, turning the surface green, all excess flux should be washed off with soapy water containing washing soda.

Bronze. This is the general name given to alloys of copper and tin. The bronzes vary greatly in composition. In addition to copper and tin they may also contain small amounts of zinc, nickel, manganese, silicon and lead to give them special qualities. Bronze is usually an easy metal to solder by the same method used in the case of brass.

Cast Iron. Soldering cast iron never produces the strength that welding does. Cracks in cast iron cylinder heads can often be soldered so that a leak in the water jacket is stopped.

In soldering cast iron be sure of the following:

1. Remove all paint, grease, dirt and rust from the part to be repaired.

2. If an iron is used, use one large enough and hot enough.

In soldering a crack in an iron casting, the top of the crack must first be widened into a V groove, deep and wide enough to allow a good inlay of solder. The groove can be filed, chiseled or ground.

If the casting is large, preheat it with a torch.

The best results are secured by using one of the special fluxes made for cast iron. Most of the fluxes made for aluminum may

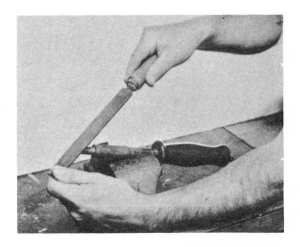

To tin an electric iron, file the tip surfaces bright while the iron is cold. Turn on current. As iron heats, rub flux-core solder over the tip facets every 20 seconds. When the temperature has risen enough, solder will spread smoothly and evenly.

be used for cast iron. Heat the casting until it can melt solder. (A large iron will heat small castings. A blowtorch must be used to heat large castings.) Then apply the flux to the groove and the area adjacent to the groove. As soon as the flux smokes, apply the solder and rub it in the groove with a hot iron until the surface is well tinned.

Iron castings are porous and sometimes are so oil soaked that it may be necessary to flux the groove more than once in order to obtain a properly tinned surface.

Use fine steel wool to scrape off any dirt and oxides which may come to the surface of the molten tinning. Then fill the groove with molten solder, using a hot iron to spread it and pack it in.

Copper. Copper is easily recognized by its red color. It tins easily and consequently is readily soldered. Any of the fluxes will be suitable for copper. Zinc chloride acts best but its corrosive property makes it objectionable for some work. Electrical parts and wires made of copper should be soldered with rosin only.

Galvanized Iron and Steel. This is the general name for iron and steel castings, steel forgings, and steel and iron sheets coated with zinc in a bath of the molten metal. The zinc coating, which protects the steel and iron from rust and corrosion, crystallizes and forms a characteristic spangle or flower by which galvanized materials are readily recognized.

131

Galvanized surfaces are easily tinned. There is no danger of melting iron or steel with a soldering iron. Either rosin or zinc chloride may be used as flux. The latter must be washed off after soldering to avoid corrosion.

An excess of rosin flux will do no harm but, if its appearance is objectionable, it may be wiped off with a cloth saturated with denatured alcohol.

Iron. Iron can be soldered with ordinary tin-lead solder but the joint will not be as strong as the material. Spot welding, bronze welding, brazing, or silver soldering, whichever is suitable, should be used instead of soft soldering, if a strong joint is desired.

An iron surface which is to be tinned for soldering must be scraped, filed or ground bright and clean. Zinc chloride is the most satisfactory flux to use for soldering iron.

Some of the commercial aluminum solders and aluminum fluxes will produce better results than either tin-lead solders or zinc chloride in soldering iron castings.

Lead. Lead is easily recognized by its weight and color. It is the heaviest of the common metals, is soft and has a bluish gray color. It is bright when the surface is newly cleaned or cut. Storage battery plates and connectors are made of lead.

The covering on cables and wires known as "lead covered" consists of lead containing a small percentage of antimony as a hardening ingredient.

Lead is an easy metal to solder if certain precautions are taken: 1. Do not allow the iron to become too hot. 2. Use a solder with a low melting point. Lead melts at 621 degrees F. This is so close to the melting point of half and half solder (370 degrees F.) that without skillful handling the lead may melt.

The iron must not be very hot and it must not be allowed to rest on one spot but should be kept moving to prevent melting the lead. A beginner should practice on scrap lead in order to determine the proper temperature of the iron.

In order to solder lead, the joint, as in all soldering, must be scraped bright and fluxed. The best flux to use for lead is ordinary tallow.

Anyone inexperienced in soldering lead can avoid the risk of destroying the work by using a low-melting-point solder, which is made especially for use on lead, pewter and other low-melting-point white metal alloys. A good one can be made by melting one portion of plumber's half and half solder and adding twice its weight of bismuth. When the bismuth melts, the mixture is stirred with an iron rod and then poured out on a flat stone.

If the ladle containing the molten solder is moved along while the metal is poured slowly, the solder can be beaten into bars and wires. The flux for this solder is ordinary tallow.

Magnesium. A solder for dow metal and alloys containing a high percentage of magnesium is composed of 18 parts by weight of pure tin and 7 parts by weight of pure cadmium. Use an aluminum-type flux which, after soldering, should be washed off to prevent corrosion.

Nickel Silver. This name is applied to the copper-nickel-zinc alloy formerly known by the name of German silver. It can be soldered with lead-tin solders and zinc chloride flux, but when great strength is required the joint should be made by brazing or silver soldering.

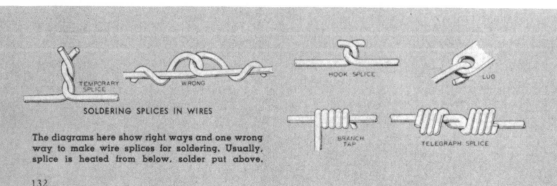

SOLDERING SPLICES IN WIRES

The diagrams here show right ways and one wrong way to make wire splices for soldering. Usually, splice is heated from below, solder put above.

Pewter. Pewter is the name of a tin-lead alloy which has been used for dishes and ornamental articles ever since the time of the Romans. The ancient Roman pewter usually was 30% lead and 70% tin. Modern pewter is likely to contain some zinc and antimony and less tin.

The highest grade of modern pewter consists of tin, antimony, bismuth and copper. Good pewter has a peculiar bluish-white luster when polished.

Pewter has a low melting point. The safest solder is one of those commercially prepared especially for this material. These solders are tin-lead-bismuth alloys and have a low melting point. Instructions for making a solder of this type are given in the section dealing with soldering lead. The iron should be no hotter than is necessary to melt the low temperature solder freely. The best flux is common tallow.

Stainless Steel. The bright surface of stainless steel generally distinguishes it from all other metals except Monel metal.

There are several commercial fluxes prepared especially for soldering stainless steel, but ordinary hydrochloric acid is excellent for the purpose. It should be used undiluted, brushed on thoroughly and allowed to bite into the metal for two or three minutes before soldering is commenced.

Ordinary plumbers half and half can be used on stainless steel but a solder containing a higher percentage of tin will give better results. A solder consisting of two parts tin and one part lead is excellent.

The trick of good stainless steel soldering lies in the knowledge that this metal is a poor heat conductor. Use a large iron and hold it in one place on the stainless steel longer than would be necessary in the case of another metal. Raising the iron itself to a higher temperature than usual does not solve the problem but proves an actual disadvantage. Overheating will discolor stainless steel and may even warp and buckle it.

After soldering with hydrochloric acid or any of the commercial stainless steel fluxes, wash off the excess flux with a solution of washing soda and soap in water.

Steel. The instructions for soldering iron also apply to ordinary steel.

Tin. Tin is a silvery-white metal with a bluish tinge. It is soft, malleable and resembles silver in appearance.

"Tin" cans used as containers are not made of tin. They are really tinned sheet iron or sheet steel. Tin is not magnetic; a tinned can is attracted by a magnet.

Pure tin or "block tin" pipes are used in soda fountains and for certain chemical and food manufacturing purposes. These are not tinned or coated but are solid tin. Pure tin is difficult to solder because of its low melting point which is 450 degrees F. Consequently there is only a very small margin between the melting point of any of the tin-lead solders and the melting point of tin.

For example, the heat required to bring half and half solder to the proper working temperature would melt the tin and ruin the work.

A special solder containing tin, lead and bismuth is required. The presence of bismuth in the solder lowers its melting point. A combination of these three metals called Wood's alloy is frequently used as a solder for tin. It consists of bismuth, 8 parts by weight; tin, 3 parts by weight; and lead, 5 parts by weight, and melts at about 200 degrees F.

Tinned Copper. Tin-coated wires, terminals, lugs and other parts of electrical circuits are easily soldered. Rosin is the only flux which should be used. Practically all other fluxes have a corrosive action which will ultimately cause trouble in an electrical circuit. •

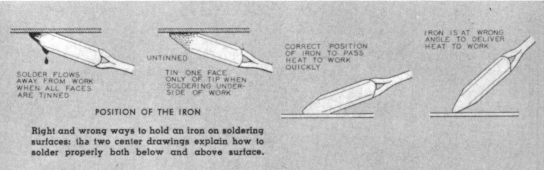

SOLDER FLOWS AWAY FROM WORK WHEN ALL FACES ARE TINNED

UNTINNED

TIN ONE FACE ONLY OF TIP WHEN SOLDERING UNDER-SIDE OF WORK

CORRECT POSITION OF IRON TO PASS HEAT TO WORK QUICKLY

IRON IS AT WRONG ANGLE TO DELIVER HEAT TO WORK

POSITION OF THE IRON

Right and wrong ways to hold an iron on soldering surfaces: the two center drawings explain how to solder properly both below and above surface.

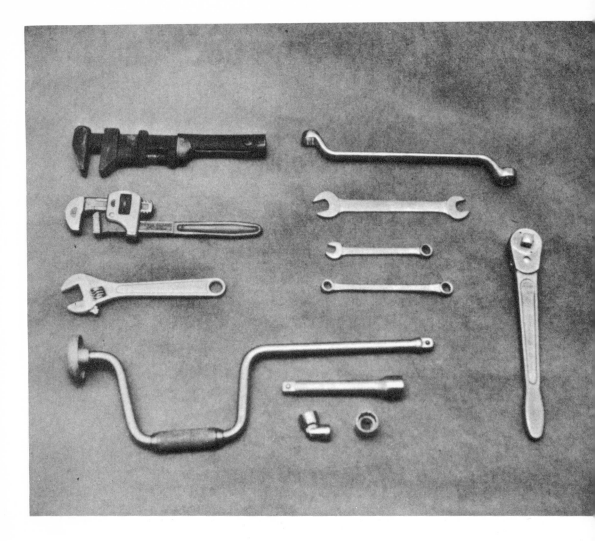

wrenches

There are many tricks to handling wrenches, but you can figure out every twist by reading these pages.

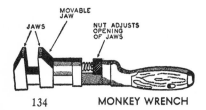

Drawings show right and wrong way to use monkey wrench. If pull is exerted on the wrong side of handle, it's easy for wrench to slip. Always adjust the wrench so that it fits the nut snugly.

MOVABLE JAW

JAWS

NUT ADJUSTS OPENING OF JAWS

MONKEY WRENCH

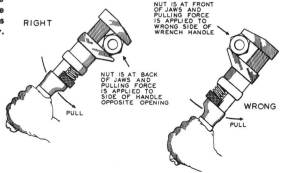

RIGHT

NUT IS AT BACK OF JAWS AND PULLING FORCE IS APPLIED TO SIDE OF HANDLE OPPOSITE OPENING

PULL

NUT IS AT FRONT OF JAWS AND PULLING FORCE IS APPLIED TO WRONG SIDE OF WRENCH HANDLE

WRONG

PULL

WRENCHES are tools for twisting or turning bolts, nuts, pipe, etc. A monkey wrench is probably the most familiar form. This is adjustable and can be made to fit a wide size range of bolts and nuts. It is not suitable for turning pipe, rods or other round objects; its jaws grip flat surfaces only. Why it is called a "monkey" wrench is a mystery.

Although a monkey wrench is very convenient at times, it is not intended for constant use in place of an open-end, socket or box wrench of suitable size. It is used principally for an odd sized nut or bolt which the open-end or socket wrenches on hand will not fit.

The common monkey wrench often has a handle lagged with wood. A very similar all steel tool supplied in the tool kits of a new automobile is known as an "auto wrench."

There are two important points to remember in using either an auto wrench or a monkey wrench:

1. Always place the wrench on a nut or bolt so that the turning force is applied to the back of the handle, that is, the side of the wrench opposite the opening. This will relieve the strain on the weakest part of the wrench, the adjustable jaw, and make slipping less probable.

Gripping action of the Stillson wrench, above and below, makes it necessary to apply turning force to back of wrench or the jaws won't grip the pipe.

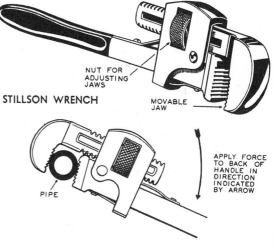

STILLSON WRENCH

NUT FOR ADJUSTING JAWS

MOVABLE JAW

PIPE

APPLY FORCE TO BACK OF HANDLE IN DIRECTION INDICATED BY ARROW

Close-up below shows adjustable end wrench in action. If you use a hammer on the handle of the wrench, the adjustable jaw may be damaged.

An adjustable end wrench is not as strong as an ordinary end wrench, but both are used in nearly the same way. You can easily strain an adjustable wrench by using it improperly as at the far right.

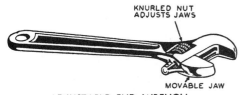

KNURLED NUT ADJUSTS JAWS

MOVABLE JAW

ADJUSTABLE END WRENCH

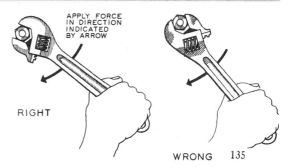

APPLY FORCE IN DIRECTION INDICATED BY ARROW

RIGHT

WRONG   135

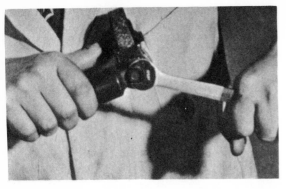

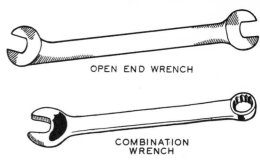

OPEN END WRENCH

COMBINATION WRENCH

Open end wrench, above, and combination open end and box wrench are of chrome vanadium steel.

2. Before turning a nut or bolt, tighten the adjusting knurl so that the wrench fits as tightly as possible. If it does not fit closely, it will slip, which may result in an injury to your hand and which may also round the corners of the nut or bolt head. It is very hard to break loose or snug down a nut or bolt which has rounded corners.

Apply a little light oil to the moving parts of a monkey wrench or auto wrench occasionally. This will keep them working freely and will help to prevent rust.

Adjustable Wrenches

These are similar in shape to the common open-end wrenches but have one adjustable jaw. They are not as strong as opened wrenches and are not intended to replace them entirely. It is easy to strain an adjustable wrench by using it improperly. Don't hammer on it to break loose a tight nut or bolt and don't slip a piece of pipe over the handle in order to increase the leverage. Some part of the wrench may bend or break if you do.

Use an adjustable wrench in the same manner that you would use a monkey wrench. Always place the wrench on a nut or bolt so that the force used to turn it is applied to the stationary jaw side of the handle. After placing the wrench in position, tighten the adjusting knurl so that the wrench fits the nut or bolt snugly. Oil the movable jaw and adjustable knurl occasionally.

There are seven or eight sizes of adjustable wrenches. The average mechanic, unless he is constantly servicing engines and other machinery, will usually find a 4", 8" and 12" adjustable wrench sufficient for his tool kit.

Pipe Wrenches and Stillson Wrenches

These have toothed jaws and are the only wrenches which will take a bite on round objects such as pipe and shafting. They will work in one direction only. To loosen a pipe the open end of the wrench must face the direction opposite that which tightens it.

The teeth on the jaws always leave marks on the work. There is no way to prevent

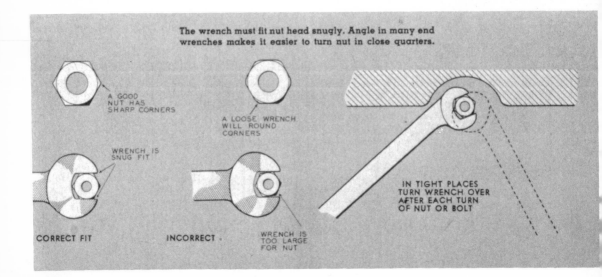

The wrench must fit nut head snugly. Angle in many end wrenches makes it easier to turn nut in close quarters.

A GOOD NUT HAS SHARP CORNERS

A LOOSE WRENCH WILL ROUND CORNERS

WRENCH IS SNUG FIT

CORRECT FIT

INCORRECT

WRENCH IS TOO LARGE FOR NUT

IN TIGHT PLACES TURN WRENCH OVER AFTER EACH TURN OF NUT OR BOLT

Box wrench won't slip off. It's ideal for turning nut or bolt hard to reach with open-end wrench.

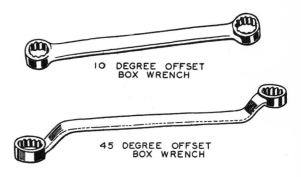

IO DEGREE OFFSET BOX WRENCH

45 DEGREE OFFSET BOX WRENCH

this. Never use a pipe wrench on a nut or a bolt head unless the corners have been rounded so that you cannot turn it with any other type of wrench. A pipe wrench will turn a nut or bolt but will also chew it and disfigure it so that it cannot be used again. A few drops of oil should occasionally be applied to the moving parts of the wrench to keep them working freely.

Box Wrenches

The opening in a box wrench consists of 12 notches arranged in a circle. It is an ideal wrench to turn nuts or bolt heads which are hard to get at with an open-end wrench. A swing through an arc of 15 degrees is sufficient to continuously loosen or tighten a nut or bolt. Unless there is room to swing a box wrench in a full circle, it is lifted completely off the nut when it comes to the limit of its motion and placed in a new position which will permit it to be swung again.

Since a box wrench cannot slip off a nut, it is ideal for breaking loose tight nuts and bolts or for setting them up. To set up means to give already tight nuts or bolts their final tightening.

After a nut or bolt is started, it can usually be worked more quickly with an open-end wrench than a box wrench. For that reason combination wrenches consisting of an open-end wrench at one end and a box wrench at the other are very popular with mechanics. The box end is used to break loose a tight nut or bolt or to set up one which needs a final tightening, but most of the actual turning is done with the open end.

Special Open-End Wrenches

Some special types of open-end wrenches are made with the head and angle straight with the body. Other special open-end wrenches may have the head and opening at an angle of 75 degrees or at 90 degrees. But the common open-end wrench is made with the head and opening at an angle of 15 degrees to the body. This makes it possible to turn a nut or bolt in limited quarters where there is little space to swing the wrench.

By turning the wrench over after each swing so that the other face is down, the angle of the opening is reversed. Thus a hexagonal nut or cap screw can be turned continuously although the actual swing motion of the wrench is limited to a 30 degree arc.

When using an open-end wrench, make sure the wrench is a good fit—that both jaws rest squarely against the sides of the nut or bolt head. Then, if possible, place yourself so that you can *pull* on the wrench to move it in the desired direction. To push on a wrench is dangerous. If the wrench slips or the nut or bolt breaks loose suddenly you may knock the skin off your knuckles and be thrown off balance.

There are times when the only way you can move a wrench is to push it. In that case don't wrap your fingers around it. Push it with the palm of the hand and hold your hand open—you won't be so likely to hurt yourself.

End Wrenches

Open-end and socket wrenches are the tools used most frequently in servicing automotive vehicles, motors and machinery in general. Open-end wrenches are solid, non-adjustable and have an opening between the jaws. They are usually double-ended wrenches.

Modern open-end wrenches are forged from chrome vanadium steel and heat treated. They're light, strong, tough tools.

The size of the opening between the jaws determines the size of an open-end wrench. A wrench with a ½" opening in one end and a $\frac{9}{16}$" opening in the other is called a ½ x $\frac{9}{16}$ wrench. The size of each opening is usually stamped on the side of the wrench. Actually, the openings are from .005" to .015" larger than the size marked on the wrench so that they will easily slip on bolts or nuts of that size. In this instance the size of a bolt or nut does not mean the bolt diameter but refers to the distance across the flats of the nut or bolt head, upon which the wrench fits.

It is important for a wrench to be a good fit on a nut or bolt head. If it is too loose, the wrench will slip and round the corners. Make certain that the wrench fits *squarely on the sides* of the nut or bolt head.

Open-end wrenches are made in many different sizes. An average set for automobile and general work usually contains about ten or twelve wrenches with openings ranging from $\frac{5}{16}$" to 1".

The wrenches with the smaller openings are shorter in over-all length than those with larger openings. This relationship between length and opening provides the correct leverage. If wrenches which fit small nuts were made as long as wrenches which fit large nuts, it would be easy to apply too much force and strip threads or twist a bolt or stud in two.

12-point Socket Wrenches

Socket wrenches are time and labor savers. They are extensively used in assembling machinery and in making automotive repairs. On some assembly lines socket wrenches turned by compressed air are used. These save the worker much muscular effort and fatigue.

However, the socket wrenches discussed here are hand tools. The modern socket wrench kit consists of several sockets made of high strength alloy steel and one or more handles. Each socket fits a nut of given size. There are two openings in the socket, one a square hole which fits the handle and the other a circular hole whose sides are notched.

There are 12 notches which slip over a hexagonal nut or the hexagonal head of a cap screw in the same manner as the notches in a box wrench. There are T handles, hinged offset handles, handles with a universal joint, ratchet handles and sliding offset handles to fit the sockets.

To use a socket wrench select the size of socket that fits the nut or bolt to be turned and push it on the handle which is best suited to the job. If there is room to swing it, the ratchet handle is preferred. The handle may be made to ratchet in one direction to tighten a nut and in the other direction to loosen it. It is necessary only to swing the handle back and forth in order

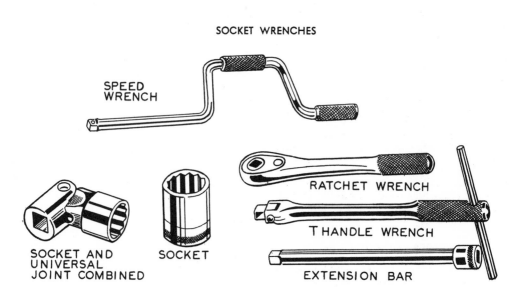

SOCKET WRENCHES

SPEED WRENCH

RATCHET WRENCH

T HANDLE WRENCH

SOCKET AND UNIVERSAL JOINT COMBINED

SOCKET

EXTENSION BAR

to turn the nut in the desired direction. The socket need not be raised from the nut at the end of each swing.

The hinged offset handle is also a labor saver. When a tight nut is to be loosened or a nut is to be set up, the handle can be swung at right angles to the socket to provide the greatest possible leverage. At the point where the nut turns easily, the handle can be swung into a vertical position and twisted rapidly between the fingers in the same manner as a screw driver.

The universal joint handle makes it possible to turn nuts where a straight wrench could not be used unless some part of the engine or machine is removed.

In some plants assemblers are furnished with a torque handle to fit sockets. Torque means turning force. A pointer or dial on the wrench indicates the amount of force being applied to turn a nut.

Nuts on the cylinder heads, connecting rod bearing caps and in other places on automotive and airplane engines should be tightened only to certain limits. The manufacturer's instructions specify these limits. A torque wrench enables you to set up a nut and stop when the force applied to the handle reaches the specified limit.

Six-Sided Socket Wrenches

The first socket wrenches to be used on automobiles and machinery had a hexagonal opening for the bolt head or nut. They were superseded by the 12-point socket wrenches in automotive, airplane and machine-shop work. However, radio and instrument assemblers and repairmen still use small hexagonal socket wrenches on small nuts and bolts. These wrenches are fittted with a wooden handle similar to that on a screw driver. Small nuts (8-32, 10-32, etc.) can be removed or replaced rapidly with this wrench.

Allen Wrench

These are L-shaped bars of tool steel having a hexagonal section. They fit the hexagon socket in Allen cap or set screws.

There are also two types of L-shaped set screw wrenches made from round bar stock with ends to fit the little flutes or splines in the two other types of headless set screws.

Headless set screws are used to fasten in place pulleys, collars and other moving parts on a revolving shaft where a protruding screw would be objectionable. The Allen type screw and wrench is the one most widely used. The short end of the wrench is inserted in the head of the screw when the latter is to be tightened or broken loose. After loosening, very little leverage is required and the screw can be removed more rapidly if the long end of the wrench is inserted in the head. •

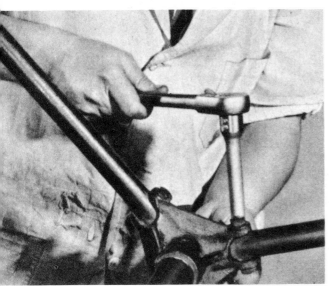

Photo shows use of ratchet wrench. This is one of the socket wrenches pictured on page 138. Below is the Allen wrench made to turn Allen set screws used on moving parts where a protruding screw is not practical.

ALLEN WRENCH

ALLEN
SET SCREW

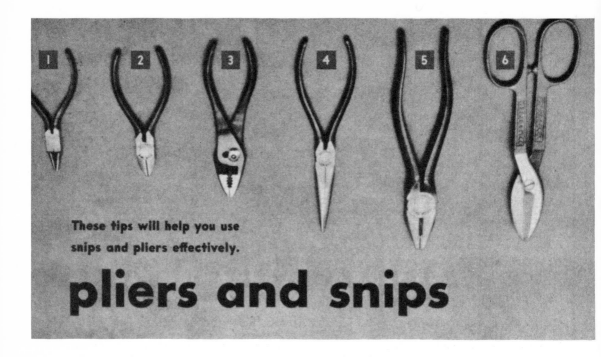

These tips will help you use snips and pliers effectively.

pliers and snips

PLIERS are useful tools in any tool kit. There are many types and sizes, each one best suited to some particular purpose. Like all other tools, pliers should be kept clean and free from grit and rust. Put a drop of oil on the joint pin occasionally. Avoid using pliers on hardened surfaces as this dulls the teeth, causing the pliers to lose their gripping power.

Round Nose Pliers are meant for bending and holding curved wires and strips. They are used to bend curves. Eyes and chain links are easily formed with this tool. Because both jaws are round and tapered toward the end, curves of small radius are bent with the tips of the jaws and curves of greater radius are bent with the base of the jaws.

Chain Nose Pliers taper to a blunt point at the tip of the jaws. The gripping surface between the jaws is flat, making this tool useful as a small wrench for bending angles in strips and wires and for holding parts too small to be handled with the fingers. Long chain nose pliers are often useful in tight spots for recovering washers, nuts and other parts which have fallen where there is not enough room for the fingers to pick them up.

Flat Nose Pliers have a flat gripping surface between the jaws but do not taper to a point like the chain nose pliers. They may be used as small wrenches as well as for holding and bending angles in strips and wires.

Diagonal Cutting Pliers or sharp nippers, usually referred to as diagonals, are designed for cutting small wires, nails, pins, screws, rivets, etc. The angle of the jaws makes it possible to cut close to a surface. Diagonals are handy for pulling out cotter pins, especially those in the castellated nuts used on the connecting rods and main bearing caps of automotive engines. This plier

Top photo shows: 1. Round Nose Pliers, 2. Diagonal Cutters, 3. Combination Pliers, 4. Long Nose Pliers, 5. Lineman's Pliers, 6. Common Hand Snips. Below are Bernard Side Cutting Pliers having compound leverage and jaws which always remain parallel.

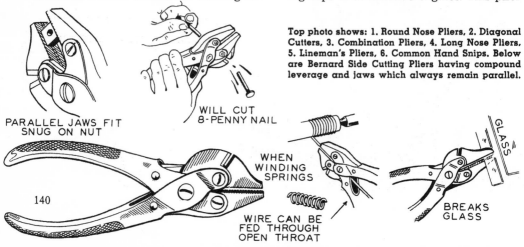

WILL CUT 8-PENNY NAIL

PARALLEL JAWS FIT SNUG ON NUT

WHEN WINDING SPRINGS

WIRE CAN BE FED THROUGH OPEN THROAT

BREAKS GLASS

GLASS

is also useful, when cotter pins are inserted, for cutting the pins to the correct length and spreading the ends.

End Cutting Nippers usually have long handles or a compound leverage which makes them more powerful and able to cut heavier materials than the diagonal type nippers.

Side Cutting Pliers, commonly known as side cutters, are essentially an electrician's tool used for cutting and splicing wires but are handy for general use. They have hardened steel knife jaws at the side for cutting small wires and rods of soft metal such as brass, copper, aluminum and soft steel.

Cutting pliers should never be used on piano wire or tempered steel. The cutting edges will be nicked and spoiled.

Combination Pliers are useful in many ways, especially in automotive work. There is a slip joint which permits the jaws to be opened wide at the hinge pin for gripping large diameters. Careless mechanics sometimes use combination pliers for loosening or tightening nuts. Not intended for this purpose, they knock the corners off. Wrenches are made for nuts. Small rods, studs, and pipes can be gripped firmly in the jaws of combination pliers, enabling them to serve in place of a small Stillson wrench on occasion.

Bernard Side Cutting Pliers are so designed that they are useful for many purposes. Their compound leverage gives great holding and cutting power. The 6″ pliers will cut a 10d nail with ease. The parallel jaws hold flat objects without wedging so that the pliers may be used as a vise and as a wrench. A wire can be fed through the open throat and springs wound with the aid of this tool. Be sure to include a set of these pliers in your tool kit.

Pictured below are a recommended group of pliers which fulfill most needs for your home workshop.

Lineman's side cutters are designed for electrical work.

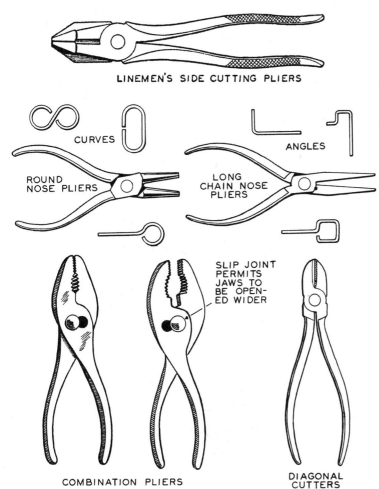

LINEMEN'S SIDE CUTTING PLIERS

CURVES

ANGLES

ROUND NOSE PLIERS

LONG CHAIN NOSE PLIERS

SLIP JOINT PERMITS JAWS TO BE OPENED WIDER

COMBINATION PLIERS

DIAGONAL CUTTERS

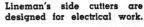

Combination pliers can be adjusted for wide gripping.

Round nose pliers give good control in wire bending work.

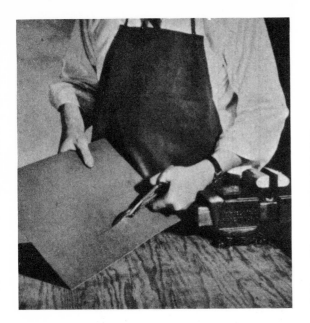

Snips for Sheet Metal

Thin sheet aluminum, brass, copper, iron, steel and Monel metal can be cut to size and shape with hand shears usually called snips. The terms sheet iron and steel in this list include tinned and galvanized iron and steel, stovepipe iron, cold rolled steel and transformer steel, but not tempered steel. Thick sheet metal can be cut only with

At left, common snips are used to cut straight lines but aren't suited to cutting sharp curves.

Below is the group of metal cutting snips which are most commonly used for sheet metal shop work.

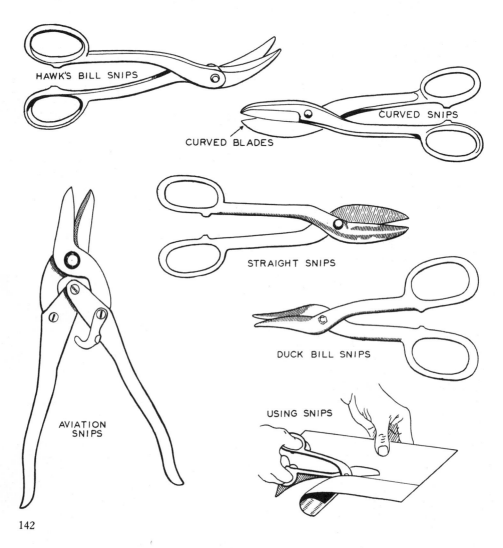

HAWK'S BILL SNIPS

CURVED SNIPS

CURVED BLADES

STRAIGHT SNIPS

DUCK BILL SNIPS

AVIATION SNIPS

USING SNIPS

power shears, metal saws, cold chisels and cutting torches.

The common sizes of snips vary in length from 6″ to 16″. The nature of a metal and its thickness determine the size of the snips required to cut it. Small snips are used for cutting thin sheet metals which are only a few thousandths of an inch thick. Steel is harder to cut than aluminum of the same thickness and requires larger snips.

The temper of a metal must always be considered in choosing the snips. For example, hard brass cannot be cut as easily as half-hard or soft brass and requires larger snips for the best results.

Kinds of Snips

Bench snips or shears are larger than the ordinary hand snips and are used for cutting heavy sheet. When in use the lower prong is inserted into a hole of the proper size cut in the top of the workbench for this purpose. The mechanic is thus enabled to bear down on the upper handle with his weight and exert great force to close the shears for heavy cutting.

The common hand snips are made with straight and also with curved blades. Straight blade snips are used for cutting straight lines. They can be used for cutting curves of large radius but not for sharp curves. Snips with curved blades are made especially for cutting curves.

Duck bill snips will cut straight lines and curves in either direction.

Aviation metal snips have a compound lever action which gives them great power. They will cut thicker metal with the expenditure of less muscular effort than is necessary with other snips. The beveled blades permit easy cutting of sharp curves in either direction. This tool will fulfill practically every requirement made of snips in the home workshop.

Hawk's bill combination scroll and circular snips have narrow, sharp pointed blades which will cut straight lines or will easily follow sharp curves. Sheet metal workers use this tool for cutting openings in furnace pipes and ducts. The offset handles make them useful in tight places such as in cornice work where ordinary snips would be cramped.

How to Cut with Snips

Snips are used to cut sheet metal in the same manner that scissors are employed to cut a sheet of paper. Place the cutting edge of the upper blade exactly on the guide line scribed on the metal sheet. The sheet should be inserted between the blades as far back as it will go.

The snips should be held so that the flat sides of the blades are at right angles to the surface of the work. If the blades are not at right angles to the surface of the work the edges of the cut will be slightly bent and burred.

Snips should be kept sharp and in adjustment. The pivot should be oiled frequently and the nut on the pivot adjusted so that the handles can be moved easily. However, the blades should not be so close that they tend to chew the metal instead of making a clean cut.

Cuts, especially for curves, should be continuous. Stopping and starting at different points on a line result in rough edges and sharp slivers of metal which will injure the fingers.

When cutting shapes from sheet metal with straight shears it is important to make the cuts in the right direction. Several different shapes are shown in one of the illustrations. X indicates the starting point and the arrows show the direction in which the cuts should be made.

When a hole or opening is to be cut in sheet metal with snips, lay the metal on a lead or hardwood block. Use a hollow punch or small cold chisel to make a hole in the metal large enough so that the point of the snips can be inserted. The lead or hardwood block should be directly under the metal at the point where the hole is punched. Drive the punch or chisel with a heavy mallet or hammer.

The mistake most frequently made by the novice is to cut slightly beyond a stopping point. This can be corrected by making it a habit to complete a cut with the point of the snips. •

Arrows show proper way to make cuts in forming the patterns below: X indicates starting point.

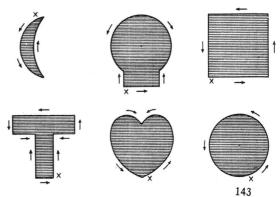